BLUEJACKET:

MEMOIRS OF A U.S. NAVY SAILOR

Vietnam, The Cold War & Beyond : April 1969 – May 1993

by

AE Kirkpatrick OSC/USN., Ret.

DORRANCE
PUBLISHING CO
EST. 1920
PITTSBURGH, PENNSYLVANIA 15238

The contents of this work, including, but not limited to, the accuracy of events, people, and places depicted; opinions expressed; permission to use previously published materials included; and any advice given or actions advocated are solely the responsibility of the author, who assumes all liability for said work and indemnifies the publisher against any claims stemming from publication of the work.

Dorrance Publishing Co
585 Alpha Drive
Pittsburgh, PA 15238
Visit our website at *www.dorrancebookstore.com*

ISBN: 978-1-4809-9485-0
eISBN: 978-1-4809-9442-3

DEDICATION

To my family.........both past and present!

INTRODUCTION

This book was written as a tribute to my fellow shipmates and sailors serving during the span of time covered by this work. More specifically, it is to and for the average sailor who got up at all hours to "stand watch," "pitch-to" on "working parties," mustered for his daily work assignment and met the daily challenges of life at sea. Fire aboard ship, the perils of working on a flight deck, and the heat, sweat and drudgery of working in the engineering spaces and bilges are always inglorious. It is to and for the guy who tended the garbage grinder, who stoked the incinerator, who filled the myriad other stations and who performed so many tasks that were necessary, the jobs the rest of us would shudder to think of being assigned to. It is for the cooks, boiler techs, boatswains mates, gunners mates, plane captains, purple shirts, redshirts, parachute riggers, EOD personnel, radiomen, yeomen and all the other ratings that compose a ship's crew. This book is for all their variety: the quiet, refrained types and the noisy, profane extroverts; the bookworms, card sharks and "operators;" the know-it-alls and the guys that didn't seem to have a clue; the slackers and the hard-chargers and the ones in between just trying to keep pace and get along. They were all there and they still are, because they are a reflection of the society they came from.

    You take a bunch of twenty-somethings and put them on a ship at sea for 30, 40 or more days straight and after working seven days a week for weeks and then pull into port, you get the stereotypical bar-room brawls and drunken sailors. But, you also get your average tourist, taking in the same sites a civilian might and taking lots of pictures of each other. You also get a lot of shoppers. Because sailors in port have back-pay to spend, the PX on base and the shops and stores in town made a lot of money in short order. With stereos, cameras, tailor-made clothes, and foreign and exotic food to sample, each port and each liberty was a race against time. And you tried to cram as much as possible into the short time the ship was in port before having to leave and go through all the boredom, drudgery and endless hours again.

Take that same bunch of twenty-somethings, then sprinkle them with "old salts" and competent, dedicated officers and put them aboard a ship preparing to go overseas. In roughly six months, through a strenuous and hectic schedule, they are trained as a crew. But, it takes more than just training to make them into one. It takes shared experiences, endless nights and days on watch and all the evolutions that occur during the course of "work-ups." They become part of the glue that makes them the heart and soul of whatever ship they are stationed aboard. In my experience, this was never something that was scheduled or expected at a certain time and place. But it was something you became aware of in due course. It could happen toward the end of training or perhaps as the ship steamed west and the deployment began. At some time or after some event, you could feel it. Everything was "clicking" and all members of the crew knew what was expected of them. Whether you were a part of a watch-section in Engineering, chocking and chaining aircraft, preparing hundreds or thousands of meals a day in the galley or solving a maneuvering solution in CIC, there emerged a bond with shipmates as well as with the ship. You became an extended family that would exist for a relatively short but finite period of time and would never be exactly replicated.

PROLOGUE

I'VE BEEN UP SINCE 4AM THIS MORNING, May 4th, 1986. Arriving aboard shortly
after 5AM, I've run through my morning duties, including checking on preparations for getting underway in CIC. Quarters for all hands is piped at 7AM and
Navigation Detail is set at 8AM. The first lines slip the quay shortly and with the
aid of the tugs, the ship noses out of the pier, backing into the channel and swinging the bow to port. In less than an hour, we've cleared the harbor and passed
Point Loma and Zuniga Point. A faint roll develops beneath my feet!

Standing at the Surface Watch Coordinator's Tactical Data Console in CIC, I
have been following the navigational and tactical picture displayed and make note
of the receding coastline now astern of the ship. Word is being passed over the 1MC
to "Secure the Sea & Anchor Detail" and to "Set the Underway Watch, Normal Underway Steaming." I can feel the change in screw count as the props bite into the sea
and propel us faster, en route to our destination. It is a destination that will take us
across the Pacific Ocean, eight time-zones, one day and 6,000 miles from home. We
are embarking on a "WestPac" deployment, not to see country, home or family for
seven months. In between my departure and return are the endless watches, countless
mundane functions and duties, and random and scheduled evolutions aboard ship
that make up a "cruise" aboard this nuclear cruiser and that will run the gamut of a
surface sailor's experience during the waning years of the "Cold War"!

I had volunteered for this assignment, and this ship. The offer presented was too tempting: a brand-spanking-new "one-off" CIC, unlike any other in the fleet. There was a truly integrated CDS (Combat Direction System), touted to be the "next best thing to AEGIS" before AEGIS dominated the fleet; a weapons suite unsurpassed by any other surface combatant; Tomahawk & Harpoon missile box launchers; dual MK 30 5/38 gun mounts; two MK-10 double rail missile launchers firing SM-2(ER) missiles; two MK-32 torpedo mounts; and MT 21 & 22 CIWS mounts. We were loaded for bear, a play on words that reminds me of our expected rendezvous with the Russian "Bear" bombers in the now-familiar "Bear Box" northeast of Guam. The "Cold War" may have been cooler, but the game would still be played, as it had been for decades.

This would be my last "WestPac"! When I return from deployment this time, I would rotate ashore and from there, retirement to the "Fleet Reserve." The experiences and the differences between my first deployment and this one are what have defined my career. The evolution of my duties, training and skill-set marks the contrast between these bookends. A shooting war has ended; the "Cold War" and its challenges have evolved. Nothing is ever the same from one deployment to the next, as this one will bear out!

I miss it and I don't! Ask any sailor and he will tell you the same!

BLUEJACKET

CHAPTER 1

ENLISTING

AFTER GRADUATING FROM HIGH SCHOOL in June of 1968, I spent the summer working at a summer camp in the Santa Cruz mountains. In the fall, I enrolled at the junior college back home. I registered with the draft board, and held a 2-S deferment so I could continue school. That lasted until around February/March of the following year. Sitting in Psych 101 waiting for class to begin, a buddy of mine sat down next to me and began opening his mail. Tim lived on campus and as this class was his first after lunch break, he had run back to his dorm to pick up his mail. He came to a brown envelope with government logo and when he read its contents, he told me it was his draft notice. "Don't you have a 2-S deferment?" I asked. To which he replied he did. Now anxious about what my status might be, I cut class and went directly to the Administration Building. One of my mother's friends and a close neighbor worked there. I found her and explained what had just happened to Tim. She shook her head and said the 2-S deferments had been stopped and that a notice had been posted on the campus kiosk close to the Student Union and hadn't I read that? Of course, the answer was no, because hardly anybody paid any attention to all the garbage that was normally posted there.

I had a cousin who was two years my senior who had been drafted and was currently "in country" over there with the 9th Infantry Division south of Saigon.

Before his going over he had spent a week visiting his mom, close to where we lived and we had spent some time together. Shortly before John left, he took on a serious tone and made it a point that I know I was not to wait to be drafted. "Even if the only option left is another branch of service, take it," he advised. Like most of my peers, I'd watched the nightly news: Cronkite, Safer and the rest, with their daily clips and stories; the shooting in the street of the VC by the ARVN officer; TET and the battle for Hue. It was a messy, god-awful waste and I personally didn't want to commit myself to a war I didn't believe was worth dying for and was impossible to win, given the political restraints in place. But, I was a product of my generation and also knew that if push came to shove, I would do my duty to my country. But, on my own terms and not the draft board's, nor the Army's!

After seeing Tim's draft notice, I heeded my cousin's advice and went downtown to the Post Office, then up the elevator to the third floor where the recruiting offices were located. Walking down the hall, I saw no signs, just branch of service seals on the glass doors and they were all open so you didn't see the seals as you were passing. At the end of the hall, the door stood open and I walked in, not knowing which service this office represented. But, behind the desk a big burly Marine (I recognized the uniform) popped tall and with a big grin asked what he could do for me. Realizing my mistake, I waved him off and mumbled something about being in the wrong office, turned and left.

Two doors up, with the door open, I glanced in and recognized the "squid suit" of the man behind the desk and walked in. After a brief discussion, the recruiter asked if I would commit to taking a basic battery test. He explained that the results would determine where I would be placed on the waiting list. "Waiting list?" I asked. "Yes," he replied and pointed to a wall chart showing how many other applicants were already on the list. So, I spent the next hour or so taking the test and when I finished, he told me they would call in a few days and let me know where the test scores placed me.

Going home and telling my parents what I had done was not fun. My mother sat for a long time, holding my enlistment papers and not saying a word. Explaining to her why it needed to be done didn't seem to change her outlook. Dad understood but didn't have much to say. Sure enough, a couple days later the recruiter called and asked me to come down to the office. When I got there, the first thing he said was "When do you want to go?" "What about the list?" I asked. He explained that I had scored high enough that I was now number three on the list and the two in front of me would be leaving in the next few days.

I told him anytime in the coming week would be fine, so we settled on that upcoming Wednesday. I was given my transportation voucher and ordered to proceed on 2 April 1969 to the Induction Center at Oakland, California. I don't recall exactly, but the Greyhound bus left at some ungodly hour and for the first few hours we traveled in the dark. Because we stopped at most of the "burgs" along the way, the trip was even longer than the eight hours it would take driving in a car. Finally, after changing buses in San Francisco we arrived in Oakland. I had been directed to make my way to the USO and to report to the active duty check-in desk for further direction. I checked in there and was given a voucher for a room close by in what I could only call a "flea bag" hotel. I was told to report the following morning to the USO for roll-call and directions to the induction center.

After eating lunch the day I arrived, I decided to call a girl I had met while working at the summer camp in the Santa Cruz mountains the previous year. She was excited when I called and asked if I could come to dinner that night at her house — she would pick me up! So, around six that night, I met her out front of the hotel and she took me home. The family lived up in the Oakland hills and was quite well to do. Her dad was an architect and developer in the local real estate market — obviously a sharp cookie! Anyway, dinner was nice. The girl's mom was really kind, but dad didn't say much, just kept giving me the evil eye! Finally, around 9PM, my "date" took me back to the hotel. When we got there she asked if she could come up! Being a sharp cookie myself, I gladly said "sure." As we went up the elevator and stepped out into the hall, I saw that the place was crawling with guys waiting for their trip to the induction center, same as I was. My date, seeing all the ogling eyes, cast a worried glance in my direction. As I opened my room door and we stepped in there must have been a dozen or more wolf whistles and cat calls that followed us. After closing the door, she became less intimidated and went for the clench! Falling onto the bed, it got hot and heavy fast. Then, the phone rang! Not thinking (with my big head, anyway), I picked it up. "Hello?" I said. It was her mom! Shit! She asked if her daughter was there and I quickly told her that she had dropped me off and I had only just walked into the room when she called. What I knew was that if she hadn't called, in another ten minutes (or less), her daughter would be more than just a few minutes late and worse for the wear. But, she certainly wasn't going to hear that from me! She thanked me and hung up. My "date" had put herself back together and was out the door before I had even hung up the phone. That was the last I ever saw or heard from her. A close-run thing, that!

At the induction center the following morning I witnessed what we termed the "cattle call" in all its assembly-line efficiency. I went through all the required medical tests, was poked, prodded, submitted to four or five blood samples, and filled out endless paperwork. One of the medical inspections was performed in a large room with us guinea pigs standing against all four walls — naked. Looking across the room, my side of the wall got an embarrassing view of some poor kid across the way that had testicles the size of large grapefruit! Whoa! He was rapidly eliminated from the process after some professional kibitzing among the doctors about his condition.

When the group of inductees I was assigned to had completed all that was required, we were taken to an office and told to wait. Shortly, a Navy officer (I've forgotten the man's rank) entered the room, followed by a couple senior enlisted types. He had us stand in ranks and told us we were now going to be inducted into the Department of the Navy and take our oaths of enlistment. Immediately after, a Marine Corps Captain and a Gunny Sergeant made an appearance and proceeded up and down our ranks, picking out eight or nine of our number and informing them that they were now the property of the Marine Corps. Just like that! At 6 foot and 159 pounds, I was a pretty scrawny looking prospect and the Captain had picked all the bigger, brawnier types. For once, I was sure glad to be skinny! We were all very surprised at what had just happened until one of the sailors in the room pointed out the fact that the Marine Corps was a branch of the Navy!

That night, I was flown to San Diego to begin Boot Camp. Arriving in the early evening, we were told at the "Navy Desk" at the airport to fall in outside the airport doors, a line of us on each side. At the next door down we noticed two lines of prospective Marine boots doing the same, though their lines were much longer. After waiting a couple hours, a bus showed up and we were herded onboard for the ride to NTC. As we pulled away, we noticed that the Marines were still there waiting.

It was now after 9PM. By the time we were led into barracks, provided with sheets and pillows and put to bed it was around 11PM. We were woken at reveille, which was 5AM and taken to the chow hall for breakfast at 6AM. *It would be a long day!* Then began the endless "hurry up and wait" that would be the hallmark of years to come and accepted as the norm: sea bag issue; hair-cut; inoculations; line up here, fall out there, double-time, quick-time, parade rest! Your life was now under micro-management!

"BOOT"

In 1969, U.S. Navy Boot Camp was conducted in two locations, Great Lakes, Illinois and San Diego (Although NTC Orlando had just opened the previous July). If you were from the western regions of the country, you would most likely be assigned to go to Boot Camp in San Diego, although I've heard that this was not always the case.

I was assigned to Recruit Training Company 69-274, the 69 representing the year and the last three numbers signifying the 274th company of that year. At the time, Boot Camp was divided into two commands. RTC (Recruit Training Command) was the first command you reported to and involved most of the basic marching & drill. You were taught how to march in formation, issued your "piece" and learned how to perform the 16-count manual at arms. One of the first tasks you had to accomplish was the stenciling of all your navy uniforms. This was done as a group in a large room where we could spread out and work. Stencils were cut with your last name outlined, all in the same "font" size. It was your job to apply the stencil in the prescribed location because each type of clothing called for a different location. On your dungaree shirt, the stencil had to be centered and applied over the left breast pocket. That worked fine for most guys, but not so much when your last name has more than ten letters, such as mine. With eleven letters in my last name, the stencil started just outside the button line and ended in my armpit!

Another lesson applied was how to fold and stow all the clothing in your sea bag, and in the limited space allotted. This entailed specific instruction given by our DI (Drill Instructor) in how to fold your pants, shirts, socks, skivvies, t-shirts, and anything else that could or should be folded. Making up your bunk in the prescribed military manner was another lesson given to us by our DI. Sheets and blanket folded and tucked at the prescribed angle and a quarter had to bounce at the expected height or your bunk didn't pass inspection.

The second command segment of Boot Camp was at NTC (Naval Training Center), which was on the other side of a waterway from the RTC and reachable by a bridge. When the boot company completed the RTC portion of training, the company relocated to another barracks across the bridge. NTC was where most of our naval classroom lessons and technical training was conducted. This included first aid, swimming, the use of sound-powered phones, knot tying, proper use of a gas mask and the never- ending marching in formation and close order drill.

Boot Camp was designed to separate you from your individuality and drill into you the fact that you were a "cog in the wheel" of an organization that required you to react instinctually to orders. In this, our instructors were proficient! Before the time of "training time-outs" .... and sensitivity training, there were blanket parties (in the middle of the night, a selected group would throw a blanket over an offender and deliver their bruising form of punishment) and shower room bristle brush parties (for those people who avoided personal hygiene). These involved hard scrubbing brushes used in washing clothes, applied by a group of peers until several layers of skin had been removed from the offender's body. Group punishment administered by DIs for an infraction incurred by an individual, and sundry other minor ordeals, were designed to remind the individual and the collective that if one "cog" failed, the whole "wheel" failed. For more serious infractions, there was also 20/30, which was a punishment detail where the offending individual carried two buckets, one on each arm, and a shovel. He would proceed to a pile of sand (at the double), fill up his buckets in rapid time and then double-time to a designated area where he was to deposit the sand and repeat the process until the one pile was gone. He would then commence to remove the sand from the new pile and displace it back to its original site! This was both humorous and scary while watching – humorous because you weren't doing it and scary because it *could be you*!

As a company, our performance sucked. We couldn't get to our next assignment on time, we had a high failure rate of personnel not passing tasks assigned, and we couldn't march in formation worth beans. The third week of boot, our

8

DI was transferred out and we got a new one. This guy had been "pushing boots" for a couple years and had graduated companies with top ranking performance marks. And, he immediately informed us that we would too. The first thing he did was to call out one of the Filipinos in our company and, as we stood by watching, barked out marching orders and cadence to which our tough little shipmate executed flawlessly. We were thoroughly impressed and collectively embarrassed. Our new DI next informed us that this man would now carry the company guide-on, which would place him out in front of us, and that we were to observe him as a means to execute our marching orders. We rapidly improved our performance while marching in formation. Later, in barracks, some of us struck up a conversation with our Filipino shipmate and asked him how he was able to perform so well. He told us that back in the Philippines, he had spent weeks enduring a "prep" course for our Boot Camp, which was much tougher than what we would experience. We were even more impressed.

Most days consisted of "rifle drill" (to the 16-count manual at arms) on the "grinder" (the asphalt drill field), which we later learned, comprised our entire routine during our graduation ceremony. You carried your "piece" about four hours a day and it was often incorporated into one of the DI's favorite forms of punishment for minor infractions. This little number was performed as a push-up, with a twist. Done with the butt and muzzle perpendicular to the ground, you couldn't keep your wrists from rolling the piece onto your knuckles and against the asphalt. Everyone had skinned up knuckles. When you weren't running through the 16-count manual at arms, you were in class studying that day's agenda: seamanship, communications, first aid, etc. Early on and during one of our morning formation marching drills, the company came to a quick halt at the bark of the DI and those of us up front could hear him chewing out one of our shipmates at the back of the company. Like a dumb ass, I swiveled my head around to see who the guilty party was. Bad move! In seconds I found myself on the receiving end of a boot being applied to my butt and sending me sprawling out of formation. Now, I was the one receiving the ass chewing for rubber-necking in formation. Lesson learned!

MAIL CALL

Also included in the curriculum were trips to the rifle range, fire-fighting mock-ups, swimming and the dreaded "gas chamber." This bit of training was designed to instill fear and enforce familiarization with the correct donning of a gas mask. First, we were all herded into the chamber, packed in tightly. Then, a light concentration of tear gas was released while we all stood counting off, as instructed. Upon command, we were then instructed to don our masks while the instructors went up and down the ranks, ensuring we had put them on correctly and obtained a seal to prevent further exposure to the gas. Once everyone had passed their inspection, we were ordered to proceed, in a calm and orderly fashion, out the door of the chamber and into ranks outside. A hurdle passed and thankfully, not repeated.

An observant person, seeing how the boot company hierarchy was arranged, could lobby himself into a position of minor importance and thereby find himself excluded from some of the more distasteful and mundane of the company's duties. A key point was to take one of the lesser positions and thereby still maintain some semblance of obscurity. Higher positions were subject to more scrutiny. As I was "in tight" with the RCPO (Recruit Chief Petty Officer), who happened to be an ex-Marine, I was able to secure the company assignment as EPO (Education Petty Officer), which entailed very few actual duties and was one or two steps up from the bottom of the company management organization. Obscurity is good — right?

It was around our third week in boot when news of the "Hong Kong Flu" virus made headlines. Although the civilian population hadn't been provided with an approved serum, the DOD or DON (Dept. of the Navy) was given one for their use and we being guinea pigs were directed to a building where the shot was to be given. As instructed, we lined up into two columns to go through the two front doors to the building. As we made our way through the line, we came up to a table, provided name and service number and moved past the table with the instruction to get to the next station with pants already down, bent over and obligingly poked in the ass with the needle! After being patted on the butt with a cotton swab, we were directed to pull up our pants and hustle out the back door to form up in company formation and await further orders. Back at the barracks that night there was a lot of bitching and moaning about how we had been treated, but what could you do?

Later into our boot tour we were loaded onto buses and driven over to the Balboa Naval Hospital complex. Ordered off the buses and into one of the buildings, we found out we had "volunteered" to give blood — Vietnam demanded it. Anyway, after we had all donated our pint to the cause, we were marched over to the hospital "chow hall" and served steak dinners. They could have kept the steak! Going down the serving line I discovered they had an ice cream machine. I made more than one trip, as did quite a few of the other guys!

About the fourth week of training, our company was selected to perform its mandatory "'service week," which for us meant Galley Duty. The first day of our service week, reveille was at 0330 and fall-out at 0400 for muster in the "loading dock" area of the galley. Other assigned companies were also mustered there with us. As we all stood in ranks, a person standing on the loading platform in front of us introduced himself as the person in charge of this particular area and began talking to us about what to expect and how we would be formed into squads to be assigned to various locations and duties throughout the galley. At the end of this short introduction, he said he wanted a volunteer before any further assignments would be made. We all stood silently, no hands were raised. Somewhere a neuron fired off and a synapse farted and my hand went up. And, a voice in my head was screaming, "Who the hell authorized that?" A couple of the guys standing close to me looked at me like I was crazy. I mean, didn't everyone know that volunteering was what put us into this situation in the first place? The man on the loading dock saw my hand and told me to move forward and take a place next to him. When I had done so, he informed me and everyone standing below in formation, that I would be his relief and take his place in charge of the galley loading dock area. Our company's "service week" ended up becoming two weeks and so, for that period, I was charged with mustering all the boot company personnel providing manpower to the galley and ensuring that assignments were parceled out and requirements met. I was provided with an office and desk and was told to pick three people for my "staff." I couldn't believe my good fortune. The down-side was that I was expected to account for shortages in personnel, even when that shortage was not within my authority to correct or address. So, I robbed Peter to pay Paul on a daily basis. I guess I kept enough people happy because I wasn't canned. Or maybe, they couldn't find another sucker like me to volunteer. Yep, I had definitely violated my own rule-of-thumb regarding obscurity.

During the latter part of my stay at RTC, the company was marched over to the NTC side of the base and into a large classroom for further aptitude tests that would determine where the Navy would place you upon graduation. Lower scores typically dictated that you would immediately join the fleet aboard ship as a "deck hand" and an "undesignated" seaman apprentice. Higher scores would mean you could be sent to a Navy school for further training in one of the technical rates. When the scores came back you were individually called in to an interview with a detailer who would tell you the results and your choices of assignment. I must have done pretty well because I was told that I could attend "nuke" school, ET school or RD school. I found out, during the interview, that RD "A" School was at Treasure Island, California, and that pretty much settled that as far as I was concerned. I would be on familiar turf and about 90 minutes flying time from home!

I was graduated from boot camp on June 17, 1969. It was just four days after my 19th birthday!

TREASURE ISLAND & RADARMAN "A" SCHOOL

28 July '69 to 14 Nov '69

RD "A" School, Treasure Island, CA

Upon graduation from Boot Camp, my orders read that I had two weeks leave and was then to report for duty at Radarman "A" School, Treasure Island, California for the 16-week COI (Course of Instruction). After checking in at personnel and being assigned a barracks, I was told my class would not commence for another week. During that time, at morning muster, those in the same status as me were given work assignments by the mustering Petty Officer. One job I recall was waxing and buffing the floors in one of the barracks assigned to the Vietnamese Navy personnel who were there attending U.S. Navy schools in their specialties. The first thing you did when entering their barracks was open every door and window you could, because the smell of "fish sauce" would overwhelm you. They had little "hot plate" stations in the barracks where they could cook their own meals and, boy, did it ever smell like it. Once my class commenced, we were still on rotation with everyone else in our barracks to clean the heads (bathrooms) or wax and buff the decks (floors).

I didn't do too well the first two weeks of school, which happened to be electronics; I was having too much fun and not studying. So, I failed the first two weekly exams. They brought me up in front of the "Academic Review Board" and told me to "shape up or ship out" and if I failed another exam, it would be the latter. They set me back two weeks to another class and I began over from the Week One curriculum. I started studying a couple hours a week, took better notes and didn't go off base except on weekends after that. My lowest test score from that point on was 87% and most of the exams I either aced or scored 90%. I surely didn't want to be sent to the fleet as a boatswain's mate or gunner's mate (even though I wasn't exactly sure what those were). No thanks

As I mentioned, the first two weeks of the course was dedicated to basic electronics and later was a couple weeks studying radar theory, application and propagation, including the effects of atmospherics such as attenuation and harmonics. Then, it was on to the lab, which was a large room full of radar repeaters so that individual students could be seated at each repeater for practical experience on the mechanics of how to use that particular model. In our case, this was the SPA-8 and SPA-25 repeater models. The SPA-8 were configured with "joysticks" (left and right handed) to manipulate the range and bearing indicators, and the SPA-25 used dials to perform the same function. And, of course one of the areas of practical experience — and obviously on the low-tech end of the training — was learning to write backwards on a Plexiglas status board with a grease pencil. This skill allowed the "plotter" stationed to receive data over his sound powered phones or an R/T circuit and plot that data on a status board for decision makers to see and use. Mostly this procedure has been overcome by technology, but there is still a requirement to maintain these types of status boards, with data that is infrequently changed for specific, extended periods or is currently not configured to be loaded into digital displays.

A few more weeks of class time were spent on tactical signals and their publications. The primary publication used for preparing and sending these tactical signals was ATP-1 (Allied Tactical Publication). We were informed by the instructor that owing to the publication's possible compromise when the USS Pueblo was captured by the North Koreans in January 1968, that by the time we got to the fleet, the publication succeeding it would probably be in effect. So we should expect changes to what we were being taught at the time.

Another area of study involved the use of the maneuvering board to plot and solve maneuvering problems of multiple ships in formation, including formation changes and course and speed changes. One mistake anywhere during the multiple maneuvers and your final solutions would be wrong. Although you felt confident after solving each evolution, at the end of the test, you were left to wonder!

Weekends spent on liberty were some of the best. I was only 250 miles from home and the Bay Area was home to family friends and many of the people I had met while working at the summer camp in the Santa Cruz mountains the previous summer. Because it was summertime I spent many of my weekends in Orinda, a small town just east of the Hwy 24 tunnel. These were friends of my parents and they had a pool in the backyard and their daughter, Shelly. I had known Shelly since my early teens when the family had lived in my hometown. They also had a summer place at Lake Berryessa up in the foothills northeast of Napa, and it was there that summer that I learned to water ski. Shelly would take the MG, drive me back to T.I. and drop me off at the gate Sunday evenings. Shelly was a sweet kid and I did like her a lot. But I confess to having a phobia and just couldn't get past all those freckles. A couple of the guys in my class saw me one time as she dropped me off and really put the elbow on me to "hook them up, too." Sorry, guys! When I wasn't with Shelly in Orinda, I was hopping a "stand-by" flight to home on Air West (or Air Worst as everyone called it back then). As my pay didn't allow me to do this too often, my parents would subsidize my fare. I would pay for the trip up and they would pay for the trip back. Riding military stand-by (meaning that you had to show up wearing your swabby suit) was $50 round-trip back then. My pay checks were around $35, every two weeks.

Another favorite activity, when we could afford it, was a trip into "San Fran" with a classmate and buddy from Boulder, Colorado. We would set aside $20 (more than half our pay) and spend the preceding days picking out a restaurant or agreeing on a type of food. It had to be within our means and of a different cuisine from any we had tried previously. And, in S.F. that was easy to do. Chinese, Russian, a steak house, smorgasbord, Irish, Hungarian — it was all there and we really enjoyed ourselves. One of these trips was the first time I ever ate octopus and escargot. Call 'em what you want, *they're still snails*!

During the last couple weeks of school occurred an incident that would make evident the Cold War was right out there on our doorstep. A call had gone out from the *USS Twining* (DD 540), which was berthed at T.I., for bodies to fill out her reserve crew so that it could perform its assigned mission to get underway for the Pacific Missile Range and persuade an invasive Russian intel ship to leave the vicinity. This NRF (Naval Reserve Force) ship hadn't time to recall her reservists and needed "warm bodies" for CIC to assist the core crew. The class that preceded us was selected for "volunteers" and those numbers necessary went aboard and got underway with the ship. Well, the next day the *Twining* was back in port due to a mechanical problem and could not fulfill the assignment. But, the students that had been sent aboard told of the ship's transit. Most of them "rotated" over the railing (seasick) and had a miserable trip. We were all glad our class had avoided that one!

USS Twining DD 540 @ Treasure Island, CA

I must mention here that *Twining* was a "stud"! Tried, tested and true, a WWII Fletcher class destroyer that had seen plenty of action both in WWII and Korea. She was awarded eight battle stars during WWII and five battle stars during the Korean War.

IN TRANSIT TO SOUTHEAST ASIA

Upon graduating from RD "A" School, my orders read that I had two weeks leave and then would proceed to my assigned duty station, the aircraft carrier USS *Constellation* (CVA-64), then on deployment off the coast of Vietnam. The leave I was granted meant that I would be home for Thanksgiving, but also that I would be leaving the following day. My orders stated that upon completion of leave I was to report for travel overseas at Travis AFB.

Now, from 1969 to the present, modes of travel really haven't changed all that much and so the means by which I made my way overseas weren't all that different from those of today. The difference was that there was a war on and your orders also stated "at the convenience of the government," which meant you'd get there when they got you there, no matter how long that took. In my case and for this trip, it took close to a week. Checking in at Travis AFB was like checking into a busy terminal at LAX: people in uniform running and walking from here to there, people sleeping in corners on the floor or on their sea bags or duffel bags, long lines and short tempers on both sides of the counters. Early that evening we boarded a Tiger Airlines flight taking us to Hickam AFB, Oahu. We made a brief stop for a crew change (we weren't allowed off the plane) and then it was off to Wake Island. While they refueled the plane, they let us off for about an hour and we all stood around outside the small, stuffy terminal area until it was time to re-board the aircraft. From Wake Island, we flew into Clark AFB, Philippines arriving in the dead of night. After waiting around the terminal for a few hours, the group I was with was told to board a bus outside that would take us to the Naval Station at Subic Bay. About an hour into the trip and somewhere up in the mountains, the bus pulled over, the doors opened and two heavily armed Filipino's in uniform boarded. No one said a word, us or them. You could feel the tension in the air. What the heck was going on? After walking the full length of the bus, the two departed, the doors closed and the bus pulled out. The guys up front quizzed the driver about what had just happened. Word came back through the bus that the Filipino Army was looking for Huks (Filipino insurgents)! What the hell Huks would be doing aboard a U.S. Navy bus loaded with American servicemen was beyond us. We were now very anxious to get where we were going and out of the mountains.

By the time we finished the trip across the Zambales Mountains and made it onto Subic Bay Naval Base it was around two in the morning and we were all groggy from being up so long and traveling all day and night. Someone assigned us bunks, gave us sheets and pillowcases and told us reveille would be at 0500! So, we made up our bunks and climbed in for a "nap."

The next thing I remember is someone trying to wake me, shaking the rack (bed) and in a not too soft voice telling me to "get your ass" out of bed! That was when I met Rudy Pantoja, (also en route to the *Connie*) with whom I became best friends and still see from time to time. Once dressed, I was directed to the "chow hall" which was pretty small and only served personnel assigned to the "transit barracks" which I was assigned to. Finishing breakfast and walking back over to the barracks, we were directed to "fall in" on numbered circles on the asphalt in front of the barracks. Muster was held at 0600 and we were given instructions from the mustering Petty Officer about what our duty assignments would be for that day. The next three days were spent doing some of the nastiest jobs I would ever experience in the Navy: cleaning bilges and cleaning garbage cans! If it stunk or was dirty, we cleaned it. All in the oppressive heat and humidity of the tropics. It was something that would take some getting used to!

Coming off leave and not having been paid for more than two weeks, I didn't have much coin in my pocket for any "night on the town." I think I had five or six dollars to my name. But the second night Rudy talked about going into town and said we could "pool" our funds. Well, that didn't amount to much as he didn't have much more than I did. But we did manage to spend a couple hours "outside the gate" before our funds ran out. So much for my first "liberty" in a foreign country.

However, for those few dollars and during that limited exposure to such a foreign environment, I made some observations that would stand me in good stead on following liberties in that port. I've never been there, but I've been told that Naples, Italy in the fifties and early sixties was the MedCruise equivalent of the WestPac experience at Subic Bay. Wild, fun, anything goes, adult Disneyland….all those adjectives and comparisons. But, also, unpredictable and dangerous if you didn't "play by the rules." Subic Bay could be that way and it was up to you to learn and play by the rules: don't take advantage, don't act like an "Ugly American," don't go on liberty alone, and don't drink to the point that you do any of the above. "Shit

River" separated the Naval Station from the town and was so named because it stunk to high heaven and was noted as being a disposal area for much of the refuse of Olongapo and American sailors who didn't follow the rules. When you walked past the Marine Guard on the Naval Station side of the river, you had to be aware that everything on the other side was designed to separate you from your money, legally or otherwise. As soon as you crossed the bridge your senses were assaulted and overwhelmed with the noise, smells and sights of a place like no other: Jeepneys and motorcycles with sidecars spewing smoke and noise up and down the street, belching claustrophobic exhaust into the already stifling tropic heat and humidity; hawkers and shills on every street corner competing for your attention and dollar; neon signs flashing above every venue (restaurants, bars, money exchange cages, whatever); the smell of BBQ coming from small vendor stands every few yards; security guards at every door armed with shotguns and looking bored; drunk sailors staggering down the street; bar girls dressed to entice and stationed at the doors trying to lure you inside; the sour smell of someone that couldn't handle his liquor and contributed his deposit right there, multiplied and drying on the sidewalk; music blaring from every doorway, seeming to compete with the other senses and beckoning for your attention. That was Olongapo in 1970.

The third day after our arrival, we were put on a bus and taken back to Clark AFB for further transfer to the ship. This was another twisting, turning, hair-raising journey through the Zambales Mountains but with the added benefit of making the trip during daylight and being able to see the sheer drop-offs and chasms we had missed on our way to Subic in the dead of night. Arriving in mid-afternoon at the airbase, we checked in and commenced to "hurry up and wait" for our flight to be called. By late afternoon we were looking for a place to eat and get away from the crowd at the air terminal, so we checked with the counter. The airman told us we still had enough time to make a trip to the Enlisted Men's Club for a meal and if we remained there we would be able to hear our flight being called over the club's PA system. So, that's where we were four hours later, when they called our flight. When the club PA system called out "All personnel manifested on Flight Number XXXX, destination Da Nang, the place erupted in cheers and clapping as those of us taking that flight stood to leave. As we walked out of the club to catch the waiting bus back to the terminal, I could tell everyone else felt as self-conscious as I did and couldn't shake the feeling. Later, in the terminal, one guy joked that maybe the send-off was because they were glad some-one else was going and not them! Maybe it was because this type of full-voiced patriotism conflicted so much with the mood of the country we had just left.

Our aircraft was a C-130 MAC (Military Airlift Command) plane. The seat-ing was nylon webbing and polyurethane, in rows mounted in rails embedded in tracks on the deck. Directly behind us, piled high above our heads and held in place by nylon webbing was our baggage and whatever supplies could be squeezed in by the loadmaster.

Compared to the previous legs of our journey across the Pacific, this one was relatively short. Arriving in the early morning around 4AM we USN person-nel were transported over to the Navy compound and left sitting in a large open-bay plywood structure. Shortly after 5AM we were directed to a small screened plywood "chow hall" that seated about 50 and had black-out curtains. When you opened the door, the lights inside went out and when the door closed the lights came back on. When this happened while eating, we rookies froze in place, food or drink frozen in space on their way to our mouths or the table, until the lights came back on! Bussing the tables were native women and it struck me that so many of them couldn't have been more than 4-foot-8, appeared to be in their late teens and just about all of them were 5 or 6 months pregnant!

After breakfast, we went back to our "hangar" area and melted in the heat as the temperature rose with the sun. Before lunch and probably around 10AM, we were roused from our sweaty seats on our sea bags and hustled back over to the airstrip. We were delivered to a two engine prop aircraft and boarded as our names were called. Funny though — all the seats were facing toward the back of the plane!

As we approached the *Connie* and "on final," you could feel the pilot making minor adjustments to the controls as the aircraft slipped and slid slightly. The sound of engines and props changed pitch and RPMs. As he "followed the ball" from the Glide Slope Indicator, your gut tightened and did a little pirouette as you waited for the "trap" in anticipation of the aircraft hook catching a wire. Then there were weak, relieved smiles all around as the arresting gear made for quick deceleration. This was my first and only landing on a carrier. Then and there, my opinion was formed that the pilots and flight deck crews more than earned that extra little stipend from Uncle Sugar!

For a detailed description of the process, here is a good link:

http://www.airspacemag.com/how-things-work/the-meatball-8421491/

(Keep in mind that the system used back in the '60s and '70s was not the same as that being used today, but the basic principles are the same.)

Grumman C-1A COD "On Final"

CHAPTER 2
WESTPAC 69 & 70
(11 AUGUST 1969 – 8 MAY 1970)

USS CONSTELLATION (CVA-64)

Days Deployed: 270

Days "On the Line": 128

Seven aircraft lost; One man taken **POW**, but no men died.

USS Constellation CVA-64

On Yankee Station: 7 - 22 December 1969; 5 -30 January 1970; 12 February 1970 -1 March 1970; 26 March 1970 -17 April 1970

LIFE ABOARD A CARRIER AT SEA

The first week aboard ship was spent "checking in" with all the various offices aboard ship and in the process learning how to get around on such a large ship as the *Connie*. First stop in the process was at the Personnel Office, where they took your "service jacket" for their records (excluding those portions of your record that were needed elsewhere during your check-in). You were then handed a "Routing Sheet," which contained a list of all the places you had to go for check-in and a spot for that office to sign off on that you had completed checking in with them. The list filled the sheet! So, off I went with a couple other guys, one of whom seemed to know the "lay of the land" and was able to get us around to quite a few locations in the process. Lunch break was over and I was at it again, but this time without a tour guide! So, I only managed a couple more signatures that afternoon.

When I had been taken to OI Division that first day, I had been assigned a bunk in a five-rack tier that was used for newly arrived personnel because there were more people than there were regular three-tiered "coffin racks." So you had to wait your turn and would be reassigned once someone else left. The five-tiered racks were not conducive to sleeping because they were canvas stretched over aluminum tubing with a mattress about two or three inches thick. The bunk above you was only about 14 inches from yours and by the time you horizontally wormed your way into your rack, you only had a few inches to spare. Because people above you climbed in and out, there were feet and hands intruding into your rack at any and all hours.

During the check-in process, I was required to be present at the division morning "muster," which was usually held inside one of the CIC spaces. After that, I was turned loose to pursue more signatures. So each morning, the LPO would check my routing sheet and see what progress I had made and, in turn, I could ask for some directions on how to get to or find any of the places I had not been able to locate through my own efforts. Some of the more "out of the way" places on the routing sheets were giving me a headache trying to locate. The ship's Library? *Give me a break!*

After finally completing the check-in process, I was assigned to watch rotation in CIC, where the Watch Supervisor would assign rotation stations during my eight-hour period on watch. Eight hours on, eight hours off! Seven days a week, four weeks a month or until the ship pulled into port! No weekends, no holidays, and the only exception was if you were in sick-bay and physically unable to perform your duties. Even though I had completed "A" School, aboard ship in CIC I was still considered a "boot" and I was told that much of what I had learned in "A" school would be pretty much useless "in the fleet." Actually, nothing at the school house could prepare you for the steep learning curve that CIC on a carrier would require. *Connie's* CIC was outfitted with Naval Tactical Data Systems consoles, which I had seen in pictures at the school, but pictures were all I really knew of it. Now I was expected to learn how to use one in a variety of roles and functions, during the course of a watch period. A typical watch rotation for me, during my first few weeks aboard ship, consisted of being woke up an hour prior to the beginning of my watch period so that I could wash up, get dressed and rush down to the chow hall for a quick bite to eat. Then, back up to CIC by quarter-to the hour watch turn-over was expected (so you could get a "pass down" on what was happening at that watch station). The Watch Supervisor made up the station rotation for that period, so you first had to find out which station you were going to start at. This might be manning a radio circuit at a comms table in D&D and writing in a log book everything that came across the circuit. I would do that for a couple hours and be relieved by someone else and then I would proceed to my next station, which might be a NTDS console manned and used to track aircraft. After a couple hours of that, I would be relieved and then proceed to my next assigned station, which might be the (NTDS) Airtrack ID Console, where you would use the IFF device installed to establish identities of the tracks that the "air tracker" was entering into the tactical data system. And, so the rotation would proceed until your eight hour watch period was over. Midwatch was the exception to the routine because around 2AM, the lights would be turned on and the junior personnel would grab brooms and dustpans for a quick 20 or 30 minutes exercise at moving the dirt around. Trash receptacles would be emptied and a quick swab job would wipe away coffee or soda residue on the rubber safety matting. Done with watch, you would again make a trip to the chow hall for whichever meal was being served and then back up to OI berthing. Write some letters, do some reading, take a shower, play some cards, watch some CCTV (if it was on the air) and then "hit the rack" because your next eight hours in CIC were coming up all too soon.

IN PORT SUBIC BAY, R.P.

24 Dec. '69 – 3 Jan. '70

Connie departed Yankee Station and proceeded en route Subic Bay, R.P. for a port call that would encompass Christmas and New Year's, a rare occurrence, given our normal tasking. All the ship's in port were decked out in traditional Navy Christmas lighting and *Connie* was no exception, although, I found it a bit incongruous watching shoppers at the Exchange wearing Christmas apparel with their shorts and flip-flops. One of the first things I did when we pulled in was to arrange for a phone call to the folks. Back then, you went to the Telephone Exchange, signed up on the roster for your name to be called and took a seat and *waited*! The first three minutes were $8 and I usually tried to keep my calls to less than ten minutes so it wouldn't take too much of my pay. I recall one time my bill was almost $30 and I vowed never to do that again. You could also call by HAM radio, but few of us did. Who wants to have a conversation with an audience and have to say "Over" all the time? I did enough of that aboard ship manning the various R/T circuits.

Because this was my first liberty ashore with "shipmates," I had departed the ship with a group of four or five guys that had "seen the elephant" and I figured that it would be best to be in company of guys who knew their way around. After leaving the ship, we headed for the PX building that housed all the stereo, sound and recording merchandise to do some shopping. As we were coming out and walking down one of the busier streets on base, I was introduced to a new sport by one of the "saltier" guys in the group. He had spied a group of Ensigns across the street, and he pulled us up short and asked if we wanted to have some fun. Sure thing! So, he told us what was up and we all agreed to go along with his plan. We crossed the street about half a block in front of our "targets" strung out in a line. The young officers had been deep in conversation as they walked and hadn't noticed us. But, as our leader approached them he called out "Good morning, sirs" and rendered a snappy salute. This brought them to attention and they answered the salute, each of them breaking off an answering salute as they passed. Each of us following our ring leader, followed his example and by the time the last of us passed, you could tell that the Ensign's had caught on and were not very happy that they had been "had" by a bunch of E-2s and E-3s! I guess you had to be there. Anyway, it made for many exaggerated re-tellings over beers out in town!

During our in-port period the command scheduled a full dress uniform personnel inspection, to be held on the flight deck. Of course, our tropical dress uniform was blouse and bell-bottom "whites." The morning of inspection everyone was in berthing tweaking their uniforms: a last-minute touch up to their shoe-shine; standing in line to use the ironing board to eliminate any stray wrinkles; checking and double-checking for any "Irish pennants;" and generally standing by for the word to be passed to muster on the flight deck. Inspection was to commence at 0800 and so everyone was mustered on the flight deck 30 minutes prior. Each division's officers and senior enlisteds nervously moved up and down the ranks, checking for anything out of the ordinary and aligning and re-aligning ranks or reordering personnel by height. By this time, it was after 0800 and, even at this hour, the sun began to take its toll. You could feel the heat from the flight deck already coming through the soles of your shoes. It was too early in the day for any breeze off the water and the air was still and heavy. Another, 15 or 20 minutes passed and the shoe polish we had worked so hard on, started melting and the sweat running down your back went from a trickle to a steady steam. We had been standing at attention for about 40 minutes when the first one hit the deck. A guy in the row in front of me, to the right. Heat stroke! It wasn't long before he was joined by another. Now, the officers began to get concerned and they held a discussion out in front of the formation and one of them went off to find the "inspection party." It wasn't long after that the "inspection party" arrived, moved up and down the ranks in short order, saluted, and left! We found out later the game plan for the inspection had to be modified (more inspecting officers designated) and accelerated (walk faster?) to get everyone off the flight deck before things got worse!

An added discomfort while in port at Subic was that this was a working port and the primary tasks while there were maintenance and repair. This required the air conditioning plants to be rotated off-line for upkeep. Occasionally, this meant that more than one unit would be down at the same time, leaving just enough A/C available for keeping critical spaces cool. This did not include most of the living spaces. Sure, you had the blowers going full bore, but that was just moving hot air around. On the mess decks, with so many hatches open to the outside and with all the foot traffic in and out, there was no way the place could be kept cool even with all A/C units on-line. With one or two down for maintenance, the mess decks were practically dripping from the humidity. Berthing was less humid, but also much hotter. You turned the blower in your rack to hit you between your face and chest and hoped you were tired enough to get to sleep on sheets wet from sweat. Once or twice, I made up a bedroll and headed up to the forward, outboard catwalk late at night (when no one was likely to run you off) and squeezed in a few quality hours of sleep with the breeze off the water serving as air conditioner.

As has been custom in the Navy for generations, when the ship's Deck Log closes out the year and a new Deck Log is opened and started, the first entry is loosely referred to as a *poem*. The deck log entry for 1 January 1970 aboard *Connie* is provided below. You be the judge! I'm sure Longfellow, Keats and the rest would have been amused. Well, maybe not!

Warchief on Yankee Station

"HOT MIKE!"

There were four of us young rookies seated at the "comms table" located in "D&D" (Display & Decision) at the center of the adjacent compartments that composed CIC (Combat Information Center). We were posted there in rotation during our watch because we were too new and untrained to man but just a few of the many stations within CIC. We had departed Subic the day before and, being so new to it all, we were excitedly jabbering away about our recent experiences in that port. In front of each of us was a log book in which we were to transcribe transmissions coming over the radio net to which each of us were assigned. We sat, headsets on, one ear for the radio net and the other listening to the chatter going on in the background (officers seated behind us at their assigned stations). To respond to radio traffic addressed to our ship, we had a "key" in hand, which we pressed before sending a response or generating a message to another ship or station within our transmitters' range. As the banter between us went back and forth, one of the guys was asking Charlie, the guy seated next to me, about how he made out during liberty in Subic. With his thick "New Yawk" accent, Charlie launched into a very vivid and animated description of his time ashore and specifically of his trysts with one of the female "bar hostesses." Just as he was describing how she could remove chrome from a trailer hitch, someone yelled from behind us "HOT MIKE, HOT MIKE!!" The four of us quickly glanced down to check our "key" to ensure it wasn't us and we all busted up laughing when Charlie let out a very New York "Awww shit!" Realizing he had been transmitting the details of his liberty to the entire Gulf of Tonkin, he knew he'd never outlive the story and we ensured it was told often and to everyone who'd listen. Needless to say, all four of us got our asses chewed out for grab-assing on watch and, of course, Charlie got the lion's share of that and honorable mention in the weekly COMSEC message!

"GENERAL QUARTERS, GENERAL QUARTERS, MAN YOUR BATTLE STATIONS"

Connie CIC, D&D Comms Table

One of the first "evolutions" that you experienced aboard ship was the call to battle stations. The majority of GQ Drills occurred during "Work Ups" and Ref-Tra as you were training for deployment overseas. The WQSB (Watch Quarter & Station Bill) dictated what your function was during each and every "evolution" (Normal Steaming; Navigation Detail; Abandon Ship; etc.) and during GQ you filled the task assigned to you on the WQSB for Condition I (GQ). If you were on watch in CIC and GQ sounded, you had to wait to be relieved by the person assigned to the station you were manning before you could leave and make your way to the station you were assigned to for GQ. If your relief took too long to show up, you could very well end up trapped between compartments if your station was outside CIC, such as the status board located on the Bridge, because all the hatches and scuttles had been closed and you weren't allowed to "Break Zebra" to continue on your way. Zebra was a "material condition" of watertight integrity requiring the closure of hatches and scuttles during the GQ drill and actual GQ. You had four to six minutes to get from point A to point B or you were stuck in between. On a carrier this is much more difficult because of the distance you may have to travel to get to your assigned GQ station. And, of course, on a smaller ship this wasn't as much of a problem. Because each manned space had to submit a verbal report to DCC (Damage Control Central) stating the space was "manned and ready," the longer it took for personnel to get to their stations, the longer it took for those people relieved from their work stations to get to their GQ stations, the longer it took for DCC to report to the Bridge and the CO that Zebra was set and GQ was manned and ready shipwide. Fresh out of the shipyards and during the first few evolutions, it was always a cluster fuck and the ship could never attain the minimum time limit required to get all reports in and stations manned. Personnel turnover from the end of the previous deployment and up to the period where pre-deployment training began meant that a large percentage of the crew had either not been aboard ship before or worked at their assigned stations. Or, being transferred from another ship or shore station, they would still have to learn the configuration and traffic patterns of their new ship. Arriving at your assigned GQ station, you had your long sleeve shirts on, rolled down and buttoned up and top button on your shirt buttoned (for flash protection). You also had your gas mask. And your pants legs had to be tucked into your socks (again, for flash protection). You verbally relieved the man at your GQ station if that station was manned during normal steaming. If not, you manned your assigned position and reported "manned and ready." Keep in mind that if there was a body already manning your station prior to GQ, that poor soul now had to make his way, amidst the mayhem and confusion, to his own assigned station and he now had less time than you did to get there. I cannot recall ever going to GQ for real (except as mentioned later due to a fire). It was always a drill and, during Refresher Training (RefTra) when the trainers were aboard it was twice a day for the duration, with the exception of the "Final Battle Problem" at the end of RefTra that lasted until the trainers were done. When they finally departed, you could practically hear the collective sigh of relief!

But, that wasn't the end of it because you still had command scheduled (and impromptu) GQs that occurred throughout the work-up cycle and during transit overseas. Even after the ship "chopped" to 7th Fleet, you continually had "training" GQs to keep everyone on their game and ensure the process didn't fall out of familiarity.

NTDS Console, circa mid to late 1970s (IFF Interrogator to the operator's right)

I had been assigned to the Surface module in CIC and was standing watch (eight hours on and eight off) in what was referred to as a "Port & Starboard" rotation. During the eight hours per watch cycle, you were rotated through the various stations in an effort to ensure that no one got bored to the point of dozing off and also to give you a broader exposure to what skills were needed and what tasks had to be performed at each station. These were composed of Maneuvering Board, the DRT (Dead Reckoning Tracer), Surface Search, SSSC Plot, Surface Tracking (NTDS Console) and Log Keeper. At times, when manpower allowed, the watch section would have a "floater" who would fill in at certain stations when things got busy. An example would be "MoBoard" when tracking a lot of surface contacts or SSSC Plot during the period when all the positional updates were coming in over the R/T (Radio Telephone) circuit. With the exception of the "MoBoard" station, all other station assignments required the watchstander to don a pair of Sound Powered Phones or an R/T headset. On occasion, we would have to "snatch" a body from one of the other modules in CIC when a floater wasn't available and it was so damn busy you couldn't think straight! Hour upon hour of boredom and one or two hours of being so busy you swore you just came on watch when your eight hours were up! I was learning that this was SOP (standard operating procedure) just about anywhere the ship traveled. There is a good article preserved on the internet from an "All Hands" issue dated March 1964 and titled "What Goes on in CIC" and it describes the predecessor facility to the Radarman "A" School that I attended at Treasure Island. Here is the link: http://www.hullnumber.com/ALL-HANDS/what-goes-on-in-cic-navymen-find-out-at-school

My first Christmas away from home and the good ole USofA, passed without much fanfare. There were Christmas cards from home, a couple "care packages," Christmas Dinner on the Mess Decks and it was over. The "care packages" disappeared fast, whether you intended to share them or not, and you got your share of theirs (for the most part). Funny though, not too many guys were very enthusiastic about the smoked candlefish package I got from my grandmother. Mmmm, good stuff! They sure did like my mom's "rum balls" though. I think I only got a couple of those for myself.

We new guys in OI Division invariably got assigned the most menial of tasks needing to be performed. So, if the "Coffee Mess" needed tending, or the "Soda Mess" needed re-stocking, or sweeping, swabbing or polishing "bright work" was needed, you were in the group selected to accomplish that. I'll mention more about the "bright work" here, though. "Bright Work" referred to anything metallic and shiny in CIC. And, in CIC there was *plenty* of that — telephone headset cradles and junction boxes scattered throughout the various modules that composed CIC and most of these were brass. Back then, brass was polished using a cleaner called "Ever-Brite" that was an un-spun cotton-like material packed in a chemical compound and preserved in a round tin with an airtight lid. You would tear off a piece and use that to polish whatever brass you were working on. After wiping it on the brass, it would form a whitish film and once dry, you wiped it off and the brass looked shiny as new. In CIC, while in port, if the workload was not sufficient to keep all hands engaged, this was a favorite "make-work" task that would be used to fill in the hours. Of course, everyone understood that, so you took your time and stretched it out. But, make-work was also, as an example, scraping and painting bulkheads and decks that had only shortly before been refurbished. Such waste of manpower was looked down on by many, but still a favorite form of keeping everyone busy by those less imaginative minds in control! Not even a year later, Zumwalt was in and Ever-Brite was out! Unfortunately, not everyone got the memo, or in this case the "Z Gram" and bad habits died hard.

Shortly after arriving aboard ship, I experienced my first "payday" while deployed. It was quite different from those I had previously had. Following instructions, I went down to the hangar bay, amidships on the port side, where the Disbursing Officer had set up a couple tables. Marine guards lurked in the background. First, you were pointed to all the sheets of computer printouts posted on the bulkhead behind the pay line. Arranged in numerical order, you found your SSN and read across to your pay amount and your "account balance." Here, you could elect to take all monies due you or you could choose to only take enough to get you by until the next payday. Next, you got a "pay chit," a small piece of paper with lines for name, SSN, amount you desired to receive, and signature on the bottom. Proceeding through the line, the disbursing clerk would compare your "chit" to the computer printout in front of him while checking your ID card to verify who you were, the amount "on the books" and the amount you were requesting to be paid. Once this was done, you moved to the next station, where the Disbursing Officer again checked your chit, the amount requested, your ID card and then started counting out the cash for you. The chit and the cash were then handed to a disbursing clerk for him to count out and then you were handed the cash and your ID was returned to you. Like most of my shipmates, I elected to only take what I needed to get by until the following payday as the ship would not be going into port any time soon, and I let the balance "ride" on the books until then. This being the first pay period for me while on Yankee Station, I was surprised at the amount displayed on the computer printout because it reflected my new status of being in a "combat zone" and entitled to "combat" pay ($128 per month) and my entire pay was exempt from withholding taxes. Instead of the usual $35 per pay period, I was now taking in a little over $200 a month, a considerable sum in those days, by comparison.

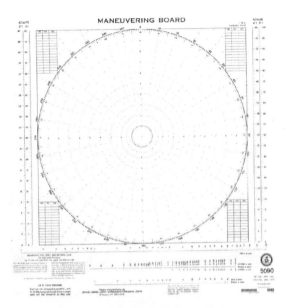

Maneuvering Board Plotting Surface

The Logarithmic Scales paralleling the bottom of the plot are for Time; Speed & Distance. When any two of those factors are known, solve for the third by running a line through the two known points of data on the scale.

Dead Reckoning Tracer.

At the time, the used paper "trace" on top of the DRT was kept for a designated period as a possible legal document that could be presented at Boards of Inquiry or Courts-Martial (for such cases as the ship running aground or a collision)

CRANKIN'

In the Navy's wisdom on how to employ an individual it had just spent $50,000 (1969 dollars) training, it deemed that after a short time spent in your parent division (mostly to get you checked in and familiarized) you were transferred (temporarily) to the Supply Department and S2M Division. For me that meant going from OI Division and my work in CIC to S2M Division, a move that also meant moving my belongings from OI Division Berthing to the S2M Division Berthing. I was to be a Mess Cook for about three months; the duration depended on when your parent division supplied a replacement for you. I was assigned day shift as most of us were, because that covered three out of the four meals served in the aft chow hall. My daily 12-hour shift began with a muster of personnel just aft of the forward mess decks and a cursory inspection to ensure everyone was in proper uniform. For S2M that meant boondockers (ankle high working boots), white uniform bellbottom pants, a clean white T-shirt and dixie-cup hat folded and tucked between belt and waistband. The work boots had to be blackened and clean, but not shined and by the end of the shift would need to be cleaned and blackened before starting the next shift. The bellbottom pants would not be white either and a change to another pair required for the following shift. And, of course, a clean white T-shirt would be repeatedly soaked in sweat from having to work your swab over the duration of your shift. S2M would provide three extra pair of bellbottom whites; these along with the three issued you in your seabag, would cover six out of the seven days you worked. Which meant you would have to pay out of your own pocket for additional T-shirts and bellbottom whites to get through the work week and allow for laundry turn-around (two days: laundry in and laundry out). Mess cooks ate each meal before the serving line opened for the rest of the crew. Although a shift was 12 hours, you got breaks during your shift and when the chow line wasn't open you helped where needed or took it easy until the chow line opened again. But, for about nine or ten of that twelve, you busted your butt. The forward mess decks and the midnight meal (midrats) were attended to by another shift of mess cooks and the hours were staggered so that when one mess was closed, the other would be open and serving a meal.

The day I reported to the galley I was immediately handed a swab and bucket of water on wheels and assigned an approximate area of about 4 by 12 feet of white and blue tile to keep clean. Now, this may not sound like much, but this area of tile was where the chow line debouched from the serving line into the mess area, where the tables were. There were two lines, port and starboard, so the traffic on my area of tile experienced about two thousand people treading across during each meal. What you quickly learn is who the office weenies, yeoman, clerks and supply types are because they hardly leave a mark walking through. What you dread are the guys off the flight deck in their varied colored jerseys. Their boondockers were caked in a mixture of "non-skid" (a composite containing course sand), oil and jet fuel and who knows what else. These boondockers left some of the dirtiest, grimiest footprints you've ever seen. If I didn't get it swabbed up and the petty officer in charge saw dirty tile, I was in for an ass chewing! So I laid-to with a vengeance and kept it as spotless as possible......for about three weeks! At the end of that period, the PO1 in charge of mess cooks walked over to my station and mentioned how satisfied he was with my efforts and as a reward he was transferring me. To the Salad Prep Room!

I hadn't the slightest idea what that would involve, but it had to be better than pushing a swab 12-hours a day! So, he took me over to the Salad Prep Room and introduced me to the PO3 cook assigned there. He was a real likeable guy by the name of Art, and I hit it off with him right away. Art explained the daily routine and then explained how we would make it work to our advantage.

The key to the routine was to ensure that, first thing in the morning, we hand-squeezed enough oranges to make a full glass and placed that glass on the prep table next to the door no later than 7 am. This was to make sure that the Chief cook got his morning orange juice, with the unspoken understanding he would keep his nose out of our business. Sweet deal!

The Salad Prep Room was charged with maintaining an array of vegetables and salads on the serving line during meals. Sounds easy enough, but after a couple weeks at sea most of the "fresh" vegetables were not so fresh anymore. All were wilted and the lettuce was downright awful. The outer half was a brown and gooey slop, which we peeled and washed away. By then, we had about one-third a head of lettuce left. And, of course, the complaints from the crew started coming in. Not much we could do with what we had to work with, but a couple times we were able to fix that by appropriating fresh vegetables and avoiding the rotation in place dictating the order they were issued from the cooler (older first and newer last). The elevator that took all the fresh vegetables down to the store-rooms passed right by the door to the Salad Prep Room and on occasion when no one was looking we were able to "divert" a few cases of really crisp, fresh lettuce directly into the Prep Room. The crew noticed and said nothing, but Art and I felt good that we had been able to inject a change into the process. By hus-tling through our prep routines before each meal, we were able to have every-thing completed and staged in serving trays hours before meal time. So, we "dogged the watch," which meant that while one of us remained in the prep room, the other could do whatever he cared and wherever that took him. If you had two hours "slack time," you each had an hour to yourself, between meals. Not a bad gig!

The same PO1 who had taken me off swabbing the deck about a month later had me report to his office. When I arrived, he told me he had another as-signment for me and that I would be working in the S2M Berthing Compartment we were sleeping in. (When you were assigned to Mess Cook duty you moved your belongings from your division berthing to the mess cook berthing). So, I re-ported below to the PO in charge of "Compartment Cleaners" for S2M Division and he spent some time informing me of what the daily routine consisted of. When he finished, I was surprised to realize that I had been assigned to a "plum" job — the entire daily routing didn't consist of more than a half-day's work be-tween the four or five of us assigned. After the first week, the hard part was how to keep busy with all that "down time" and stay out from under prying eyes (you didn't want them finding you in your "rack" in the afternoon sleeping.)

First thing in the morning we went around the compartment ensuring all the bottom racks were "triced up" and once that was done, we swept the compart-ment. Once completed, we swabbed the deck and then broke out "the monster" (buffer) which, when the ship rolled, would take all your strength to control. Once the deck had been buffed (buffing the wax to a glossy shine), we moved on to cleaning the head. That took to lunch time. Once a week, we picked up the laun-dry bags that had been put out on each of the bunks and took them down to the ship's laundry, picking them up the following day and distributing them back to their owners.

For me, the spare time was filled by working on my advancement require-ments, hanging out in CIC or OI Berthing for an hour or two, and reading. I had even signed up with a book club and was soon receiving monthly deliveries of books I had ordered.

Something I hadn't noticed before my stint as mess cook was the fact that just forward of the aft mess decks there was a space referred to as "over-flow," meaning that when too many personnel were eating chow and the regular mess area became full, tables set up in the next space forward. Well, one day we were moving these "over-flow" tables around when elevators located next to this area started spilling out handlers pushing yellow hand carts full of bombs. After parking a dozen or so of these carts with the bombs on them, the handlers started "assembling" the bombs. That was when I learned that this chow hall "over-flow" area was in fact a designated "bomb handling and assembly area." After being aboard for a few months, it was nothing out of the ordinary to sit eating your meal while the ammo handlers were busy assembling bombs next to you.

While working as compartment cleaner during the last month or so of my mess cook assignment, a Zone Inspection was scheduled to be held and the Supply Department, to which S-2 Division belonged (and was the parent division for us mess cooks) was on the list for its spaces/compartments to be inspected. We S2M Division compartment cleaners were mustered with the Leading Petty Officer and given our compartment assignments for the inspection. Well, I was given a space on the second deck forward on the starboard side of the forward mess decks, which turned out to be a "ladder well." This is the space you step into and where a ladder is emplaced leading either to the deck above or below, or both. I was taken to the space, shown what was expected regarding cleaning and given a "crib sheet" on what I was to do when the inspection party arrived. I had the morning to get the space ready and then, after lunch, and in my pressed and cleanest dungarees, was to stand by for inspection in my space. After standing in the space for almost two hours, the inspection party finally arrived. This consisted of an inspecting officer, the division officer who "owned" the space and a junior enlisted type functioning as the "recorder," writing down all the "hits" noted by the inspector. Now, the space I had been assigned was a low-traffic space and off the main traffic patterns aboard ship, so to begin with the space didn't show the normal wear and tear of heavy traffic you would find in a lot of other spaces. My cleaning job mainly consisted of wiping down the "angle irons" (the horizontal structural ribbing) and area around the hatch (hatch combing) and taking a wire brush to the ladder treads, as well as sweeping, swabbing and buffing the deck. All this took a couple hours and I held off buffing the deck until right after lunch so it would look its best, without scuff marks. When the inspection party arrived, I "popped tall" (came to attention), stated my name and rank and "Compartment 2 – 86 – 1Q ready for inspection, sir" to which the response by the inspector was "Very well." In less time than it takes to read the above, the inspector made a couple comments, duly noted by the recorder and they departed. I stood there for a few moments wondering "That's it?" So was born my loathing of the dreaded Zone Inspection! "Do you know what a Zone inspection is, sailor?" "Yes, sir! It's a royal pain in the ass!" As it turns out, I had never been in that space before and I would never have call to be in it or pass through it during my two tours aboard the *Connie*!

Then we had "Pig Pen." When I first arrived in S2M Division, I was assigned a bottom rack (bunk) in berthing. The person residing in the top bunk was assigned to the scullery. This was the dishwashing facility positioned as you left the mess decks; it was where you scraped any food residue from your metal eating tray, handed the tray to the mess cook inside, placed your dirty utensils into a plastic tub and left. The scullery was a small, humid, squalid space where nobody wanted to work because of what I just described. At the end of a shift, you were covered in food stains, your uniform was at the least "moist" from the humidity and at the most soaking wet from the dish sprayer and slopping water around. "Pig Pen" had been stationed to the scullery shortly after I arrived at S2M and bore up under those conditions for the first month or so. But, those of us sleeping close-by started noticing he had seemingly given up on trying to stay clean; the odor coming from his rack made that all too obvious. One day, I noticed his dungaree pants had been tossed into the corner by the foot of my rack. They were so dirty that the bottom pant legs stood on their own from the congealed, caked filth. To get them out of the way, I grabbed the pants, opened the curtain to his rack and tossed them in. It was then I noticed that his bedding was in the same state. Sheets and pillow case a dark, crusty brown with a smell all their own. Naturally, I complained to the compartment cleaners, who took the matter up with the PO1 in charge of the mess cooks. Next thing I know, "Pig Pen" is gone along with his dirty laundry, and his rack had been stripped and a new mattress installed.

A few days later, I spotted him in the chow hall eating with the "brig rats". What a shock! I later learned that he had been sent to CO's mast and sentenced to four or five days in the ship's brig, where the marines had orders to ensure he was instructed in correcting his personal hygiene habits — probably with the application of hard bristle brushes for added emphasis. At any rate, he was soon released, spic and span. But, when he went back to the scullery he was soon back to his previous state. But the command was keeping tabs on him and so back to the brig he went! To my knowledge, this went on for two of three more trips to the brig before the command gave up and we never saw "Pig Pen" again. He'd been transferred off the ship, whether to the brig ashore or for processing to be discharged I never found out. Some of us were of the opinion that if it was the latter, he may have been one of the foxiest guys aboard ship!

At the end of my three-month assignment as mess cook, I returned to my parent division and started reacquainting myself with the job I had been trained for!

Steamin' Seaman, Olongapo, R.P., Feb. '70

CHAPTER 3

NAVY CHOW

DEPENDING ON WHICH SHIP YOU WERE STATIONED ON, how long you had been at-sea and how well the cook in charge of the menu managed the funds allotted, the chow varied from pretty damn good to pretty damn bad.

You had fish on Fridays, and later in my career there was always an "ethnic" meal worked into the dinner menu: Filipino; soul food; corned beef & cabbage on St. Patty's Day, etc. Some of it was very tasty and a welcome change from the norm. Once a week we got steak. At least, that's what it said on the menu; we referred to them as gaskets, they were so tough. We all believed that the only way you could get steak that tough was to run them up the Chisholm Trail to Abilene before slaughter. We all knew that the government procurement system awarded contracts to the lowest bidder and it was obvious that applied to steaks too. And, we were reaping the results of that process. Which must have been why the Navy provided A-1 bottles to every table on steak night!

While overseas in the early '70s, the menu was dictated mainly by the extended supply train that delivered the fresh and dry goods to ships on-station off the Vietnamese coast. With over 40 ships clamoring for stores on any given day, it was an impossible task to schedule delivery to each one without someone feeling short changed. Back then, we were still using WWII ships for stores delivery because there weren't enough newer ones to do without them. And, that includes the AO's (oilers) and AE's (ammunition).

After four or five days at sea, you ran out of real eggs and milk. How could you tell? When you weren't offered eggs to order and could only get scrambled eggs, you knew what you were getting. When you went to the milk dispenser and lifted the handle to pour your glass, the smell from the "reconstituted" milk made many of us nauseous; we'd wash out our glasses and go to the "bug juice" dispenser instead. "Bug juice" was our reference to the concoction made from a "Kool Aid" type blend that had so much saccharin in it the sweet taste was almost repulsive. Oh, and it also attracted any insect within a five-mile radius. So, after the fresh milk gave out you ate your cereal dry or your oatmeal without milk.

You couldn't always count on being able to get to the chow hall (located at the opposite end of the ship from CIC) or not being stuck in a long line and not having enough time to get through it before having to go on watch. Or, if they were serving a meal that didn't appeal to you, there was always Plan B. For most of us, this was hitting the ship's store and laying in a stock of "geedunk," navy slang for candy or snacks. My choices were usually canned sardines and crackers. We were allowed to snack while on watch at our assigned station provided it didn't impair our performance. On my second WestPac someone complained about the sardine smell and I was told not to bring them into CIC anymore. So, I would wolf down a snack while on break out at the division TV lounge area. When someone complained about that I told the LPO they either had to stop selling them at the ship's store or I should be allowed to eat them in a division common area such as the lounge. He agreed and the complaint died right there.

During Vietnam we really enjoyed pulling into port in Japan and one reason was for the provisioning the ship conducted off the local market. Fresh veggies and fruits were brought aboard and some were novelties to a lot of us. Case in point! I had not seen, heard of or tasted "Asian Pears" until seeing them being offered on the chow line while in port at Yokosuka, Japan back in 1972. Ever since, it's been one of my favorite fruits!

Probably the most notable evidence of local provisioning I would ever see was when I was aboard CGN-9 during our stay in Australia. "Chop" had purchased enough "surf & turf" to last more than just one meal. For those of you not familiar with the "Aussie" version of "surf & turf" let me describe what we experienced. You ate off compartmentalized plastic serving trays and drew one from the stack at the head of the serving line. After selecting our other choices we moved to the steak and lobster, where the cooks gave us one of each, the steak being so large it covered most of the other compartments on your tray. The lobster was placed on top of that and the size of the lobster almost covered the steak — biggest damn lobsters I've ever seen. And, the steaks were not previously frozen; nor were they the "gasket" type I had eaten so often while on Yankee Station, back in the early '70s.

Then there is the "pretty damn bad" version of the menu. While I was aboard the *Mount Hood* and while overseas, the food became downright unbearable: something green (and always overcooked), or white and brown! Green, white and brown! Green, white and brown!!!!! There were always complaints in the "suggestion box" adjacent to the chow line. And, isn't it an accepted norm that sailors will bitch about anything? Well, yeah!

It got to the point one day that I was pretty fed up with the lack of diversity and as I was selecting a table to sit at I overheard a bunch of guys at another table griping about the chow. After taking a few tentative bites of the items on my tray, I knew I would be going on watch hungry. As I was taking my uneaten dinner to the scullery window, I noticed the suggestion box and decided to fill out one of the "chits" that were next to the box and let the command know how dismal things were getting. This was all anonymous of course because there was no requirement to provide a name or signature to the form.

As I was filling out the "chit," I could still hear the other bunch complaining about their chow. So, I grabbed a handful of chits and walked over to their table. I threw half-dozen chits on the table and told them they should quit their bitching and submit a chit. Then, I walked around to the rest of the tables and did the same. All under the eyes of the line cooks on duty.

Yep, you guessed it. Next morning before going on watch, I was summoned to the XO's cabin. And, yeah I knew I was probably going to get my ass chewed. But I felt I was within my rights and was prepared to defend my actions.

I was in for a surprise. Stepping into the XO's cabin I saw the senior cook aboard ship was there also. The XO opened the conversation asking why I had distributed the chits around the mess deck asking the men to fill them out and stuff the suggestion box (the box was full by the end of the meal). I pointed out that I was only enabling them to act on their verbal complaints. He then explained why the senior chief was there and directed the senior chief to explain his menu. After about 20 minutes of "I have this much to spend and these provisions to buy in order to assemble the menu for that period," the XO asked if I had any questions. I told them I wasn't blaming the cooks as much as the provisions they had to work with and pointed out that some deviation from the formulated menu couldn't be a bad thing. I also mentioned that the XO had duty officers who were tasked daily with sampling the general mess meals and filling out a report that was submitted to him, with their review of the food served. And, were they too intimidated to tell the truth or weren't the chits being read and acted on? The XO got a little miffed at that but let it slide. The senior chief said he would do what he could with his next provisioning and hoped that this would satisfy my complaint. I stated that if that was all that could be done and an honest effort were made to improve the fare, that was all I could ask.

To the senior chief's credit, the chow improved markedly and during our remaining time overseas the meals weren't as bland and repetitious as they had been previously. And, because I was transferring before the ship's next deployment, I wouldn't have to go through that again! I also noticed that the junior duty officers making the daily meal sampling were spending a lot more time writing up their reviews of the meals. On a small ship such as *Mount Hood* I'm sure they were all aware of who was to blame for that! Suck it up, butter bar! (Ah, yes! One of the most dangerous weapons in the naval arsenal is an ensign with a pencil!)

While on the subject of chow, I should mention here, the various "messes" (eating areas) aboard ship, with the exception of the Officers Wardroom. As I've discussed during my stint as mess cook, there is the General Mess Area which is for crewman E-1 to E-5. Then, there is a mess area off the General Mess area specifically designated for E-6's, which go through the same serving line as the General Mess, but are seated in a separate enclosed space and between meals, served as a lounge of sorts.

Then, there was the CPO Mess, a separate messing area with its own serving line and an adjacent lounge area.

As I was a member of the CPO mess aboard CGN-9, what follows is from that point of reference. The CPO Mess could be either an Open Mess (same meals and provisions as the General Mess), or a Closed Mess (provisions and menus separate from the General Mess). A Closed Mess meant that records were kept on who ate from the mess, which was charged to each person monthly by the collection of dues (not to exceed your BAS — BAS was the Navy's Basic Allowance for Subsistence, added into your base pay and other allowances). The CMC (Command Master Chief and the senior Mess Specialist (MSCM) were in charge of the mess with one of the members serving as the Mess Treasurer. CGN-9 had a pretty posh CPO lounge, but given my schedule, I couldn't and didn't spend much time there. But, it did have its share of "lounge lizards!"

"LIBERTY" PORTS, "WORKING" PORTS & VARIATIONS THEREOF

A Liberty Port of Call meant that, with the exception of the duty section, all hands were granted liberty to go ashore, provided they hadn't been assigned a task that would prevent them from leaving the ship or were "in hack" due to a minor infraction. In either case, they would still have to secure their "Liberty Card" before actually being able to "cross the brow."

A "Working Port" meant that each day, you put in a regular eight-hour work shift, prior to being "granted" liberty. Again, this was if you weren't in that day's "duty section" or you weren't in trouble for some minor infraction.

"Tropical Working Hours" was a modification to the regular eight-hour work day, which the command was allowed to institute at its discretion and was used with the intent of avoiding some of the worst tropical heat topside for those exposed to the elements during the performance of their daily tasks. This meant that reveille and quarters were conducted an hour earlier than normal and lunch was moved to coincide with "knock off" at 1300 (1PM). So, you actually accomplished a six-hour work day. Duty section assignment still dictated if you had to stay aboard or not. "Tropical Hours" were commonly applied while in port at Pearl or Subic.

The "Three M's" (Muster, Mingle & Make It) was another variation of a working day and also at the discretion of the ship and which the division could implement if the work load allowed. Reveille and quarters were held at the usual time, but the daily work assignments could be detailed such that most tasks were completed before lunch and liberty could be granted at that time. We *loved* 3M Liberty! But typically, the only times this would occur was during the first couple weeks upon our return from deployment. The only two times that I experienced 3M liberty was upon our return from WestPac aboard the *Connie* in 1970 and 1972.

"Cinderella Liberty" was usually dictated by the mission tasking of the ship, as was the one case I had the experience of enduring while aboard the *Hood* in Subic Bay. Upon completion of the normal work day, liberty was granted to those in the crew not assigned to that day's "duty section" with the caveat being that all hands had to report back aboard no later than midnight (whence the "Cinderella" reference). Some discretion was left to the various departments and/or divisions to the point that, instead of remaining aboard until knock-off at 1600 (4PM), the department/division could allow liberty a couple hours before that, and usually case-by-case. But, we still had to be back aboard by midnight. When the ship was finally tasked and we got underway, it was a relief because we knew that, upon return to port, "Cinderella Liberty" would be no more!

LIBERTY CALL - YOKOSUKA, JAPAN

6 - 16 March 1970

Connie was detached and we departed Yankee Station the night of 1 March, en route to Yokosuka, Japan — my first of many port calls to that location. Finally arriving the morning of 6 March, we were tied up to Piedmont Pier, which was typically where the carriers moored. Rudy and I had been discussing a trip to Tokyo and worked our duty rotations so that we would both have the same two days to make the trip and spend some time in the city. So, the day we began our trip, we walked out the gate and up the hill to the Yokosuka train station. By paying careful attention to the English "subtitles" on all the signage we were able to deduce which train would get us there in the least time (red line, green line, black line all had their posted stops and travel time). Buying our tickets we stood on the platform and waited for our ride. When our train showed up (on the minute scheduled) the waiting platform was crammed full of people. As soon as the doors opened and the people getting off were out of the way, the crowd on the platform surged toward the doors and started filling up the cars. News to Rudy and me was the fact that when the cars "appeared" full, "pushers" stood behind the crowd with long batons that they used to shove everyone forward and through the doors until everyone was aboard; then the doors barely managed to close on all us sardines! Welcome to mass transit in Japan!

The trip took just a little over an hour and soon we were getting off the train and trying to find our subway connection to the Ginza district, where we would find the USO. Growing up on the West Coast, where San Francisco was considered crowded in the day, nothing had prepared me for the mass humanity of urban Tokyo. We found our connecting subway to Ginza and after a short ride, got off at that station. Climbing out of the subway tunnel and into the congestion and bustle of the Ginza District was, for a country boy like me, eye opening. I suppose Rudy was more at ease with it, being from the Chicago area, but even so, it must have surprised even him. Staying shoulder to shoulder we made our way through the throng of people to the doors of the USO. What a relief! Upstairs, we took seats at the cafeteria counter for lunch, glancing out the window frequently in amazement at the site of thousands upon thousands of people going about their business, unaware of the spectacle they created to our unaccustomed American eyes!

While at the USO we were able to get a map of the city and some advice from one of the USO counter volunteers about what to see and where to go. So, setting off after lunch, we made our way to the Imperial Palace, walking down the park-like avenues that surround the palace. Shortly, we were approached by a diminutive, weathered older gentleman riding a three-wheeled bike with a two-seat carriage on the back. He asked, in pretty fair English, if we would care to hire him for a ride around the palace! After discussing the fare, we agreed and boarded his vehicle. As he set off on his route, he began what turned out to be a running commentary on the palace grounds, the moat, the buildings within the grounds, an abbreviated history of the dynasty, and on and on! He really knew his subject and it was a very entertaining tour. When it ended, he pulled out a photo album and commenced showing us his "career," from the early 1950s right up to the present — all his past customers standing in front of his vehicle and a few pictures here and there of himself through the years. Rudy and I were both impressed and gladly submitted to him taking our picture for addition to his album.

After walking around the palace grounds a little more, in the areas our trike driver couldn't get to, we decided it was time to find rooms for the night and dinner. Not far off the palace grounds we found a hotel that would take "gaijins" (foreigners) and checked in. We ate dinner nearby and returned to the hotel where we tried watching TV. Back then, Japanese television would air 25 or 30 minutes of a show followed by about 15 to 20 minutes of commercials. After the novelty wore off, we decided that was enough for us and hit the hay early. After breakfast the next morning, we made our way across town to the Tokyo Tower, another tourist spot that had been recommended to us. Taking the ride up the glass elevator to the first observation deck was quite the experience and after walking around the observation deck and taking in the sights, we hopped back on the elevator for the ride back down. Exiting the elevator, we asked for directions to the nearest "benjo" (toilet) and were directed to a large, circular structure standing off to the side of the tower. We walked around it until we found the entrance, a common opening in the wall that led to both the women's and men's facilities, partitioned down the middle, by the wall. On the men's side, there were toilets on the right (the typical Japanese hole-in-the-floor style) and urinals on the left against the partition. Rudy and I made for the urinals and commenced our business. While doing so, I happened to look up and found that the wall only came up to my neck and I was now returning looks with some surprised women, squatting over toilets. Now, there is nothing titillating or sexy about watching a female squat over a hole! Rudy heard the women, saw that I was looking across the wall and asked what was going on. He couldn't see what I was seeing, because his eye-line was below the top of the wall. I didn't explain until we were on our way out the door, and when I did we both busted up laughing.

Because we had to make our way back to Yokosuka that day, we only had a couple hours to spend window shopping in the complex of stores below ground, under the tower. After eating lunch, we made our way to the nearest subway station and started our ride back to the base. All in all, a short but fun trip!

As you would expect, the area around the main gate to the naval station held many diversions specifically designed to a sailor's taste. The Alliance Club was the enlisted men's club located just outside the gate, across the street and down a couple blocks. Walking inside you were immediately impressed by the sheer size of the place — it took up two city blocks! Dancing, eating and drinking were all available and at navy base prices. If I recall, a beer was 25 cents and lunch would run you about $2.00. But, if you wanted local "flavor" you could always go a couple blocks up and into "the Honcho" or "Honch" for short. There were girlie bars, western bars, dance bars and a few I won't mention here. Even though the currency exchange rate back then was 360 yen to the dollar, the price of a beer could run up to $2 and if you bought one of the hostesses a "ladies drink" that would cost you $3 to $5. At those rates you would soon find yourself broke and heading back to the ship. However, there was a way to stretch your money as we found out from some "station sailors." What you did was go to one of the little mom-and-pop mini-marts, pick up a "warclub" of Acadama wine for about $8 and check it in to a bar. You paid a nominal fee to the bar called a "set-up fee" and they served you from your bottle for as long as it lasted. The "warclub" of Acadama (not so fondly referred to as Acadoo) stood about 2 feet tall and must have held over a half-gallon of the surly brew. A buddy and I had split the cost of the bottle and the fee for checking it into the bar and when we called it a night, there was still some left. Given the absolute misery we experienced the next morning, you can understand why we never went back to finish the bottle. Once was enough!

"The Honch," Yokosuka, Japan 1972

An incident that occurred on a different trip to Yokosuka involved a return train trip from Tokyo. It was late at night and I was with a group of four or five other sailors, coming back to the ship after a day spent in the "big city." There weren't many people riding that time of night, and sitting across from us were two locals. One was nicely dressed and well kempt and the other was a street person who was obviously drunk. As we traveled along, the drunk became obnoxious, ranting on about something in the local dialect that we obviously couldn't understand. But, the well-dressed gentleman seemed highly embarrassed by his behavior and in his limited English he continually apologized for his inebriated countryman. After about 10 or 15 minutes of this, the train came to a stop, the sober man gathered up the drunken one and gingerly took him off the train, sat him on a bench and returned to his seat. As he sat down and looked across to us, he asked if that was OK! But, what has stuck with me for decades is that he wasn't embarrassed for the drunk. He was embarrassed for his culture. I doubt many Japanese tourists to the states get a glimpse of the skid rows that inhabit so many of our towns and cities!

BACK TO YANKEE STATION

Connie departed Yokosuka 16 March '70 en route back to the Tonkin Gulf, but not before some local ops in the Okinawa OpArea. There we performed some formation maneuvering, touch-and-gos to qualify (or, re-qualify) some pilots (Car-Quals). We arrived at Yankee Station 27 Mar and commenced strike operations, as usual. But, this "line period" would have its share of trials and tribulations. On 8 April, one of our pilots ditched shortly after take-off and the following day, a *USS Coral Sea* E-2 went into the water about 17 miles from *Connie*, which dispatched a helo to assist in the SAR (Search & Rescue).

1000. COMMENCED MANEUVERING AT VARIOUS COURSES AND SPEEDS WHILE LAUNCHING AND RECOVERING A/C. 1348 PILOT EJECTED FROM A-7 A/C SIDE NUMBER 300 OF VA-97 BEARING 210° 8 MILES FROM CONSTELLATION. DISPATCHED HENDERSON AND HELO 005 TO MAKE RESCUE. 1353 PILOT VISUALLY SIGHTED BY HELO 005. 1403 PILOT ABOARD HELO 005. 1419 COMPLETED LAUNCHING AND RECOVERING A/C. SET COURSE 310° SPEED 20 KTS.

08-12 UNDERWAY AS BEFORE. 0800 HELO 005 OVER WRECKAGE. DOWNED A/C 180° 7.5 MILES FROM CONSTELLATION. 0810 DOWNED A/C IDENTIFIED AS E-2 A/C FROM CORAL SEA. C/S TO 10 KTS. 0819 C/C TO 150° C/S TO 6 KTS. 0832 FIVE SOULS REPORTED ABOARD DOWNED E-2 A/C. 0900 C/S TO 13 KTS. 0910 DISPATCHED MCKEAN TO SAR AREA. 0920 C/C TO 175° C/S TO 9 KTS. 0936 C/C TO 135°. 0940 POSSIBLE MAN OVERBOARD REPORTED BY HENDERSON. 0953 DISPATCHED HELO 005 TO ASSIST HENDERSON. 0959 C/C TO 350° C/S TO 15 KTS. 1030

Aircraft Lost During Operations at Sea: 8 & 9 Apr '70, respectively

CHAPTER 4

USS CONSTELLATION RETURNED TO SAN DIEGO
8 MAY 1970

OUR RETURN STATESIDE was marked by the command allowing maximum liberty for the crew and unless you had duty that day, you were allowed liberty. So, four out of five days, you were "on the beach." The drawback was that it was very short-lived because the ship was underway for local SOCAL Ops during 15-21 May. With preparations proceeding for our upcoming move to Puget Sound Naval Shipyard, there was a lot of hustle and bustle considering the ship had only been stateside a few short weeks.

Ashore on liberty for the first time in San Diego, I checked into signing up for any excursions that the YMCA had on offer. The big draw at "the Y" was the slot car track. It was the biggest I'd ever seen, then and now. You could rent a slot car and run it on the track for hours and never spend $5. You could eat in the cafeteria (burger & fries) for less than $3. Or you could go up the street a couple blocks and hit the many arcades. One of my first outings back then was to Balboa Park and the Zoo. This was spendy for my budget back then, but I really enjoyed it. I spent one day at the zoo and another wandering through the exhibit buildings in Balboa Park (Museum of Natural History, Aerospace Museum and the rest).

During duty days aboard ship, you mustered with the OI Division duty section and were given assignments for the day. In my case, that meant helping in the berthing compartment sweeping, swabbing and buffing. It was similar to my stint with S2M division while "crankin'."

A function assigned to OI Division personnel while in port (any port where we were tied up to a pier and phone line hook-ups were available) was to man the telephone switchboard in the aft IC Room. Your first time you were assigned to be UI (under instruction) with a person that had stood the watch before and was familiar with the equipment and how to go about getting outbound and inbound calls connected. After a couple hours, my instructor patted me on the back and said "it's all yours" and departed. Now, it wasn't a terribly complicated function, but it did have its challenging moments — mostly from the callers, not from the equipment! Stateside, a typical call would come in from an outside line with some female on the other end asking "Is Johnny there?" (Yes, sweety, there's about 40 or 50 of 'em!) So, you'd ask for his last name and too many times they couldn't tell you that. So, you'd ask what his job aboard ship was and they usually couldn't tell you that, either. At this point you had to explain to them that without further information you wouldn't be able to help them. Overseas, this exchange took on a whole different slant because you had to try and understand a person that was not speaking in their native tongue and your ear wasn't tuned to the local accented version of the English they were trying to speak.

On 30 May *Connie* departed San Diego, making the transit north to Washington State.

SHIPYARD OVERHAUL, PSNSY BREMERTON, WA.,

June '70 thru April '71

Being in the shipyard during an overhaul is never the best experience. Noisy, gritty and grimy. Umbilicals strung out everywhere and you were constantly ducking your head or stepping over or around welding leads, air ventilation hoses, compressed air hoses, etc. In some passageways, you walked in a perpetual stoop! You were constantly bumping and banging your hard-hat into one thing or another. Getting around was a real chore in many places. Naturally, being" in the yards" meant you would be temporarily assigned to one of the "collateral duties" such as SFOMS (Ship's Force Overhaul & Maintenance System), which was tasked with performing functions of the overhaul within the capability of ship's personnel. For example, the ship and SFOMS Department provided personnel support for "Fire Watch" duty. This entailed supplying the shipyard welders with a body and a CO2 Extinguisher to stand by the welder and be ready to apply the CO2 if the welding caused a fire, which was common. That was my assignment! All of us had learned CO2 Extinguisher use during our Firefighting Training at Boot Camp, but that didn't mean we remembered much. So it was decided we would get a "refresher" course — about 30 minutes' worth! Yep! Now, we were experts!

Every morning you mustered with your section PO at the Fire Watch Desk in the hangar bay and awaited your assignment to a shipyard welder who would stop by to pick up one of us. Welders could not weld without a firewatch attending his work. We were to ensure his work area was free of fire hazards and that any burning slag did not have the opportunity to turn into a fire or transfer to another fuel source.

As with any job, once you get familiar with the routine and the people, you find ways to "work the system." In Fire Watch, this meant that if you and a welder hit it off, he would help to ensure that you were signed out to him as often as possible. In my case, it was a TIG **(tungsten inert gas)** welder named Robert who was a full-blooded Navajo. We spent many hours together, mostly with him welding and me watching. But, if he had a dentist appointment or someplace else he had to be in the afternoon, he would not expect me to go back down to the Firewatch desk and make myself available for the remaining couple hours. This meant I could "caulk off" somewhere until quitting time. Another possibility was the hole in the bottom of the ship! While in dry-dock and in order to facilitate the removal and replacement of equipment from the lower engineering spaces, a large hole had been cut in the bottom of the ship. If I wanted to leave the ship to go to the exchange or whatever, I could stash my CO2 bottle and nip out the hole, climb the dry-dock ladder and catch a bus to the exchange. But, I only did that a couple times because for such a short period, it was too much of a trip back and forth to make it worth the effort. Still, that hole would provide opportunity!

After six months of hauling that steel cylinder CO2 extinguisher around the ship, five levels up, four levels down, forward and aft I was sure glad to transfer back to division and get rid of that damn thing!

ECHO WHISKEY

During our voyage back to the States I had been called into a meeting with the CWO2 in charge of the EW "Shack" and told he'd like to offer me a position working there. It sounded interesting and another field of the rate I could learn, so I agreed. That settled, I was soon sent, during May 1970, to Electronic Warfare Operators School at FAAWTC (Fleet Anti-Air Warfare Training Center) at Point Loma, San Diego. The *Connie* would still be in Bremerton for overhaul at the end of the course. I attended the two-week "crash course" in the operation of the primary signals detection device aboard *Connie.* By "crash course," I mean they stuffed so much information into two weeks that your head was spinning by the end of it. Snooptray, HeadNet, Fansong and on and on! These were the NATO designations of the threat emitters we needed to memorize. We were told we should know the launch platform's capabilities, the weapons envelope, the firing and homing emitters and what countermeasures to use to defeat them. Our primary piece of equipment aboard *Connie* was the WLR-1, an Over-the-Horizon Detection device, which required manual tuning through nine bands of the electromagnetic spectrum covered by this equipment. Advantages were that with a trained and sharp operator you could detect "threat emitters" at ranges far exceeding the launch envelope of the threat platform. Disadvantages were that if the operator didn't continually cycle through the bands most commonly associated with the high threat emitters, he might miss a threat signal or find it too late to have adequate reaction time to defeat the threat. To keep your "head in the game" you lived and breathed NWP-33, which was our reference publication for all things EW. All this, of course, is "ancient history" in the evolution of the current systems now deployed aboard Navy ships. But, they have their own shortcomings as any EW person will admit to — but most likely, only to another EW! (P.S.: EWs have since been merged with the CT rate in 2003.)

There were eight of us watch-standers assigned to work in the EW module of CIC, four per watch section, eight hours on watch and eight hours off watch, as was the norm in the rest of CIC. As each person also had his assigned collateral duties and maintenance of equipment that supported the gear inside the module — there was a lot to learn before we deployed back to WESTPAC. The detection and proper identification of enemy emitters was our primary duty. Once that had been done, we notified the officers on watch in D&D (Display & Decision) about the emitter and its threat level. Search emitters were no threat, but targeting and homing emitters could possibly require immediate countermeasures. For the highest-level threat emitters, the ship's reaction time to defeat the threat was measured in seconds, so our process of evaluation had to be almost instantaneous and notification up the chain-of-command would necessarily require that be done as or after the threat was defeated.

I didn't really develop much of a rapport with the guys in the EW shack and still played cards and went on liberty with the buddies that I had made during my other assignments in CIC. There were some strange dudes in that EW shack, so that may have been why.

In October 1972, the Navy split the Radarman rating into two NECs (Naval Enlisted Classifications). A radarman would become an Operations Specialist (OS) and someone working in the EW shacks would become an Electronic Warfare Technician (EW) – the person had a choice. Six or seven months before the rate split it was decided that personnel assignments be adjusted early to allow for training time should the personnel shuffle require it. Of course, the CWO2 tried to talk me into choosing the EW rating, but I politely begged off and was allowed to move back into CIC as an OS, so the EW shack had to train another body, that is, someone who would remain an EW after the rating split happened. But, I'm getting ahead of myself.

After EW school, it was back to the *Connie* and straight to "Fire Watch" for most of the remaining time the ship was at Bremerton. But before our return to San Diego, I was told that I and three others from OI Division would be sent to San Diego for NTDS Operator's School. By the time the course was over, the *Connie* would have arrived from Bremerton.

When the four of us walked aboard the ASW Training base on Harbor Drive, San Diego we checked into the Personnel Office expecting to be housed in the barracks there and transported up to the training center on Point Loma each morning for class. But when we stepped up to the check-in counter the lieutenant there asked us if we were electing to be assigned to barracks or would we be requesting per-diem. What? We had a choice? We asked her why and she told us that the barracks being relatively new still lacked carpet and air conditioning and were classified as being incomplete, thereby requiring the Navy to offer per diem if we declined the barracks "as is." Well, we took a couple steps back from the counter to discuss the option. We hurriedly agreed that per diem was the way to go, provided that we pooled our funds for housing off the base. That settled, we went down the street to a hotel on the corner of Harbor Drive and Rosecrans Avenue to see what we could afford. We were told that for a "double double" (two large King beds) we could get by on a quarter of our per diem. This meant sharing a bed with a shipmate but after agreeing this wasn't a problem, we secured the room for the duration. Next problem was transportation. We would have to catch the bus up to Point Loma each morning from the base, which meant a four-block walk from the hotel each morning. But after the first day, the bus driver agreed he would pick us up on the corner across from the hotel as it was on his route anyway and drop us off each afternoon at the same spot. We just had to make sure we weren't late or we'd miss the bus and really be in trouble. The entire two weeks settled into a routine which included arriving back from class and changing into our swim trunks for a dip in the hotel pool each day before dinner. Sweet!

As you've read in previous sections, I spent a lot of time in class going to one navy school or another. For the most part I've only mentioned the ones more noteworthy and pertinent to my work in CIC, but there were dozens of others that ranged from a half-day to upwards of two weeks. I'll mention a few of these here, to reflect that school-house training was an on-going proposition for many. Much of this, of course, was driven by billeting requirements, and if the BOM (Battle Organization Manual) or WQSB said a warm body had to fill an assigned billet number, a body was provided.

It was necessary for each Work Center (WC) to have trained maintenance personnel for their equipment, which meant those people would be required to attend 3M (Materiel Maintenance Management) training either at the user level or the supervisor level. Once back aboard ship, your recent training was put into practice and you fulfilled tasks assigned to the division as required by their 3M Maintenance Schedule.

Also, in the realm of training driven by rank, I was sent to LMET (Leadership, Management Enlisted Training) and the NavLead CPO course.

A ship undergoing an overhaul and extensive shipyard work would allow the department and division a good opportunity to ensure that as many personnel as the budget would allow be sent to Navy schools, thus filling requirements needed when the ship was undergoing training and filling those specialty billets that are necessary before a ship "chops." In the Pacific, "chop" refers to a ship transiting from EastPac, to WestPac. There were shipyard periods during my career where I would end up spending a large portion of my time in school and not in the shipyard, which obviously was fine by me!

Another course given to junior as well as senior enlisted and QMs (Quartermasters) as well as OSs was the Nautical Rules of the Road COI, which lasted a week. While in Bremerton during overhaul aboard CGN-9, the command sent a half-dozen of us to attend the course, which was being given at the Naval Submarine Base at Bangor, Washington. The only other time I had been aboard Bangor was on the *Connie* when we went to off-load weapons prior to going into dry dock in 1970. Back then, it was primarily a Weapons Station and the Submarine Base did not exist yet. When I was with the group attending the Rules of the Road" course, I was amazed at how much the base had grown and all the relatively new infrastructure built to accommodate its new requirements. But, I digress.

The school curriculum, of course, stressed the rules governing navigation at sea. Reference texts were Bowditch and the USCG Nautical Rules Handbook. As visual aids, navigation charts were displayed and scenarios were discussed, from low visibility precautions and special circumstances to inland navigation rules. Because much of this was applicable information for those QM and OS personnel assigned to their ship's Navigation Detail, there were many lively Q&A sessions during which a couple of the instructors had a difficult time satisfying us students with their level of response. And, when the invariable "Course Feedback Survey" sheets were passed around, they took some hits for it.

Then, there were the forums, conferences, meetings and working groups that could fill a calendar all too frequently and which, for the most part, I encountered during the later part of my career. Discussions at these venues ranged from current resolutions in place to overcoming equipment or tactical deficiencies encountered or expected to occur to planning of upcoming events that would impact specific operations. Other subjects were new documentation and how they were to be employed; canceled or added maintenance requirements; reviews of current Navy operations; discussions regarding our opponent's recent operations and so on. Much of this was time-sensitive and would only apply for the period it was being briefed for.

There were also each individual's Personnel Qualifications Standards (PQS) which I've touched on earlier, but which I will briefly explain here. Typically, when a person checked aboard a ship, one of the first things issued to him by his division would be a PQS Book, which was required by him to complete, usually within a given time. His PQS Book would contain pages of functions and tasks that he needed to learn and demonstrate before those being signed as completed by a designated and/or qualified signer. Depending on the ship and its configuration in the field the crewman would be working in, the PQS Book could comprise upwards of 50 to 60 pages, with dozens of signatures (or, initials) required for each page. This effort would keep a crewman busy qualifying for months and all in addition to classroom training and military duties. Although PQS did not exist when I entered the Navy, it had become instituted by the '80s and would be a ready benchmark to judge a person's professional development.

THE APARTMENT

When I wasn't in San Diego attending school, Rudy had talked to me about going in with a couple other guys he knew and getting an apartment in Bremerton. With our pay being what it was, pooling resources would be the only way we could afford one. So, one of the guys turned up an apartment with rent that wouldn't break our budget and we moved in a few months after arriving in Bremerton. The place was a *dump*! No curtains, no bedding, and layers of paint chipping off the walls. But, it appealed to us because it beat sleeping on the berthing barge on the base. Rent was $80 per month which meant we each only had to chip in $20. Like I said, it was a dump! Immediately, we started acquiring the necessities of setting up house: bedding, curtains, cooking utensils and the like. And, to hold down the cost of all this, most of the stuff we bought came from "Sallies," only a few blocks down the street from the apartment. The two bedrooms had beds in them and the couch in the living room was a fold-out, but we were still short a bed. So, on one of our trips to "Sallies" we picked up another mattress and put it on the floor in the living room. The cook got assigned to that one! Poor guy!

One side of the apartment faced the street and had three sets of windows we had to find curtains for. Rudy solved that problem. While out on a salvage assignment aboard one of the decommissioned ships anchored in Sinclair Inlet, he located a huge Mexican flag and brought it back to the apartment. I came home one day and found that he had hung it across all three of the windows facing the street. It covered that entire side of the apartment. Problem solved!

The four of us were me, Rudy, a corpsman named Tim, and a cook, whose name I don't recall. But, the corpsman and the cook were strategic selections on our part. The corpsman and the cook for obvious reasons. Rudy was our "fixer" and he was good at it! And, my contribution was that I was the only one with a car. Shortly after arriving in Bremerton, I had gone car shopping and found a nifty little Monza Corvair for $200 and cashed that amount in savings bonds to buy it. Now, anyone with a grease-monkey background will tell you that the Corvair had a bad mechanical reputation and mine would prove to be true to that also. Luckily, I found a shipmate who could help me out and teach me some of the mechanics I needed to know to keep it running — most of the time. As my contribution to the guys in the apartment, I was able to provide limited transportation around town. But I made sure they understood I wasn't providing a taxi service and they would all have to pitch in for gas every month.

During this "yard period," *Connie* had her 9th birthday and the command pulled out all the stops. A big bash was planned at a large venue out in town, grub was laid on, bands were hired and a Playboy Playmate was one of the guests. To make her presence more democratic, a raffle was held and the winner would serve as the Playmates' escort for the evening. Wouldn't you know it, our corpsman Tim was selected. We were all green with envy! The evening of the party, Tim was driven in a limousine to pick up his date and they arrived at the party in style. And what a knock-out she was. She did a little song and dance on the stage and just below the footlights were as many of the crew as the space could hold, ogling and making fools of themselves trying to catch her eye. She loved it! Well, we found out later Tim had been a perfect gentleman during the course of his "assignment," but before they parted he was able to talk her out of her "skivvies," which he flashed around for months afterward!

A few months later, we were sitting around on a Friday night wondering what to do when one of the guys thought we should invite some girls over. We'd all been to some USO dances and made some acquaintances, so we walked to the pay phone across the street and started dialing. I called a girl I had met who lived in Port Orchard, across the Sinclair Inlet from Bremerton, and asked if she and some of her girlfriends wanted to come over. She said she'd see what she could do. After telling the guys, we all talked about what to get for our little "party" and shortly walked across the street to the mom and pop grocery on the corner to pick up some munchies. The corpsman, being the only one over 21, had us chip in and he bought some beer as well. As we were walking back across the street from the store a station wagon full of girls drove slowly by and they all hung out the windows smiling and waving. What the heck? The car stopped, turned around and came back towards us. It was then that I saw the girl driving was the one I had called. She had rounded up six or seven of her school chums and brought them along. After showing them our accommodations, which the girls were not impressed with, I paired off with the girl I knew and we were soon necking on the cook's mattress. Shortly, I felt one of the unattached girls snuggle up to my backside. What the heck! I turned over and gave her some of what her friend was getting — and, promptly got smacked on the back of the head. For me, the night ended right then and there. Never saw either girl again. Go figure!

The spring of '71 meant I could now use the car for a trip home because the roads through the mountains would be free of snow. I tinkered to get the car in as good a shape as possible for the trip and Rudy agreed to make the trip with me. Now all that remained was to pick a weekend when we were both not on the duty roster. Finally identifying the weekend when both of us would have liberty, we made plans. Trouble was, if we waited until knock-off on Friday afternoon, we wouldn't get to Eureka until 2 or 3 in the morning. So, we decided to use the hole in the bottom of the ship to make an early exit. We had to make some arrangements that would allow us to leave early and unnoticed, but everything was in place to do so by the time we got ready to leave. That Friday around 1PM, we slipped through the bottom of the ship, climbed the dry-dock ladder and made our way to my car. We had stashed some civvies inside, but didn't have a place to change right there so we drove off in our dungaree working clothes figuring on changing later at one of our gas stops. I put some gas in the car in southern Washington, down I-5, but we hadn't bothered to change clothes. I had decided to cut over from I-5 to Hwy 101 on the coast by taking the road over the mountains from just south of Roseburg to Coquille and just before Coquille, taking the turn-off to Bandon on the coast. About half-way from the turn-off to Bandon, the car started sputtering and soon the engine died. Coasting to the side of the road, we both got out and popped the hood (located in the back). We had looked the engine compartment over and found nothing noticeable and I had arrived at the conclusion that we were out of gas. As my gas gauge hadn't worked since buying the car, it was within the realm of possibility that I had misjudged the amount of gas needed to get over the mountains. No sooner had I related that to Rudy than an Oregon State Trooper vehicle pulled up in back of us. A young trooper got out of the passenger side and walked toward; we could see the driver taking down our license number. The trooper asked what the trouble was and I explained. He made a comment about our attire and that's when we found out that prisoners working on the state farms wore the same outfit. Just as quickly he told us that he'd realized we weren't "off the farm" and asked us what ship we were off of. We laughed with relief when he asked us that and quickly told him the *Connie* in Bremerton. He smiled back and told us that just over a year ago, he had been on the *Kitty Hawk* before mustering out and getting the job with the state troopers. He went back to the patrol car and explained to his partner who we were and what the problem was. Coming back to us, he said that this time of night, it being well on past 10PM, there wasn't a gas station open within 50 miles. Then he invited us to crash at his house for the night and he'd take us to get gas and back out to the car in the morning. We jumped at the offer! So, off we went. He had to stop by the station to check out from his shift and then we hopped in his car and he took us to the house. Turns out he was "house sitting" for the owners who wouldn't be back from the LA area until June. It was a large, two-story home with plenty of bedrooms and Rudy and I picked one each and were soon snoozing away. In the morning our trooper friend was good as his word and had us back out to the car, with gas, by 8AM. We exchanged addresses and thanked him profusely before driving off. We pulled up to my folks' house shortly before noon, to the surprise of everyone because they had been worried when we didn't show the night before. It was a *very* short visit though, before climbing back into the car for the long trip back north. After that messed up trip, I never drove home unless it was a three-day holiday or I had leave. Rudy and I both stayed in touch with the trooper for four or five years, exchanging Christmas cards, but after that we never heard further from him.

Also, while in Bremerton for this overhaul, I met Rose. She and her girlfriend Janet had spotted me and a friend of Rudy's at their church one Sunday and arranged to meet us. Unknown to either me or Joey, they had already decided on who would be dating whom! Rose and I became an item and we dated seriously for over six months. I was invited to her family's home for dinner one night and found out their house was just off the tarmac at Kitsap County Airport. Her dad owned Puget Sound Airlines! This was mostly small aircraft making hops between county airstrips and the islands in the sound. There was not much money in it, but if you ran a tight ship, you could make a living at it.

Other than the trip home by car, I usually managed a flight home every couple months, with the folks pitching in for part of my fare. The usual routine was for me to hop a ferry to Seattle, take the shuttle to Boeing Field (before SeaTac was finished) and fly from there. But, as I was getting set for another trip home Rose said she'd worked it out for me to fly from Kitsap airport on one of her dad's planes to Boeing field and that she would fly over with me. So, that's what we did and it saved me some time and money. Cool!

Knowing I would be leaving in a few months, I had a decision to make. I didn't have the heart to string Rose along until the last moment and then kiss her goodbye and run off. And I also couldn't bring myself to commit to anything more permanent, which she seemed to be hoping for. With over two more years remaining on my Navy contract and another deployment staring me in the face, I didn't want to be one of those guys leaving a "WestPac widow" back in San Diego while I was overseas. So, I broke it off and we were both miserable for some time afterward. I still think of her from time to time!

I mentioned previously that Rudy had been part of a salvage run on one of the decom ships. This was quite common back then as there were plenty of WWII and Korean War ships being brought into Bremerton for lay-up in the mothball fleet that was tied up close by. When the *Bonnie Dick* (formerly CVA-31) pulled in for lay-up preps and salvage, I was given an open salvage chit and authorized a Navy pick-up to go over and see what I and three others could strip off her that would be useful in *Connie's* CIC. So, off we went, with screw drivers, vice grips, hammers and the like, loaded in the cab. Driving up to her, we noticed there had been a ramp laid from the dock to one of her lowered elevators, so we drove aboard and into the hangar bay. Parking the pick-up amidships, we bailed out and headed for CIC. We ended up stripping anemometers, rheostats, Plexiglas status boards and a lot of other odds and ends that could be used back aboard *Connie*. Then we spread out and took a look around the ship. Two of us made it into the Flag spaces where we noticed that all the very well-appointed furniture was still in place. Gold Mine! We quickly rounded up the others, loaded into the pick-up and raced back over to the *Connie* to unload our stash. Then we piled back into the pick-up and made it back aboard the *Bonnie Dick* to carry off some of that furniture. You see, OI division had a newly refurbished crews lounge just off our berthing space and we were in need of some sofas and chairs. This would fit the bill nicely. We really made a haul, filling the pick-up bed to overflowing with goodies. For a few months our lounge was the envy of all the other divisions. Sadly, it was deemed too nice for us common swabbies and a few months later was re-designated the PO1 Lounge. Fully furnished, I might add!

By March the ship had reached the point in her overhaul that it was time to put her through her paces out at sea. The later part of March and the first week of April were spent doing that in the OpArea (W-237) off the northwest coast of the Olympic Peninsula. There were GQ drills, Man Overboard drills, high speed runs and crash-backs (reverses) and many more trials before returning to Bremerton to get ready for our transit down to San Diego. We had been warned that anti-war demonstrations were scheduled for the morning of our departure and it was recommended that the crew arrive onboard the night before. Sure enough, the following morning, the fence line on the hill above the shipyard and in view of the ship, was crowded with protesters. They were waving signs, making noise and generally living up to their reputation!

We departed PSNSY, 12 April and arrived at NAS North Island, San Diego on the 15th of April.

CHAPTER 5

WORK-UPS & REFTRA

MAY - SEPTEMBER '71

"WORK-UPS" AND REFTRA are a series of benchmarks that every ship must perform to required standards before being deemed operationally trained and qualified for deployment overseas. There were other material inspections that needed to be completed as well and without which the ship would not be certified in those particular fields and could prevent the ship's being qualified as materially ready for deployment. I don't profess to know the details of all these requirements and won't attempt to go beyond mention of them here: INSURV, OPPE, ORI and CarQuals, to name a few, were all important events in the course of becoming qualified and certified for operational readiness or deployment. Most of the crew were not directly involved in one or the other of these events, but to those departments that were, they were crucial. To most of the rest of us, their impacts on the daily routine were just a pain in the ass!

Work-Ups consist of a series of drills, exercises and events that are scheduled before the ship's readiness to commence Refresher Training. Battle Drills, Navigation Exercises, Fire Drills, Mass Casualty Drills, Abandon Ship Drills, Man Overboard Drills, Blue Bells (nuclear weapons handling) and more, were first practiced by the ship's crew and later observed and graded during "Refresher Training" (or whichever relevant board of observers was required). The culmination of RefTra was a battle problem lasting most of the day and with the last few hours requiring the ship to be "buttoned up" (watertight hatches, doors and scuttles closed) in a material readiness condition necessary in a combat environment. Later, more advanced exercises included an integrated battle scenario with "Red" and "Blue" adversaries, conducted in SOCAL and called COMPTUEX (Composite Training Unit Exercise). As an added measure of training and in cooperation with our allied navies, another multi-phased and progressional exercise was included during the ship's and their assigned Battle Group's transit to WestPac; this was called RIMPAC. Commenced in SOCAL, RIMPAC progressed to OpAreas around the Hawaiian Islands and culminated overseas, with various ships and navies represented and being added and subtracted as events progressed. Both COMPTUEX and RIMPAC still take place today as a means of training and evaluating individual units and their Battle Groups in the broader spectrum of integrated, cooperative tactical employment. Much of the interoperability training already completed by the USN ships is again employed during RIMPAC to better enable intra-navy communication and their ability to operate as a cohesive unit. With as many as a dozen different allied navies participating during designated portions of the overall exercise, the RIMPAC exercise was a valuable "snapshot" of allied readiness at the time. But, many of the benchmarks achieved must be re-established during each RIMPAC owing to ship type and capability changes as well as crew turnover. I'm relating my perception of RIMPAC as a direct result of my participation in three of these exercises during my career. At the upper echelon, there may be disagreement over my interpretation of the goals and achievements, but I am not attempting to portray RIMPACs from that point of view. I confess that much of this, in the earlier RIMPAC's I was involved in, was way beyond my paygrade. But, being stationed in CIC afforded me a better understanding of what the ship was tasked to accomplish.

During the latter part of our shipyard period and after all systems were back on line (power, chilled water, LP & HP air, etc.) NTDS was brought on-line and went through a series of element and systems tests to demonstrate upgrades to the consoles and the computer program. As a direct result of its Vietnam experience and lessons learned at the PIRAZ station off Haiphong, the navy attempted to solve the "auto detect" problems experienced. To read about the evolution of PIRAZ, NTDS and BVP, go to the following link:

http://ethw.org/First-Hand:The_Naval_Tactical_Data_System_in_Combat_-_Chapter_7_of_the_Story_of_the_Naval_Tactical_Data_System

The PIRAZ experience had shown that with the volume of air traffic in the controlled air space of this station, it was not within the current technology to maintain an accurate, up to date tactical picture. If the "auto detect" problem could be solved, it would eliminate the necessity of humans being required to detect, generate computer data and update that data. In the late 1960s that problem seemed to have been solved with the introduction of a BVP (Beacon Video Processor) CPU addition to the computer program. *Connie* received this upgrade at the tail-end of the shipyard period and a tech rep was onboard to put it through its paces. I and two other RDs were assigned to assist in these efforts and to make ourselves available to the tech rep whenever he wanted to load and test the BVP CPU. After running embedded video while in port, the system was deemed ready for at-sea testing. A limited amount of on-line time was accomplished while the ship was going through "shake down" off the Washington coast, but fully integrated operations would not be possible until we could demonstrate its inter-operability in a "real world" tactical environment. This meant SOCAL Ops! So, it was August before that could happen. What we found in SOCAL and during Flight Ops was that while BVP could detect and track multiple targets without a problem, it could not maintain track when that air track entered "marshall" or was engaged in ACM (Air Combat Maneuvers). The rate of turn was too steep for BVP to manage and the tracks would go "wild" both in course and speed. You couldn't blank out "marshall" or an ACM event from BVP and you couldn't blank out a set radius from the carrier to tell BVP to stop tracking within that area. Another thought that we all mentioned to the Tech Rep was that, while BVP detected and tracked air tracks squawking IFF, it did not detect "raw" video which would logically be the "bad guy" and *not* squawking IFF! However, the current PIRAZ problem was not with circling airplanes in "marshall" and was not with tracks *not* squawking IFF. So, in that particular scenario, BVP was the perfect solution. For carriers? Not so much!

Much later in my career and while aboard *the Beach* we ran into a similar problem with RVP (Radar Video Processing). After hundreds of hours of element
and systems testing by the contractor back in the Dam Neck, VA lab, RVP was
included with the Baseline (CDS Block 0) program. Hundreds more hours were
spent testing aboard ship, while the ship was in Bremerton. More hours were
spent in SOCAL and the Hawaiian Island OpAreas with the system online and
RVP activated. But it was not until we were stationed in close proximity to the
carrier that we discovered we had a problem. Because the CDS Tech Reps had
departed the ship in Hawaii, we had to contact them and have them flown back
and brought out to the ship so we could demonstrate the problem to them: they
could then write up a CPTR (Computer Program Trouble Report), take it back
to Dam Neck, solve the problem, load the revisions into another RVP CPU, fly
it out to wherever we were and test it.

The problem was, while our air search radar was operating in the same common air space of the carrier, RVP could not track aircraft once they had entered
"marshall" (again) and the track data would go "wild," generating heading and
speed leaders of Mach 1.5 to 2. So, the Tech Reps wrote it up and, in a week,
they had produced their solution, flown back out and loaded the new RVP CPU.
We quickly discovered they had overlooked a key component in the calculations.
While the new RVP code "nulled out" the area designated as "marshall" they had
failed to realize that "marshall" is not a fixed geographic point, but rather a moving area "slaved" and relative to the carrier. Back to the drawing board, another
week passes and they finally get the problem solved and delivered. The entire experience was partially our fault because we hadn't impressed upon the Tech Reps
that "marshall" needed to move with the carrier. We assumed they recognized
that part of the problem. I guess we were just "too close" to the problem!

One of the emergency maneuvers drilled repeatedly during work-ups was
the ship's response to the detonation of a tactical nuclear weapon within our tactical area. Those of us in CIC who plotted this reaction commonly referred to it
as "Ass to the Blast, Balls to the Wall." When the ship received information con-
cerning the detonation of a nuclear device within our tactical area of operations,
it was the Bridge team and CIC that plotted the situation and recommended the
response maneuver as an effort to minimize the effects of the blast and its expected radiation. Range and bearing of the blast were plotted on the DRT trace

and a template was overlaid on the reported epicenter of the blast, then transcribed on the plot. If the ship was inside the prescribed circle and downwind of the blast, there was nothing for it but to expect, at the very least, casualties due to the blast and radiation. If the ship were outside the circle but upwind of the blast, it was possible that the damage from the blast could be minimized and radiation avoided. Radiation exposure greatly depended on where the ship was from the blast and where the prevailing winds would take the radiation cloud. So, CIC's recommendation would be dictated by proximity and wind. In my opinion, the exercise was a rather hopeless proposition!

The ship departed for WestPac on 1 October 1971. As we made our way down the channel, anti-war protest boats were attempting to place themselves in our intended path, but Coast Guard small boats were intercepting them and herding them out of our way. Another contentious departure!

CHAPTER 6
WESTPAC 71 & 72
1 OCTOBER 1971 - 1 JULY 1972

USS CONSTELLATION (CVA-64)

Days Deployed: 274
Days "On the Line" (Yankee Station): 154
2,835,000 Meals Served
17,289 Arrested Landings
Mail 875,000 pounds
Fifteen aircraft lost, nine due to enemy action.
Six aircrew members were missing, five were listed as KIAs, one as MIA and three were taken as POWs.

ON LINE PERIODS:

4 - 21 November 1971; 30 November 1971 - 30 December 1971; 1 January 1972-1 February 1972; 9 February 1972 - 1 March 1972; 14 -22 March 1972; 9 - 30 April 1972

CHANGE OF COMMAND

Captain H.E. Gerhard: January - 26 September 1971
Captain J.D. Ward: 27 September 1971 - 11 April 1973

PEARL HARBOR & OAHU, HI

Returning from my first WestPac, the ship had not stopped at Pearl Harbor, so this would be my first liberty in Hawaii. As I was not part of the Navigation Detail while pulling into port, I was to muster topside and "man the rail" as is the custom. The divisions station for this was the port, forward flight deck and as the location of our berth would take us past the *Arizona*, the command was given and we all came to attention and rendered honors. It was a hushed, solemn and moving experience. My first trip into town touched all the usual tourist spots, Waikiki and the International Market Place; Waikiki Beach to watch the surfers and those that were trying to surf; a trip to Diamond Head and some shopping at the Ala Moana Mall. The second day a buddy and I hopped *da bus* and spent the day getting off and on as we made our way around the island. Kaneohe, Chinamen's Hat, the north shore to check out the surf and surfers. I also spent some time getting around base to the EM Club, Navy Exchange, etc., but our stay in Pearl was short and we were soon underway again. We had a schedule to keep!

D&T

D&T stood for Detection & Tracking. When the ship deployed for WestPac in October 1971, D&T was the CIC module I was assigned to work in. Your rotation on duty was the standard eight hours on watch and eight hours off, repeated daily until you pulled into port. Mixed into that rotation were your studies for next higher rank, meals, showers, letter writing, working parties and any collateral duties you may have been assigned. Your "line periods" were, on average, 24 to 30 days in length and in-port periods were rarely more than five days at a time. The pace was both grueling and filled with tedium. The tedium was in the tasks performed while on watch in D&T. The module was responsible for detecting, identifying and tracking any and all aircraft within range of the ship's air search radar. NTDS (Naval Tactical Data Systems) consoles were arrayed against the bulkheads of the module and consisted of a Track Supervisor, ID Operator, Height/Size Console Operator and two to three operators whose sole function was to update the positions of all the ship's air tracks as well as search for raw video that had not been assigned a track and enter one associated to that video. Before the age of integrated combat direction systems and auto track and detect capability, each track with video had to be updated to its current location as the video and track moved through the monitored airspace. And then, when it got too hectic, you were hamstrung by the limitations of the technology when too much data (air tracks, surface tracks, marshall, entry and egress points, MIGCAP, BARCAP, RESCAP, TARCAP, etc.) had been entered and the system simply "froze up." Re-booting the system could take 10 to 40 minutes depending on the severity of the systems overload and the personnel on watch below in Computer Central. When you had more than two carriers operating on Yankee Station, this occurred all too often. Upgrades and new technology allowing for entry of all operational data would not be available until the 1980s and even then on a limited basis as new ships and upgrades to the older ships occurred. To allow for geographic features and the "special purpose" tracks mentioned above to be displayed, the only recourse to our limitations back then was to plot many of these "reference points" on a large Plexiglas display board facing D&D (Display & Decision) in grease pencil. As these points were only relative to the "strike" being launched, the data would have to be re-plotted for each subsequent strike.

It was during this second WestPac that an opportunity arose for me to pick up some extra coin. Word went around the division that one of the guys transferring off the ship had been one of the personnel trained and carded as a projectionist and there was need of a replacement. Back then, training films (and "training films") were shown in divisional spaces using a Bell & Howell movie projector and the projectionist was a volunteer. If the film shown was a Navy training film, the projectionist did his duty. But, if the film was a "training film" of the unsanctioned type (adult movies), then the projectionist was paid with tips collected from the audience and offered to the guy running the projector. For training, you sat through a one or two-hour class and then were UI (under instruction) during a film showing. Upon completion of the class and UI screening, you received a card designating you as a trained and authorized projectionist. Official navy training films where your services were required could actually get you pulled off watch in CIC to show a film. But for the unofficial films of the adult type, you could only provide services during your off-time. In the CIC area, the place to do this was the CATCC (Carrier Air Traffic Control Center) Office, located adjacent to D&T. This was mainly due to new films arriving aboard ship through air transfer from COD flights, which meant that people in CATCC were "in the loop" for procuring them. Most of my unofficial showings and most of my tips came from providing my projectionist skills for the "airdales" in CATCC. One of the first times I did so, I found these guys really got involved in their porn. For example, usually there would be a "narrator" stationed close to the action on the screen and his job was to provide a running commentary. Most all of us would be in stitches at the comments and sound effects coming from these guys. Naturally, the pilots provided the best repartee! Many of the times my services were requested in CATCC, one of the 2nd Class POs would come looking for me to see if I were available. Eventually, he and I became tight and I always made good tips when working the projector there.

Because COD flights were manifested through CATCC, I thought there was an opportunity there and pursued that through my buddy. There were times when Rudy and I would want to travel either from Bremerton to San Diego or vice versa, but getting a seat on a plane was always the difficult part. One time, when we were looking for transportation, I talked with my CATCC friend and he said he could get us two seats on the manifest for the COD. This was when we were in San Diego and the flight would originate out of NAS North Island (NASNI) and terminate at Kitsap County Airport, just outside Bremerton. Of course, we gladly accepted the offer and made plans for the trip. The day of the flight and after departing NASNI, the COD made a stopover at NAS Alameda for fuel and passengers. The crew had all us passengers deplane and wait in the terminal while the plane was refueled. When it came time for us to load up again, Rudy had disappeared and although I quickly looked around the terminal as everyone walked out to the plane I couldn't spot him anywhere. I began to get worried. After we all loaded into the plane, I mentioned to one of the crew that my buddy was missing. Still, they had a schedule to keep and so after they pulled the stairs away from the plane, they began to close the hatch. Just then, I heard someone outside yelling and recognized Rudy's voice. The crewman at the hatch leaned out and down, grabbing Rudy's hand and yanked him up and into the aircraft. Later, when I asked what happened, he told me he had made a phone call and hadn't heard the PA announcement to board the aircraft. If he'd been left behind, he would have been in a real pickle and would probably have had to get to the Oakland airport and a flight back down to San Diego. One of the problems with taking a COD flight was that, in an unpressurized cabin, temperatures at 5,000 feet or above during the winter left you under-dressed and stomping your feet and flapping your arms. So most of our flights were on the NALCO birds out of NASNI, which flew the DC-9s. But you signed up at the terminal the day of the flight and hoped there were enough space-available seats for you to get boarded. These flights terminated at McChord AFB and on the return trip you had to get from Bremerton over to McChord and again hope there were available seats. Still, I made quite a number flights, back and forth, by one means or another.

FLIGHT QUARTERS

Before setting Flight Quarters, the disposition of one of our assigned escort ships was modified, directing them to "Take Station" as "Plane Guard." This was designated as "Station 1-SNX," which was 170 degrees relative behind the carrier, at 1000 yards in the eventuality of an aircraft going into the drink and the pilot having to be fished out of the water. It was a nerve-wracking position to be in on a moonless night. Also, before launch, the plane-guard helo was launched and assumed station off the beam of the carrier. With these safety measures in place, launch would commence once the ship had been swung into the wind and speed attained to give the aircraft a wind speed across the deck (and off the port bow to allow for the angle) of 30 knots. This was accomplished either by existing wind speed or a combination of wind speed and ship's speed into the wind and was dictated by the heaviest aircraft, when fully loaded with bombs and fuel.

In CIC, preparations for Flight Quarters began much earlier. Although the CDS (Combat Direction System) program had been reloaded at the beginning of the mid-watch, many of the Watch Officers in D&D (Display & Decision) believed this should be done again a couple hours before Flight Quarters by reason that a "refreshed" computer load would minimize the cumulative faults during the launch sequence. An hour before launch and updated at the direction of the Bridge, the Surface Module in CIC would re-work its calculation of the desired "wind envelope" for establishing a "Flight CORPEN" to give aircraft the desired "wind off the bow." This was done using both the CDS method (not relied upon due to known errors in the calculation) and the Maneuvering Board solution, which was checked and rechecked for accuracy and modification as the wind shifted. The "Foxtrot Corpen" or "Flight Corpen" is the chosen course for flight operations, based on the current true wind course and speed to achieve the desired relative wind across the deck.

Through the launch and until the aircraft departed "marshall" (a designated rendezvous point close to the carrier), each was in communication with and under the control of a CATCC (Carrier Air Traffic Control Center) controller. Checking out of "marshall," the pilots would be directed to "switch up" to an FAC (Fighter Air Control) R/T circuit manned by an RD/OS in CIC who would run through each aircraft's status (fuel state, weapons state, IFF checks and any existing equipment limitations); the pilots would then be cleared to the next controller scheduled for that mission (i.e. Red Crown or an airborne controller or FAC (Forward Air Controller)).

In D&T, we would not begin tracking the outbound strike until after the aircraft left "marshall" and were on their way to their designated assignment for that particular launch evolution. They might be part of the strike package or designated as one of the many type CAP stations, as mentioned above. In order not to overload the CDS program we would endeavor to establish outgoing tracks by grouping. If we could pick out the IFF of one aircraft in a grouping of two or three, we would only establish and update that one track. This saved labor in updating existing tracks and also minimized data entry and thus the load on the program. These TDS tracks, when the tactical picture was "clicking," would be picked up on radar by PIRAZ and tracked by them, thereby taking "control" of the TDS (Tactical Data Systems) track and making necessary updates to the TDS "symbol" as the aircraft transited toward them or went "feet dry" (over land). For launch evolutions designated for strikes into South Vietnam or Laos, there was no PIRAZ ship and once the aircraft went "feet dry" TDS tracking would cease due to radar interference from the land mass; control would be passed to the designated on-station FAC.

During Flight Quarters for the recovery of aircraft, when strike aircraft were released from PIRAZ or FAC control, they would switch up to the ship's designated FAD circuit and establish communications with the same RD/OS they had checked out with. This was to relay information about remaining fuel and weapons status and any emergencies or battle damage. D&T in CIC would establish TDS tracks on incoming aircraft or take existing TDS tracks "under local control" and track them through our airspace and into "marshall," where control would be passed back to CATCC. Given the technology of the time, these data-intensive periods too often caused the CDS program to freeze or crash and, once brought back on-line, it would take some time to re-establish all the tactical data that had been lost. This was an inherent problem that would take years and further technological breakthroughs to solve.

TRIP TO MANILA & MARYKNOLL COLLEGE @ QUEZON CITY

While stateside, one of my working buddies told me about his writing to a girl in the Philippines through a PenPal ad he'd seen. So, I thought I'd give it a go! I wrote a letter to the PenPal organization, which they sent on to one of their "customers" to respond to. Shortly, I received a reply back from a girl who was a student at Maryknoll College outside Manila. The letter was well written and lively and I was impressed, so I continued writing. We did that for five or six months before the ship was to go back overseas, and I mentioned the approximate time we would be making our first port call in Subic. We were both wondering if it would be possible to meet up during one of our periods in port there.

Well, our first time in Subic during that WestPac we hadn't been tied up to the pier for more than an hour when I got a call in CIC from the switchboard saying there was a call for me on an outside line. It was my PenPal and apparently she had gotten plugged in to the Subic grapevine and found out the date and time we were to pull in, as well as the phone number to the ship's switchboard. I was *very* impressed! We made arrangements to meet and she asked if I could bring three or four friends. I told her I'd try and after talking a bit more, hung up. I had no trouble finding shipmates eager to go. On the day of the trip we made our way to the bus station in Olongapo to catch a *Liberty Liner* to Manila. The place was a beehive of people and standing in line to board a bus showed us that by the time we got aboard the bus would be full. One of the kids hanging around the station approached us asking if we would pay him to secure seats for us on the bus and we told him yes. So, he and a couple of his cronies went around and climbed through the open window at the back of the bus and "reserved" the entire back seat. When we sat down, we gave him and his buddies a few pesos and they exited the same way they had come in. As they departed, they asked if we wanted anything to eat or drink because they would get that for us, too. One of the guys perked up and asked for a case of "San Magoo" (San Miguel beer). Shortly, two of the boys hoisted a case through the window and then proceeded to bring up a block of ice, which they applied an ice pick to and chipped it down over the warm beer. All this and the ice too, ran us about 10 pesos or about $2.50. The bus pulled out of the station and soon we all had a cold beer in hand, watching the scenery go by. Back then, the road through the mountains was just a two-lane job, at best. When two large vehicles met, they both had to move out a bit to allow passing each other. This meant that at times the outer wheels were on the edge of the roadway and you could look out the window, straight down into the jungle hundreds of feet below. We concentrated on the beer!

Once through the mountains, the roadway (I wouldn't really call it a highway) followed dikes between rice paddies, into and through small towns which got progressively larger as you approached Manila. Going through the small towns and larger ones, the bus would slow for traffic, the door would open and on would hop a bevy of vendors selling ice cream, soda pop, candies and the like. On the other side of town, the doors would open again and the vendors would hop off and wait for the next bus traveling in the opposite direction. Once or twice, while stopped in traffic, passengers got on and off to run to the side of the road, drop trou and do their business before running back to the bus. It all seemed routine and no one but us took notice. That is, until it was our turn to void some of that beer we'd been drinking. As soon as we climbed off the bus and lined up along the road to do our business, every female on the bus hung their head out the window and watched the Americans take a whiz! With a lot of giggling going on around us, we climbed back aboard and took our seats.

Arriving in Manila, we hired a jeepney, the Philippines' version of a cross between a bus and a cab, which could seat about eight people comfortably. We had the driver take us into the city so we could find a hotel for the night — our meeting with the girls wasn't until the following day. The next morning, we hired a jeepney again to take us out to Maryknoll College, where the girls attended school and where my PenPal had told me she and her friends would meet us. The college was an all-girls school and when we pulled up at the gate and tried to get in, the guard told us no men were allowed on campus unless escorted by a faculty member or a student. But he got on the phone and called up to the school telling the front desk to get ahold of my PenPals and say there were visitors at the gate. Soon down the driveway came a bevy of girls, including my PenPal. After she identified herself, she told us we'd have to come up to the main building and wait while the girls got ready to leave. Really though, I think this pause was so we could be put on display while the students paraded through the waiting area checking us out. It sure seemed that the word had got around and that our waiting area was the destination of every student on campus.

Anyway, as it turned out, while we were waiting and the girls were getting ready, they also made arrangements for our transportation for the day by contracting a Jeepney driver that would be ours for however long we needed him. When the girls were ready, we walked back down the hill to the gate to wait for our driver. When he pulled up, we were impressed. The Jeepney appeared to be brand new, all tricked out and with quadrophonic sound blasting all the latest stateside rock & roll. Cool! As we drove through Quezon City on our way to Manila, we mentioned that we'd really like to find a place to eat lunch, it being that time of day already. So, the girls told the driver the name of a restaurant they knew of and that's where we went. Very upscale, too! Lunch out of the way, the girls told the driver where we intended to go next and when we arrived we saw that we were down near the Bayshore drive and at the Cultural Center, which we toured for a couple hours. Then, it was off to shopping a mall of sorts, where just about anything and everything was available. We guys bought some knickknacks to take back with us, but mostly this stop was for the girls because they loaded up! By the time dinner rolled around we had already discussed where to go, and again the girls picked the place. It was a rather dated restaurant, but very popular — the place was packed. We finally got a table that was big enough for all of us and asked our hosts for their opinions on what was good on the menu. We also noticed that the prices were higher than usual, but we wanted to impress the ladies. We probably spent a couple hours in there, because we ordered a lot of food and finished all of it, too! When the bill came, the girls had told the waiter, in Tagalog, to leave it with them and not give it to us. We were surprised, because when we found out and insisted that we pay, they were adamant that it was their treat. The bill was almost 300 pesos! We walked a few blocks up the street and into the lounge at the Hilton, just to relax and sit and talk. That was when we learned more of the background the girls had come from and why they had no qualms about paying our tab. Each of them came from well to do and well-connected families — my PenPal's family being owners of a number of lumber mills on Palawan Island. One of the girls was even a congressman's daughter.

As the hour got later and the conversation tapered off, the girls told us they would be leaving us here because they had to get back to the school before curfew. As for us, we had to be back on a bus to Subic the following morning, so we all said our goodbyes and we saw them off. My PenPal and I exchanged a few more letters after that, but because there was no future chance of meeting, the letters stopped and I never saw her again. But she was a good kid and we all enjoyed the day given us!

"GOD, ON GUARD!"

It was Christmas 1971 and the ship was at sea on Yankee Station, which by this stage of the war was a general area of operation determined by its relative proximity to targets that might be designated for upcoming airstrikes. Watch rotation was the standard 8 on 8 off in CIC and for however many days we were to remain at sea. This sometimes went on for over a month, seven days a week! You can imagine the drudgery that this entailed. Ever go without seeing daylight for 3 or 4 weeks? It gave me an acute appreciation for the "bubble heads" and what they had to endure as a submariner.

I had been temporarily assigned to support the embarked CTF 77.7 staff to fill a seat at one of the tactical data systems computer consoles, whose internal communications circuits had been modified to allow me to talk with the "tennis shoe" types, the linguists and analysts assigned to monitor enemy tactical frequencies. Also, staff needed someone familiar with the computer consoles that could input this type of information into the tactical picture displayed on the scopes. As North Vietnamese (occasionally over Vihn) or CHICOM (over Hainan) aircraft were monitored during launch, I was fed the range and bearing to the launch site and would then enter a "Hostile; non-vehicular" tactical track correlating to the information provided. I would also enter a SIF (Selective Identification) code to denote where the information originated. "Non-vehicular" is a type of track that, once entered, could not be updated from raw radar data and to reposition the track required I be provided with updated range and bearing. Otherwise the track sat where it was initially entered until I was provided with new data or when I was directed to "drop" the track from the system due to outdated information. A few times, depending on how far north "Yankee Station" was, I was able to associate the tactical track with raw radar video. Informing staff, I would update the track to the video and the track would go "vehicular" for the time that I held video.

It was late and my watch that day was "midwatch" or graveyard for all you non-swabbies out there, that is, midnight to eight in the morning. Before coming on watch, I had gone down to the mess decks to eat "midrats" (midnight rations), which usually consisted of leftovers from the dinner meal and a few added alternatives. When I entered the mess deck area, I noticed something highly unusual. There was a long line at the "bug juice" dispenser. What the? So, I got in line and asked the guys ahead of me what was going on. In very hushed tones, they told me to hush up and don't make a fuss. OK! Now I think I understood. Someone had added some "flavor" to the bug juice for some "holiday cheer." Sure enough, when I got to the dispenser and poured a cup, my nose told me I was right. So, down the hatch! There was a senior enlisted off to the side of the dispenser that made sure the guys understood there was only one trip through the line being allowed. No one had a problem with that, though.

Because you were required to relieve your predecessor at quarter to the hour, I had already assumed the duties of the station by the time midnight rolled around. One of the radio circuits required to be monitored 24/7 was called "Guard." It was an emergency & distress circuit; a specific person on watch was always assigned to monitor this vital radio net. To ensure that nothing was missed, it was always patched into a speaker within CIC so that anyone in proximity would hear it if something were to be transmitted. The "Guard" speaker was in the "overhead" just above my assigned station. At the stroke of midnight the speaker boomed out, for everyone in the Tonkin Gulf to hear, "This is God, on Guard, it's a boy!" There were smiles all round.

Another incident during this assignment was an emergency landing of a battle-damaged aircraft. The NTDS console I was stationed at was right next to one of the CCTV monitors used for observation of launch and recovery operations by the staff. When staff was informed of the problem, we all swiveled right to take in the scene as it unfolded on the TV camera. The crash net was up and yellow gear stationed forward of that. Should the aircraft fail to be stopped by the crash net, it would be kept from moving forward and causing damage to aircraft parked on the forward flight deck by the yellow gear. The latter was *not* the preferred method for the pilot!

As we followed the camera and it panned to the aircraft's approach — it was a Phantom — we could see that the nose-wheel of the plane was not down. You can only imagine what the pilot was thinking! The plane bounced onto the deck, nose high as it caught an arresting wire. As the wire payed out and the plane continued forward, the nose started to drop. Just as the nose went level with the deck, it poked through the crash net and the aircraft came to a halt! The nose didn't even scrape the deck! We all had incredulous looks on our faces at the miracle that we had just witnessed! What a lucky SOB!

I heard later that the pilot was none other than CAG, so I would have to attribute some of that miracle to his skill as a pilot! Some! But, not too much. Whether it was CAG (Carrier Air Group) or not, I'm certain, at the moment, he would have agreed!

CHAPTER 7

PIRAZ

ONE OF THE KEY FUNCTIONS in support of air operations in the Tonkin Gulf and over North Vietnam was the PIRAZ station. Taken from Wikipedia, the following provides a relatively accurate description of its purpose and function:

"PIRAZ is a United States Navy acronym for Positive Identification Radar Advisory Zone.[1][2] The zone is defined by the air search radar coverage of a ship patrolling a designated PIRAZ station." "The PIRAZ ship requires a Naval Tactical Data System radio-linked computer installation to effectively identify and track all aircraft anticipated to enter the airspace of the zone during combat." "The concept originated in the summer of 1966 as Yankee station was established for United States Task Force 77 aircraft carriers launching strikes against North Vietnam.[3] A fixed patrol station within range of land-based aircraft made the stationed aircraft carriers vulnerable to attack. A PIRAZ station was established in the westernmost portion of the Gulf of Tonkin where air search radar coverage might extend over North Vietnam and the air-strike routes from Yankee station. This PIRAZ station radio call sign was "Red Crown." The first PIRAZ ships were USS Chicago, King, Mahan, and Long Beach.[2] Belknap class frigates began rotating into PIRAZ station assignments in 1967….."".

"USS *Agerholm* was typical of the ships providing torpedo boat destroyer "shotgun" escort for the Gulf of Tonkin PIRAZ station." PIRAZ ships carried long-range RIM-2 Terrier or RIM-8 Talos surface-to-air missiles to defend their stations. *Chicago* fired RIM-8H Talos-ARM anti-radar homing missiles against North Vietnamese shore-based radar stations.[8] Each PIRAZ ship was accompanied on station by a "shotgun" torpedo boat destroyer with quick-firing guns to defend the PIRAZ ships from torpedo boat attack.[9] PIRAZ ships provided protective radar surveillance of the remotely piloted vehicles performing aerial photo reconnaissance of North Vietnam"….. (Code named "Buffalo Hunter").

If you were an aircraft flying in "Red Crown" airspace and were not in compliance with established egress/ingress procedures or were not flying a prescribed route, not transponding the correct IFF code or hadn't been "deloused" by CAP, the next sound you may hear would be that of a fire control radar "locking on" to you! Pucker factor!

A very good account of an engagement aboard a "Red Crown" PIRAZ ship during the Vietnam War can be found at the link below. The specific incident related, while not "typical," is indicative of the high level of alertness required at such a station. The North Vietnamese, while not "built" for air-to-surface engagement, were opportunists. If they detected a pattern and that pattern revealed a weakness or created an opportunity, they would attempt to take it! As evidenced by the" Higbee" strike on 19 April 1972, as related below.

Hard Charger: Battle at PIRAZ (USS Biddle (DLG-34):
https://ussbiddle. wordpress.com/battle-at-piraz-18/

Whenever "Red Crown" came up on Navy Red or any other R/T circuit in the Gulf, everyone cocked an ear in CIC!

CIC SURFACE MODULE
& SSSC PLOTTING THE "GUN LINE"

One of the watch stations we manned in the Surface Module of CIC was the plotting table and radio circuit called "Triple SC." This was a large plotting table with a chart of the entire Gulf of Tonkin including most of South Vietnam, North Vietnam and Hainan Island. The chart was covered with a clear acetate overlay so that the plots made in "grease pencil" could be erased and updated as necessary. Our duties at this station were to plot all blue water naval units at Yankee Station, PIRAZ (Red Crown) and the "Gun Line" along the coast of Vietnam, to be updated every hour. This included units rotating onto and off of those positions. Because the R/T net was "uncovered" (not encrypted) the coordinates for each unit had to be encrypted using a hand-held encryption device provided for that purpose. This was referred to as a CAC Card (not to be confused with the acronym currently in use to identify DOD identity cards) and consisted of a group of randomly generated letters and numbers. Another hand-held operator encryption device was referred to as a SIRTCI Wheel, but this was much later in my career. So, using the CAC card meant that, as each unit transmitted its location in code, the receiving units had to use the device to decode the message into latitude and longitude and then plot that unit's location. Before the 1972 North Vietnamese "Easter Offensive," this required decoding and plotting roughly 30 or so positions hourly. Due to the rapid increase in ships stationed in the Gulf due to the NVA offensive, there were anywhere from 60 to 68 "blue water" ship's in the

Gulf daily. These could be on-station, off-station to replenish and re-arm, or en route to or from port calls. However, with so many ships present they were being assigned to task units of three or four ships and we were instructed to take updates from the OTC (Officer in Tactical Command) of each of these task units, instead of from each individual ship. This was a wise move because it would have been impossible to encode, decode and plot all of these ships during the given hour. During Operation End Sweep, the de-mining of the NVA harbors and coastline, SSSC was used to keep track of those units, as well.

During the course of the war, 29 ships were hit by NVA shore batteries, 19 seriously enough to be withdrawn for major repairs, but none was sunk. Based on the HOSTA (Hostile Fire File) record found at the National Archives and additional data found in *A Short History of the United States Navy and Southeast Asia Conflict 1950 – 1975*, there is an established record showing that U. S. Navy Hostile Fire Casualties from 1968 – 1973 were: 6 killed and 34 wounded. These incidents rarely made headlines and casualty reporting was usually relegated to the home-town newspapers where the sailor hailed from.

"WAGER"

"Wager" was the call sign of an Air Force plane stationed over the Gulf of Tonkin 24/7, one of its duties being radio relay. Wager connected shore sites with off-shore units, from the PIRAZ (Positive Identification Radar Advisory Zone) picket ship off Haiphong to any ships that might have been stationed down on "Dixie" station off the south coast of Vietnam and all the gun-line ships in between; this was done via "Navy Red," a secure R/T circuit. During the same Christmas previously mentioned, we had a USO troupe aboard for a couple days and they put on a few shows so that most of the crew had an opportunity to see them when not on duty or watch. There weren't any big name stars in the group, but they were a hit anyway as two of them were young American girls in their early twenties and very hot looking in their mini-skirt outfits. They just had to be a little careful climbing up the ladders from deck to deck and make sure none of us sailors were following too closely behind.

Anyway, I was on watch at my CTF-77 Staff tactical computer station, when they brought one of the ladies up to CIC for a tour. Of course, the Flag Staff Officers made sure she visited their part of CIC and I got to meet her. Just then, Navy Red "secure" radio circuit belched out "Warchief, this is Wager, Over." He was calling us. A staff watch officer leaned over the TDS console and told the CIC Watch Officer stationed below that he would take the call. One of the watch officers picked up the hand-set, pressed the key and asked the USO lady to respond "Wager, Warchief. Roger, Over." Which she did! There was a long silence before the reply came back, "Warchief, Wager. That's not fair, over." We all busted up laughing! It's a safe assumption that she was probably the only civilian American female ever to be on a tactical radio circuit, on a warship in the Gulf of Tonkin, through the entire war.

When I was selected to temporarily support the CTF-77 staff, it required that I be temporarily given a TSSI (Top Secret Sensitive Information) clearance. As part of the process, I was sent up to SUPRAD (Support Radio) where our "tennis shoe" types (cryptologists and linguists) worked. I sat down with an LT for an interview and briefing that entailed a description of what my prospective duties would entail. What I hadn't anticipated was the involvement of my family by being assigned to this type of work. After the ship returned to the States, I learned from my parents that they and some of their neighbors received visits from the FBI asking questions about me. One of dad's buddies asked him what kind of trouble I'd gotten myself into this time. When my parents were interviewed, they weren't given a reason. Well, being from such a small town, news and gossip made the rounds that I had gotten involved in some hush-hush work overseas and when I finally got leave to go home I got more than a few questions about what I had been up to over there! Which I had to leave unanswered!

As an aside, there was an added perk to being temporarily assigned to staff. Three of us had been issued a CTF-77 Liberty Card, which entitled us to go to the head of the line of those personnel waiting to leave the ship. On a carrier just pulling into port, this could be a real time saver, because the lines could be long and if there was a hold up for one reason or another, time consuming. But, normally the lines moved at a goodly pace and most of the time I took my place and shuffled on through.

LIBERTY CALL - HONG KONG '72

Connie pulled into Hong Kong, dropping the "hook" (anchor) a few miles out from the Royal Navy Pier. From the ship to the pier required about a 20-minute ride on a ferry shuttle. By the time CIC was "secured" and a light "field day" held, those of us allowed liberty got dressed and queued up in line to catch a ride. I was able to partner up with Rudy for liberty and we wandered around the Fleet Exchange and the Wanchai District before catching a bite to eat. Eventually, we found ourselves at the Hilton Hotel and thought we'd go in and check out their tourist literature for possibilities. As we climbed the stairs and entered the cavernous lobby, we heard some pretty good rock & roll coming from a large entrance off the lobby and down a short set of stairs. So, we thought we'd check it out! As we started down, an oriental stopped us and asked if we were with Chase Bank because this was their private party. We had just started to respond when a tall, blonde middle-aged Caucasian walked up and asked if we were off that carrier in the harbor. When we told him we were, he immediately waved off the doorman and invited us in. While he was showing us the layout, Rudy wandered off in the direction of the band, while I got the 5-cent tour. There was a long table full of food and our host said to grab a plate and have-at-it. While I was doing that, Rudy returned and excitedly told me that he'd spoken to one of the band members and turns out they were the same Filipino band that was playing in Subic at the Sampaguita Club when we last left P.I. So, he'd put in a few requests and sure enough, during their next set, dedicated the songs to him! Santana & TDG (Three Dog Night), but I'm guessing based on knowing Rudy's musical tastes!

When we had our plates loaded up and were arriving at the end of the serving line, there was an absolutely stunning oriental lady dressed in traditional garb who greeted us and asked if we wanted to buy a package of "2 for 1" coupons. Asking her what the "deal" was, she explained that in the pack of coupons there were two for one offers for tours, ferry rides and restaurants. She also showed us that each coupon had directions in two different Chinese dialects, so your cab driver would easily know where you wanted to go. Sounded good, so we ponied up the 50HK dollars (about $10US) and bought a pack. Sitting down to eat, we broke open the coupon pack and started shuffling through the different cards. We decided that to really get our money's worth we would have to use two of the coupons each day we had left in port and that's what we did. We really didn't use any of the ride or tour coupons, but picked out the restaurant coupons that sounded good. Each day on liberty, we would use one for lunch and one for dinner and we were able to get through six or seven of those coupons. We chose Polynesian, an American steak house, Hungarian, Chinese (of course) and a couple others that I don't recall. The Polynesian restaurant was a selection for lunch and when we walked in they had just opened the doors. The place was huge and probably seated a couple hundred people, but at that time of day, Rudy and I were the only one's there. And, it seemed as if the entire staff wanted their turn on waiting on us.

We showed them the coupon; they smiled, nodded and seated us at a table. The food was great, but what made the meal was an item on the desert menu that you don't often see: Cherries Jubilee! I'd had it before and so, ordered it then. When dessert finally arrived, they wheeled over the cart, gave Rudy his ice cream and then started to work on my fare. When they "fired up" the Cherries Jubilee, it startled the heck out of Rudy and he asked what the hell that was. I explained and he promptly ordered some for himself!

That night, we took in the Hungarian restaurant. I don't recall much about it, but I do know that when you're in a Hungarian restaurant you order goulash and that's what I ate. Between the meals, Rudy and I spent a lot of our time going to various clothing shops and ordering tailor-made jackets and pants. Compared to the States, these were real bargains. I also ended up buying a Canon QL-26 camera with a wide angle lens; aboard ship, I spent many hours with it and became pretty proficient.

The next night we selected a Chinese restaurant in Kowloon, which meant a ride over on the Star Ferry. Once there, we hailed a cab and showed the driver our coupon; shortly he pulled up in front of the place. At the top of the stairs was a large assembly of fish tanks with various types of fish inside and from which you selected if you were going to have fish for dinner. But we didn't want to get ahead of ourselves before seeing the menu, so we proceeded inside. We showed the maître de our coupon and he nodded, smiled and took us to a large round table that probably could have seated six or eight diners comfortably. The place was packed and the table we went to was the only one available. It was then we noticed we were the only non-Orientals in the room. We hoped that wouldn't pose a prob-lem. When our waiter showed up with the menus we were slightly intimidated –

the menus were huge and had dozens of items listed (both in Chinese and English). Rudy and I exchanged bewildered looks and then asked the waiter "what's good?" He quickly recommended the Peking Duck dinner for two. Sold! Not too long after and as we finished our first libation, here comes our waiter with a serving dish that you would put a Thanksgiving turkey under. Whoa! Placing it on the table, the waiter removed the lid and sure enough there was a very big bird surrounded by garnish, water chestnuts, rice and vegetables. He produced a carving knife and fork and commenced to make short work of our bird; within a couple minutes he had the bones separated from the meat. We were impressed and later talked about making sure that was a guy we'd want on our side in a knife fight!

Well, there was absolutely no way the two of us could eat the whole damn thing, but we made a go at it anyway. Finishing our aperitif, the waiter asked if we wanted a "to go" box. But, we just laughed and told him no and to just bring us the check! While waiting for the check an English (judging by the accent) couple took a table directly next to ours. After a few minutes looking over the menu, the male leaned over to us and asked "what's good?" With a big smile, Rudy and I highly recommended the Peking Duck dinner for two! Our waiter overheard us as he approached our table with the check and he broke into the biggest grin of the night.

For our last day in Hong Kong and based on the recommendation of a British "swabbie" while at the Fleet Exchange, we headed for Aberdeen. Located on the southwest coast of Hong Kong island, Aberdeen, we were informed, was a good place to buy jade jewelry as well as uncut pieces at prices much reduced from those found in the downtown shops or the Fleet Exchange. We spent a few hours wandering the jewelry shops, picking out some nice pieces of jewelry and some stones. A trip well worth the round-trip bus ride!

TYPHOON

During one of our line periods on Yankee Station, we had the unpleasant experience of having to ride out a typhoon at sea. I believe the CO had been released by the TF command to be allowed to maneuver the ship to best advantage during the storm or had interpreted his orders to accomplish the same thing. Whatever the case, by the time we were detached to do so, we were pretty well boxed in and had no choice but to be exposed to quite a bit of the storm. Now, you can maneuver a ship into the wind and avoid taking the brunt of the wind on the beam, but not forever. Sooner or later, you're going to have to change course due to landmass or other shipping considerations. In a "bowl" like Tonkin Gulf, there aren't a lot of choices so you do the best you can. While the bow was in the wind, the ship rode pretty well, beam to beam, but if you were toward the front of the ship you really got a roller-coaster ride with the bow rising to the top of the swell and then falling like a stone down into the trough. When you came to the bottom of that, the front end of the ship shuddered from the impact of the bow striking down into the water.

Hours before the effects of the storm had begun and in anticipation of the worst, all aircraft and "yellow gear" that could be lowered from the flight deck and squeezed into the jam-packed hangar bay had been moved. The hangar bay doors were shut, which usually wasn't the case due to air ops requirements and the fact that the air flow made the hangar more tolerable in the tropical heat. All exterior hatches, scuttles and doors were closed and dogged down or sealed with instructions to the crew that no one was allowed topside until further notice. Word was passed over the 1MC to "secure for heavy weather," which meant that if anything in a space wasn't chained down, welded down or locked down, the personnel responsible for that space were to secure it so it wouldn't become a flying missile when we hit the heavy seas. Although everyone tried to ensure that happened, invariably something was overlooked and accidents happened. With that big of a ship and our lack of exposure to such situations, we could never be 100% sure something had been secured!

CIC and OI Berthing, being located toward the forward part of the ship, our experience was a little wilder than for, say, the guys berthed or working back aft. And, there were two deck divisions berthed forward of us. The first night we could hear some of their gear crashing around as the ship rose, fell and shuddered through the storm. The following morning was the worst when the ship was maneuvered onto a new course and in doing so our beam exposed to the wind and the ship turning through the trough. Heavy mountains of stormy seas slammed into the ship as she made the turn and if you were trying to walk down a passageway during that, your feet were on the junction of the bulkhead and the deck while standing upright. An experience that a "tin can" sailor would feel right at home with, but to us was *way* out of our comfort zone! The ship seemed to hang there in the wind, taking body blows every minute or so until finally we started coming out of the turn and getting the weather off our beam.

During the storm, I had been working in CIC on regular watch rotation, but it was a little different with the ship pitching and rolling as she was. Wherever your watch station assignment, you did your job with one hand because the other hand was busy keeping you from falling off your stool or being thrown out of your chair or just plain being knocked off your feet! I recall looking at the radar plot and seeing our plane guard destroyer disappear off the screen for minutes at a time while they were down in the trough of the waves and then popping up on the radar screen again for a few brief moments before plunging back down again. As rough as our ride was I couldn't even imagine what they were going through and was thankful that I was on a "bird farm!"

When the storm eventually let go of us and normal routine returned to the ship, we were able to see some of the damage. A large section of the starboard bow catwalk had been torn and mangled by one of our plunges into the trough. As is evident in the picture below, even a big ship like a carrier is not immune to the power of an angry sea!

CVA-64 @ Pier 3, NAS Alameda 30 June 1972

Note typhoon damage on the starboard bow; catwalks damaged or torn away were replaced while still deployed.

CHAPTER 8

Working "Parties"

WHILE ON YANKEE STATION, the demands of the ship's air operations required that the ship be re-provisioned every three to five days depending on weather and availability of the necessary replenishment ships via Underway Replenishment (UNREP). One night an ammunition ship would come alongside for transfer of bullets and bombs. The next night a "reefer" (refrigerated stores) ship would be alongside to transfer food. The third night an oiler would pull up and pump Navy Distillate and JP-5 (jet propulsion fuel). Occasionally you would do two of these evolutions at the same time: an oiler on one side pumping fuel and a "reefer" on the other side passing food stores. Then the process would repeat. To keep up with these transfers, manpower had to be provided from the ship's company for two of them: transfer of bombs and bullets and taking on food stuffs, which included frozen foods, fresh vegetables, canned goods, dry goods and whatever else "Chop" had on his list — "Chop" was sailor slang for "Pork Chop," which is what everyone called the Supply Officer. Every division aboard ship had to provide a commensurate number of bodies to the effort. Based on the manning of each division, those bodies were likely to be from the lower ranked personnel such as E-2s & E-3s. While Mess Cooking, I wasn't assigned to these Working Parties, but on subsequent deployments, I certainly was assigned my share. Even during the deployment in 1973 when I was an E-4 I was not exempt. It just depended on how many of the lower ranks were available and if they weren't, E-4s and even E-5s could be put on the list. Not as frequently, mind you, but, you were still "in the running," so to speak.

Much of the transfers involved movement by "highline" strung between davits on each ship; the other means of transfer was by helicopter shuttles between the two ships (VERTREP). In either case, pallets of fresh stores or explosives would be staged on the flight deck of the supply ship for wire hook-up and delivery to the deck of the carrier. These would then be moved by "yellow gear" from the drop point to the designated elevator for transfer down to the hangar bay, where they could be broken down, stacked and moved to the designated elevators and stuck below into store rooms. Being assigned to an "ammo" working party meant that you mustered with the Petty Officer in charge of the working party at a designated area in the hangar bay at the appointed time. Your may have just been relieved off watch in CIC, but until you were released from the working party, there would be no sleep. If the working party lasted three or four hours, you had four or five hours left before going back on watch in CIC.

Ammo for the planes' guns came in cans stacked on pallets. These were either broken down for distribution to different elevators or store rooms or put on one of the ship's forklifts and moved as a whole to wherever required. The bombs came in two parts: The fins were enclosed in lightweight aluminum casings and each casing had to be broken away from the fins before the fins were stacked on hand-carts to be moved for storage. The business end of the bombs were loaded a couple at a time onto hand-carts and moved to elevators then struck down below into ammo storage bunkers. The most common bombs were the 250-pounders; two fit on a hand-cart, and then it took two of us to manhandle the cart. If you weren't careful while when trying to move the cart, the pitch and roll of the ship could cause you to stop and start a lot because you didn't want to try moving it "uphill" and you didn't want to let it get up too much headway on the "down slope."

During most of the ammo working parties I was assigned to, I tried to get on the portion assigned to breaking the bomb fins out of their casings and stacking them on the hand-carts; I really wasn't built to muscle around the bombs themselves. Usually there were close to two dozen of us working at it, with stacks of encased fins in front of us and more being deposited around us. You had to be careful because as you broke the casing away from the fin, you would toss it over the side and if you were in front of someone doing the same, you were asking to get smacked in the legs, butt, back or head with sharp pieces of flying aluminum. This happened all too regularly, but usually only ended in heated verbal exchanges between the dumb-ass standing out front and the dumb-ass who hit him! I'll admit to being one of those, but only once! By the time the working party was over, you were a walking-talking puddle of sweat, your muscles ached, and you were tired and hungry. Although you may have been able to get some food, a shower and sleep may not have been possible depending on when you had to be back in CIC and if "water hours" were in effect!

WATER HOURS

On a carrier, the steam catapults to launch aircraft had priority over the fresh water supply to the detriment of the crew's ability to take a fresh water shower! The command's solution to the problem was "water hours." This meant there were designated shower facilities with specific times when they would be available for personnel to take a monitored "navy shower" not to exceed three minutes of running water per person! During these times, designated petty officers would be placed in the shower area to ensure that no one took a "Hollywood shower" exceeding those three minutes. After some trial and error, it wasn't that hard to do but you had to work at it to stay within the limits. Actually I didn't care to take a longer one anyway, because the water was tainted with JP-5 jet fuel. JP-5 entered the fresh water supply because when the ship transferred JP-5 for ballast or just shifted it from one storage bunker to another, they often times had to use the same piping used for transfer and storage of fresh water. Taking a shower on a carrier meant the water coming out of the tap usually reeked of jet fuel and when it hit it formed an oily sheen on your skin. Washing it with soap didn't matter because you had to rinse with the same stuff. You got out of the shower, toweled off and joined the rest of the shiny, smelly bodies gathered in front of the mirrors applying deodorant and shaving lotion in the hope that it would mask the stink, but instead, creating a funky mix of the two (JP-5 and English Leather — P U !).

Another "residual" of using the common piping was that your coffee and Kool-Aid also tasted and smelled of JP-5 and the "scuttlebutts" (drinking fountains) gushed water that also reeked. Flushing the piping mitigated the problem for a time, but was never expected to last long due to continual demands to move water and fuel through those common pipes.

This problem led to an amusing incident shortly after I had reported aboard the *Hood* in '77. While taking my first shower aboard that ship, the first thing I noticed was there was no JP-5 in the water! Wow! The next thing I noticed was that the other people showering were taking those long, luxurious "Hollywood" showers and didn't seem concerned about how long they left the water running. So, after finishing my shower and while shaving I struck up a conversation with one of them and mentioned how we were always on water hours when I was aboard the carrier and didn't they practice that here? He laughed and said the ship produced a lot more water than we consumed and that during some of our Un-Reps we actually transferred fresh water to some of the ship's that needed it. I took long, hot, JP-5 free showers after that!

FIRE

Fire: One of the most dreaded four-letter words on a ship at sea! If you were on duty in CIC, you would hear the word passed over the 1MC, make note of its location and continue your duties. If updates were announced or additional personnel required, in the back of your mind you made note of that just so you were aware of the progress of efforts to put it out. The closer the fire was to you, the more attention you paid to the updates! I'm sure everyone else did the same.

Fire being an ever-present threat aboard ship plus experience gained and lessons applied from WWII and more recent events such as the massive fires that broke out on *USS Forrestal* (CV-59) on 29 July 1967 and *USS Enterprise* (CVN-65) on 14 January 1969, the navy invested heavily in the installation of the latest fire-fighting equipment and ensured that as many personnel as possible were adequately trained in that science. FIRE was one of the conditions that could trigger a "real world" GQ! If that happened, it was bad and, by then, most everyone was aware of it!

My own experience in that field started in Boot Camp and involved classroom as well as mock-up training (buildings constructed to resemble compartments aboard ship). While *Connie* was undergoing upkeep and overhaul at PSNSY Bremerton, a number of the crew, me included, were sent to a three-day local fire-fighting school that was created at Bremerton during WWII. There were two days of classroom instruction broken up with one- to two-hour periods during which we would either be tasked with putting out a fire set in a large tank or directed to make entry into a burning mock-up of a ship's structure using equipment and procedures in which we had recently been schooled. Classroom instruction included use of the Foam Application Nozzle & Spray Nozzle, PKP Applicator, AFFF, the CO2 Extinguisher, various pieces of equipment used in dewatering, and the OBA mask & canister replacement. Most of them were put into play when the "out of the classroom" demonstration was performed. Classroom time was also when we were shown films from the two carrier fires mentioned above. To watch the gritty, black and white films of these ships in crisis and see men disappear in explosions and flame was sobering. To be on the same type ship as those on which these fires occurred was even more so, because you were relating to the spaces and locations of where those fires took place in your daily routine aboard *Connie*. It suddenly got a lot more personal!

Once I had completed this course and reported back aboard ship, as a collateral duty I was assigned to one of the repair parties and put in charge of a piece of equipment, which if the need arose for my repair party to fight a fire, I was to deliver to the scene and apply the equipment to its purpose. I was assigned a 4-inch eductor, which was to be used in de-watering. Now, for a skinny kid like me, carrying that damn hunk of brass any appreciable distance was not within the realm of possibility, not to mention the fact that getting up or down ladders from deck to deck would have proved laughable. But none of the senior enlisted assigned to my repair party seemed to notice there was a problem with me being able to handle the eductor and I sure as hell wasn't in a position to "whine" about it. Luckily, I was never called upon to find out, except during drills!

During Vietnam and while aboard *Connie* the statistics dictated that a fire of one sort or the other occurred three times a day. Most were electrical and confined to breakers and circuits that never "transferred" to other materials and were put out by personnel assigned to that space; there would not be any announcements over the ship's PA system (1MC) and did not involve designated fire-fighting personnel. Fires were designated Alpha, Bravo and Charlie by their ignition or fuel source. Alpha were fires fueled by wood, paper, etc.; Bravo was fueled by oil and Charlie was ignited by electricity. Fires that warranted were announced over the 1MC, as were the type, location and assigned personnel. A typical call was: "Fire, Fire, Fire, Class Alpha Fire in compartment 01-123-L, Away the Flying Squad Away." The "Flying Squad" was composed of designated personnel whose primary duty was in response to these calls and all other duties were subordinate to that call. Once the "Flying Squad" had reported on scene, the scene leader would determine if any additional personnel or equipment were necessary to fight the fire. If so, the Fire & Repair Party whose area of responsibility the fire resided in would be called out as well. Fire & Repair Parties were assigned a contiguous group of spaces/compartments within the ship for which they were responsible and would therefore know when a fire fell within their boundaries.

Two fires of particular concern stand out in my memory, both having occurred aboard a carrier. The first was aboard *Connie* and was particularly nasty because it was located under the angle portion of the flight deck and only had two direct paths of access: from the catwalk and from the port outboard 03 level off the main passageway. The fire was discovered late at night while I was on duty, while assigned to the ship's MAA (Master At Arms) Office, and while the ship was in dry-dock at PSNSY, Bremerton. Shortly after the alert was passed, those of us on duty at the MAA Office were directed to specific locations and told to set up restrictive access from those points (traffic control). This was to keep personnel who were unaware of the danger from wandering into an active fire-fighting scene and also to keep "looky-loos" out of the way of fire-fighting personnel. As the scenario developed some of us were called upon to assist the fire-fighting parties by securing firefighting boundaries and directing additional firefighting personnel to where they were supposed to go. We were also directed to draw OBA masks and canisters for our safety and in case it was necessary to employ us directly. General Quarters was called away during the early morning hours, which set in motion the reaction of further designated firefighting personnel, including the PSNSY Base Fire Department By the time I was relieved of duty at 6AM, my "salt & peppers" (white shirt & black trousers) were "pepper & peppers!" It took over four hours to extinguish the fire and the re-flash watch lasted most of the following morning.

The second most memorable fire occurred aboard "*The Big E*," which was also at PSNSY and involved spaces on the second deck, port side just forward of the general mess area. The fire had been started in some of the overhead vent ducting but rapidly spread using bulkhead paint for "transfer" fuel (during WWII and prior to going into the combat zone, all internal spaces had their paint removed to avoid such hazards (a lesson the current Navy hasn't taken to heart). Damage from the fire was limited to the immediate area, but still involved an inordinate amount of time and personnel to defeat.

As you can well imagine, while being stationed as a crew member aboard *USS Mount Hood* (AE-29) — an ammo ship — your attention to ANY fire was more acute. A fire in the wrong place and that was it! Luckily, during my time stationed aboard, I cannot recall any fire that was not put out in less than 15 or 20 minutes and none that were located close to the ammo storage holds.

CHAPTER 9

PORT CALL - *REPUBLIC OF THE* *PHILIPPINES*

GRANDE ISLAND

Grande Island sits at the mouth of Subic Bay, RP and was used for R&R when ships were in port. When a carrier like *Connie* pulled in, the island was exclusively for its use. Activities provided included swimming or snorkeling, water skiing and movies. Movies were 10 cents, renting gear was 25 cents and signing up and standing in line for your turn at water skiing was 50 cents.

While I was working as a mess cook and if I was on-duty, I would be assigned to assist loading food and beverages aboard whatever craft was being used to transport material and activities equipment over to the island. I would then be tasked with following the stores to the island, unloading them and helping with preparation and serving. The usual fare included hamburgers and hot dogs with potato salad or slaw. And also big tubs full of beer on ice! Stuff I'd never heard of before (Schlitz, Bergermeister, Fallstaff) all tempered to over-seas use with plenty of "preservatives" injected into the brew! If it weren't for the fact that it was "free" I doubt any of us would have drunk it! Well, maybe!

Also provided on the island were barracks where you could get a bed for 50 cents a night, but were usually sold out as soon as they were made available.

Nightly entertainment was provided at a disco/dance club also located on the island. There were bands provided and a "shipment" of local female dance partners were brought out nightly in a landing craft. As you can guess, toward the end of the night, with the alcohol flowing, you couldn't walk around outside the club without noticing the bushes moving and the hushed moans of the ill-concealed activities taking place. But, when "last call" was made, a Shore Patrol sweep of the grounds rounded up stragglers and ushered everyone aboard the departing landing craft back to the base.

SUBIC BAY NAVAL STATION

Unlike at Hong Kong or Singapore, when the ship pulled into Subic Bay, RP it wasn't designated as a "liberty" port, but rather a "working" port. With all the necessities attendant to what needed to get procured, repaired or replaced, Subic was the place to do so and you had five days to do it. Port calls when "line periods" were on your schedule meant you rarely spent more than five days in port, including any liberty port you may have been in. OI Division spent much of the time in Subic involved in maintenance of our assigned spaces that were out on the weather decks, that is, exposed to the elements. Chipping and painting in the heat and humidity of the tropics was not a favored task! A way to avoid this nasty duty was to volunteer to assist the "Chart PO" with a trip or two to the local DMA (Defense Mapping Agency) Office to procure navigational charts. Prior to deployment, the ship was provided with its allotted "library" of charts, but when arriving in 7th Fleet, we would find we had been assigned additional charts, most usually necessitated by changes in scheduling that would take us where our library of charts didn't account for. Subic had a DMA Office and it presented an opportunity, if you could weasel your way into the process. If you were the RD assigned as "Chart PO" you, of course, had to make a run to that office for "updates." In a working port, during normal working hours it was no easy feat to get off the ship for an "authorized" task, but this was one of them and you took advantage of that! So, the Chart PO took an assistant or "trainee" with him and a laundry bag of "dirty" uniforms that you could say you were dropping off at the cleaners on base. But, what you were really doing was disguising a liberty uniform in the laundry bag so that you could make your DMA run and pick up charts, then turn that job over to your assistant/trainee, go to the bathroom at the Fleet Exchange and change into the liberty uniform that was inside your laundry bag. Then you dropped the rest of the bags' contents off at the cleaners. You hoped your uniform wasn't so wrinkled it wouldn't pass inspection by the Marine sentry as you walked out the gate and into town. The drawback was that this ruse was only good for one or two uses during a deployment without making the higher-ups suspicious.

These days all chart libraries and updates are provided via the NOAA web portal and the ship's designated "library" is downloadable to the ship and then displayed on designated TV screens on the Bridge and CIC (and other spaces as dictated by the command). Paper libraries are still a requisite, but day to day use has progressively moved to digital displays. This makes me wonder if anyone aboard knows how to "cut a fix" or calculate "set & drift." Judging by groundings and collisions during recent years, I would venture the answer is NO!

One of my first purchases at the NEX in Subic was a small cassette player that would fit inside my racks locker aboard ship. With headphones on I could lie in bed and listen to some righteous tunes and tune out the reality of being aboard a carrier overseas, if only for a few songs. I learned the base had a "recording library" up the hill from Cubi Point pier and after buying some blank cassette tapes and purchasing the requisite hook-up cords, I would make frequent trips up the hill and spend hours recording cassettes from the huge library of songs. I don't recall what the fee was, but the time spent was well worth it!

Aboard ship, "knock off" was passed through the division and by 1630 liberty was usually granted for those of the crew not designated as part of the duty section. In a working port, the ship was usually on a three or four section duty status, meaning you would have to stay aboard as part of the duty section every third or fourth day. After leaving the ship, many of us wanted to get a good meal and then knock back a couple cold brews at the Enlisted Men's Club before charging out into town. The EM Club (called the Sampaguita Club) was what could be best described as a smaller version of what you now experience by going to one of the many Indian Casino's scattered throughout the States nowadays. The eating and drinking areas were pretty large and the gaming area was primarily populated with "one armed bandits." The main attraction was that you could eat, drink and gamble through the night and still walk out with money in your pocket. Everything was inexpensive, even the gambling because those machines were the friendliest one's you'd find anywhere. One night, on one of my earliest liberties in PI, a buddy and I left the ship with just eight bucks between us. We knew we couldn't afford going "out the gate" with that paltry sum, so we settled for the EM Club. After a cheap meal and a couple beers, we wandered into the gaming area with the foregone assumption that we would just donate the rest of our funds to the machines, call it a night and go back to the ship. Well, about 15 minutes later, we walked out of there with twenty bucks apiece and right on out the gate. Time's awastin'!

OLONGAPO CITY & BARRIO BARRETTO

For one of the best descriptions of the "entertainment" available outside the base gates in Olongapo, along with some great nostalgic photos, Dennis Clevenger's Blog covers it quite well and can be found at: https://dennisclevenger.wordpress.com/2012/02/21/liberty-call-olongapo-city/

However, we all have our own recollections and unique experiences that make our memories special and different for any others. Mine are no exception, so here goes!

With the exception of the one trip out the gate I made while in the transit barracks at Subic, I was new to the "game." When *Connie* pulled in for the first time after I arrived on board, I had not been assigned to "Crankin'" yet, so I went ashore with a "pack" of RDs (radarmen). The more experienced guys in the group (most everyone but me) headed for the Florida Hotel about halfway down "the gut" and upstairs, to get rooms. With more than a dozen of us, that took up one wing of the hotel. Then it was back downstairs and across the street to the "New Florida Club" for some brew and entertainment. The club always hired all-girl bands that could really belt out some of the best rock & roll from the States. And they were always cute as hell, too! A couple hours later, we would "up anchor" and move down the street, over and up to the Sierra Club, one of the largest nightclubs in that area of Olongapo. They always had some great Filipino bands playing and if you closed your eyes you couldn't have told the difference between a sound track from the States or the band playing on stage. They were that good! Because curfew was then in force in P.I. and we were all below the rank of E-5, we had to be off the streets by 10PM. So, usually after one more stop we would all return to our rooms at the Florida Hotel, pay the desk clerk to secure us some food and drinks and then wander from room to room (wherever the bull session or card games were going on) and hit the sack sometime after midnight. The next morning, if you didn't have to return to the ship for duty, you would make it down to Kong's Restaurant by 9 or 10AM where they had a back room that had A/C and could seat our group at a large table. Breakfast was always noisy with everyone laughing and recounting the previous night's events and never seemed to end before noon! After my assignment to "mess cooking," the shipmates I went on liberty with were usually other mess cooks and not OI Division buddies — guys from engineering, bomb handlers, air wing or flight deck personnel, etc. One such steamin' buddy was an "airdale" E-3. He was a tall, gangly guy with the typical Navy issue black rimmed glasses. He was easy to get along with and not of a gregarious nature, which I preferred. He and I had gone out in town one night and at the end of the night he found himself going home with one of the bar girls that would not take no for an answer. The next morning we spent the day out at Grenade Island doing some snorkeling and water skiing and, he being more pasty white than I was, he had a pretty toasty sunburn going on as a result. After this, I didn't see or hear from him until after we got underway a few days later. That's when I noticed he wasn't sleeping in his rack and wasn't working his usual shift on the mess decks. So, I asked one of the petty officer's in charge of us about him and was told he was in sick bay. *What the hell???* After I got off shift I went over to sick bay and asked around and found him in a bed with his feet propped up and swollen to twice the normal size. He told me that when he went home with the girl, they had done the "nasty" in a bed that was way too short for him. So, while he's boinkin' the babe in the bed, the front tops of his feet are being rubbed raw on the footboard. That, combined with our trip to Grande Island, and his immersion in salt water of dubious sanitation quality, had resulted in his condition. Of course, at first, I was really worried about his feet, given their abnormal size. But, as the days progressed and the swelling went down, I had to start ribbing him about the whole thing. I mean, come on! Something like that can only happen to a sailor, right?

"The Barrio" was located a few miles up the bayshore outside Olongapo. By my third WestPac, I was avoiding downtown due to the prices and all the hustle and bustle of the place. Barrio Barretto was more laid back and had considerably less Shore Patrol, and the prices were like night and day. A beer would cost you half of what you'd spend in town and what hotels were available were also less expensive. The added feature was being able to get out on the bay in a banca boat or do some swimming at White Rock Beach Resort, an attraction that had three or four swimming pools, diving boards and water slides. When I was aboard the *Hood* and if I was going "out the gate," I spent most of my liberty time out there. My last WestPac aboard CGN-9, I planned on staying out there and brought along a bunch of guys from the division. As is typical, from the end of the '84 WestPac to our deployment in '86 we had experienced a considerable amount of personnel turnover. The '86 WestPac was no exception and we had about 25% of our division personnel that had never been overseas before. Now, normally as a Chief I would not go out in town with the guys from the division, but as these kids were FOB (Fresh off the Boat), I wanted to make sure they knew the rules of the game. Olongapo can be a dangerous place if you don't. They all wanted to stop at the first place in town that looked promising, even though I told them we should continue out to the Barrio where their money would last longer. Not to be dissuaded, they insisted and I went along. Every time someone told them how much a beer was they'd look at me and I'd let them know if that was too much or not. One of the kids took a fancy to one of the bar girls (B-girls) and when she told him how much the "bar fine" was (allowing her to leave during her shift), he asked me if that was too much. And, it was! Well, that was it! The other B-girls came over and voiced their displeasure at my interference and we all got up and left. We piled into a jeepney and I told the driver which place to take us to, out in Barretto. Off we went, but not before it started pouring rain, as only it can in the tropics. About half-way to the barrio one of the guys said he had to take a leak and some of the others chimed in. We stopped the jeepney and the guys piled out. It was pitch black outside by then, so I couldn't see them even though they were only a couple feet outside. One, two, three piled back in, but we were one short. About then, the missing shipmate pulled himself aboard, soaking wet with scrapes and bruises. And, minus his prescription eyeglasses. What the heck? He told us he'd slipped off the lip of the drainage ditch and fell in, losing his glasses and getting the bumps and bruises he now wore. When we got to the barrio, we got in out of the rain and over a brew discussed what he intended to do. He didn't want to go back to the ship because it would be days before he would be able to replace his glasses and if he did go back he would be asked about his bumps and bruises and even maybe restricted to the ship. So, I told him the following day, we'd go back into town, find an optometrist, and get him a new prescription and new glasses. He sounded relieved that he wouldn't be subjected to any scrutiny from the command because of a dunk in the drainage ditch. He got his new glasses the next day and we all stayed out in the barrio until we had to get back aboard ship. By then, the news of his little accident had made the rounds and he took a good ribbing about it!

J.D.'S TAXI SERVICE

One night while on liberty in Subic, about four of us were upstairs in a bar when closing time occurred and we'd had enough to drink that we believed we shouldn't stop just because martial law dictated that we had to be off the streets at curfew. So, taking an inside stairwell down to a cafe that was below the bar, we were able to take a table in the back and order some food to go along with the beer we'd brought along. What we didn't allow for was that, even though we were seated in the back, we still stuck out like a sore thumb because all the people up front were locals and we squids were much taller than they were. So, Shore Patrol had no hard time spotting through the large windows up front heads that didn't belong there. As soon as they came walking in we knew we'd been "made" and promptly got up and walked towards them. They "escorted" us to their panel van and we joined the others inside for the ride back to the base and Shore Patrol HQ.

What we didn't know was that our CO had standing orders with SP HQ that any of his sailors picked up for minor infractions and without incident were to be delivered to the ship with no further penalty or prosecution either on the Shore Patrol's part or by the ship's command. We fell into that classification! So we were given a ride back to the ship in the ship's van, which had on its side the lettering "J.D.s Taxi Service," J.D. being our Captain's first two initials. We came back aboard ship, changed into our dungarees and went below to eat midrats. We came back up to our compartment and showered, played some cards, changed into clean "civvies" and were back out at the main gate to the base when it opened at 6AM. Sweet!

"THE SHADOW"

A carrier in the Gulf of Tonkin usually warranted an attendant Russian spy ship, which the fleet referred to as an AGI (Auxiliary, General Intelligence). During the mid to late 1960s these craft would ply the waters off the coast of Vietnam with the thin guise of being a "fishing trawler," booms, nets and all. However, after they had been around a few years and everyone knew what they were and what they did, they dropped the fishing nets routine and just tagged along with the fleet whenever and wherever needs be. In CIC, after the AGI had been around a few days you got the sense that he was "taking station," because they always seemed to conform to whatever tactical formation we would be ordered into. Rumor was that they had a copy of our signals book! Actions speak louder than rumors!

An AGI "in trail" would become an accepted norm for my deployments on the *Connie* and even become involved later while I was on the *Mount Hood*. More about that later!

CHAPTER 10

APRIL '72: YOKOSUKA & HOMEWARD BOUND - NOT!

"GOOD MORNIN' GENTS. THIS IS THE CAPTAIN!"

CONNIE EXTENDED (3 APRIL - 14 JUNE '72)

The morning of what was to have been our last day in Yokosuka before departing for home, the Captain came up on the 1MC (ship-wide announcing system) with "Good mornin' gents. This is the Captain!" He then proceeded to fill us in that our WestPac had been extended and we were needed back on Yankee Station, telling us about the NVA "Easter Offensive" and its impact on South Vietnamese forces (some of this news we had heard from sources around the navy base). Even before the announcements, preparations had begun to meet our new tasking. The motorcycles that so many of us had purchased and helped load and stow below were being off-loaded. New provisions were added to those already taken aboard for what was to be our trip home and many of the crew started scrambling for any means available to relay the bad news to their loved ones, before we pulled away from the pier. That evening, 3 April, we were underway and headed south with our escorts, *USS Sample* (DD-1048) and *USS John Paul Jones* (DDG-32) in company. As the ship's deck log indicates, *Connie* arrived back in the combat zone the afternoon of the 7th and was soon launching and recovering strike aircraft. On the following day, we took on more fuel and ammo to replenish our stocks.

NAVPERS 3100/2 (1-66)
(Formerly NAVPERS 719)

DECK LOG—REMARKS SHEET

S/N-0105-404-1560

USS _CONSTELLATION (CVA-64)_ ZONE DESCRIPTION _-8(H)_ DATE _TUESDAY 11 APRIL_, 19 _72_

(Day) (Date) (Month)

AT/~~PASSAGE FROM~~ _SOUTH CHINA SEA_ TO _____

POSITION	ZONE	TIME		POSITION	ZONE	TIME		POSITION	ZONE	TIME		LEGEND:
0800				1200				2000 a				1-CELESTIAL
L 10°54.4N BY 2				L 10°54.2N BY 2				L 11-07.8N BY 2				2-ELECTRONIC
λ 109°10.8E BY 2				λ 109°06.0E BY 2				λ 109°23.9E BY 2				3-VISUAL
												4-D.R.

REMARKS

00-04	STEAMING IN COMPANY WITH TASK GROUP 77.4 COMPOSED OF USS
	CONSTELLATION (CVA-64) AND USS JOHN PAUL JONES (DDG-32)
	CONDUCTING AIR STRIKE OPERATIONS FROM THE SOUTH CHINA SEA
	WHILE OPERATING IN ACCORDANCE WITH CINCPACFLT FOURTH QUARTER
	EMPLOYMENT SCHEDULE. OTC AND SOPA IS C.O. USS CONSTELLATION
	(CVA-64) SCREEN COMMANDER IS C.O. USS JOHN PAUL JONES
	MATERIAL CONDITION YOKE AND READINESS CONDITION THREE
	SET. SHIP DARKENED EXCEPT FOR RUNNING LIGHTS AND RED
	FLIGHT DECK FLOOD LIGHTING AFT. BASE COURSE 050°T BASE
	SPEED 12 KTS. ALONGSIDE USS ASHTABULA (AO-51) WHILE
	RECEIVING AMMUNITION BY CONREP.
0100	COMPLETED TRANSFERRING AMMUNITION
0106	ALL LINES CLEAR
0108	COMMENCED BREAKAWAY FROM PORTSIDE OF USS ASHTABULA.
	MANEUVERING ON VARIOUS COURSES DURING BREAKAWAY.
0112	C/C 230°
0113	C/S 13 KTS.
0114	C/S 12 KTS.
0117	DETACHED USS ASHTABULA TO PROCEED ON DUTY ASSIGNED
0130	RECEIVED DRAFT REPORT. DRAFT FWD 33'7" AFT 37'3"
0146	CALLED AWAY THE FLYING SQUAD TO INVESTIGATE A CLASS
	CHARLIE FIRE IN COMPARTMENT 03-186-1M
0149	FIRE REPORTED OUT AND WAS REPORTED TO BE A SHORT IN A
	400 CYCLE POWER TERMINAL BOX.

J.R. HALL LTJG USNR

04-08	UNDERWAY AS BEFORE
0400	OBTAINED RADAR CONTACT ALPHA BEARING 028°, 39,000yDS
0528	CONTACT ALPHA AT CPA BEARING 045m Range 5,300yds
0607	C/C 035°
0615	COMMENCED LAUNCHING STRIKE AIRCRAFT
0618	C/S 15 KTS
0620	C/C 045°
0621	COMPLETED LAUNCHING AIRCRAFT HAVING LAUNCHED
	16 STRIKE AIRCRAFT
0643	C/C 225°, C/S 12 KTS

A.I. KING, LT, USNR

08-12	UNDERWAY AS BEFORE
0800	C/C 045°
0815	COMMENCED LAUNCHING STRIKE AIRCRAFT
0820	COMMENCED RECOVERING AIRCRAFT

EXAMINED

Just Another Day at Work: Ammo UnRep,
Radar Contacts, Class Charlie Fire & Launching Aircraft

LINEBACKER I (APRIL - OCTOBER 1972)
ON LINE FROM 7 APRIL TO 18 MAY 72

By the time we arrived off the Vietnamese coast, the news filled us in on the "Easter Offensive." Accordingly, we expected to be employed off the north coast of South Vietnam because news reports were predominately about the battles in that area. However, when strike operations commenced, we in CIC could tell before being told that we were not there in support of the action up north. Without having to look at the tactical plot or read our latitude and longitude, we could tell by checking the radar screen that we were south in the general area of "Dixie" station and flying strikes in support of the action occurring around Loc Ninh and An Loc. We would remain employed there and further north from 4 April until the end of the month. The move up the coast meant we could support requested air asset tasking around An Loc as well as in the Central Highlands. But by the end of that period, we would join carriers up north in the conduct of Linebacker 1 and Operation Pocket Money. During Linebacker ops, you knew it was going to be a busy day when you could see chaff clouds blooming on the radar scopes off the coast of Haiphong.

Connie was finally released from Yankee Station ops on 18 May for a short in port period in Subic Bay and before our port visit to Singapore as related below.

An excerpt from CAG-9 history states that "From 25 through 30 April, *Constellation's* VA-146, VA-147 and VA -165 hit areas around the besieged city of An Loc in support of South Vietnamese troops, some only 40 miles outside the capital of Saigon. Targets attacked included artillery fire bases, enemy tanks, bunkers, troop positions, ammunition caches and gun emplacements."

BATTLE OF ĐỒNG HỚI 19 APRIL 1972

USS Higbee (DD-806) suffered battle damage; *USS Sterett* (DLG-31), *USS Oklahoma City* (CLG-5) and *USS Lloyd Thomas* (DD-764) were other units engaged in the battle. In late May, *Higbee* would visit Singapore as one of the *Connie's* escorts.

Damage to USS Higbee's aft Gun Mount

If the reader desires to delve into the more nuanced aspects of the engagement, there are technical discussions of the capabilities of both operator and equipment that can be found at the following link, http://www.navweaps.com/index_tech/tech-088.htm

At approximately 17:00, USS *Sterett* detected three hostile aircraft approaching the navy ships. After two failed attack runs, one of the MiG-17Fs, flown by NVAF pilot Nguyen Van Bay scored a direct hit on USS *Higbee's* aft 5-inch gun mount with a BETAB-250 (250 kg/551 lb) bomb. The explosion destroyed *Higbee's* gun mount which was empty because the 12-man crew had been evacuated following a "hang fire" (a round stuck in one of the barrels). The MiG was then shot down by a *Terrier* surface-to-air missile fired from USS *Sterett*. A second MiG flown by Le Duan Xi made an attack run and then headed back toward land. *Sterett* fired two more *Terrier* missiles at the aircraft; the MiG and a missile simultaneously disappeared from the *Sterett's* radar, indicating a probable kill.[1]

The link below is taken from Wikipedia and details the evolution of the MiG-17 as well as the modifications made to the two MiGs involved in the air battle that enabled them to function in a "fighter/bomber" role.

https://en.wikipedia.org/wiki/Mikoyan-Gurevich_MiG-17

Roughly in the same geographic area and one hour after the MiG's damage to the *Higbee,* the action continued with a surface threat, as recounted below and continuing the Wikipedia account.

"At approximately 18:00 as the US ships withdrew to the northeast, USS *Sterett* detected 2 surface targets shadowing the US ships, after 30 minutes, *Sterett* opened fire on the targets with its 5 inch guns destroying 2 suspected North Vietnamese P 6-class torpedo boats.[1]"

However, having been on watch with CTF-77 staff aboard *Connie,* I can inject the following. Upon noting hostile air tracks entered into the NTDS system by *Sterett,* the staff watch officer contacted VADM D.W. Cooper (CTF-77) and shortly the admiral arrived at the CIC Staff Watch Officers station next to my NTDS console. By then the air threat was over and the admiral was brought up-to-date. As mentioned in the Wikipedia report and around the 1800 time period,

I noticed surface hostile tracks being entered into the NTDS system in the general area of *Sterett* and her ships in company. Informing the staff and identifying them as *Sterett's* track data, I was directed to contact them via *Navy Red* and verify the validity of the tracks. *Sterett* did indeed confirm that these were hostile tracks and their intention was to engage them by "taking with guns." Approximately 10 minutes later, these tracks were dropped from the system by *Sterett* whereupon the admiral and staff directed me to query *Sterett* as to the status of the "dropped" tracks. All this took place over *Navy Red* and on the speaker in the overhead. *Sterett's* response was that the tracks were "scrubbed" because the targets had been sunk. At this VADM Cooper let out a big war-hoop and slammed his fist on the desk, exclaiming "Hot damn! Hot damn!" and the Staff Watch Officers broke into big grins, as did I! We had just been witness to the only *named* naval battle of the Vietnam War!

During Linebacker I & II, the "Gunline" would grow to around 60 surface combatants (in rotation), stationed along the coastline in groups of three or four; it ran from the Red River Delta in the north to south of the DMZ.

During "Linebacker I," *Coral Sea, Midway, Hancock, Kitty Hawk* and *Connie* were present on Yankee Station and eventually composed a total of six carriers rotating on station in support of the Linebacker operation.

On May 10, 1972, Lt. Randy Cunningham and Ltjg. Willie Driscoll of Fighter Attack Squadron 96 became America's first fighter aces of the Vietnam War by downing three MiGs while dog fighting over North Vietnam. During egress from the North, they were struck by a SAM and forced to bail out shortly after becoming "feet wet." Both were picked up by a SAR helo and transported safely back aboard *Connie*.

1420 RECEIVED REPORT ONE F4-J SIDE NO. NG 212 BUNO 155797 WAS SHOT DOWN OVER ENEMY TERRITORY. PILOT H.L. BLACKBURN, CDR USN AND RIO RUDLOFF, S.A. LT USN REPORTED MISSING IN ACTION.
1425 RECEIVED REPORT ONE F4-J SIDE NO. NG 100 BUNO 155800 WAS SHOT DOWN OVER WATER SOUTH OF HANOI. PILOT CUNNINGHAM R.H. , LT USN AND RIO DRISCOLL W.P. LT JG USN WERE RECOVERED BY SAR HELO FROM USS OKINAWA (LPH 3)

Above: Cunningham & Driscoll returned aboard as the first air aces of the Vietnam War; Blackburn was declared KIA & Rudlof a POW

OPERATION POCKET MONEY

The *Connie* had pulled off the line and was headed along our usual route to P.I. In the middle of the night as I was getting ready to go on watch, I could feel that things were not as usual. The throb of the ship indicated that we were making high speed and as flight ops were not occurring, this was not normal. Hurrying into CIC and D&T, I could see by the radar screens that we weren't in our usual location. Asking around, I was told we were headed for P.I. to allow designated aircraft to fly off and be loaded with mines and then to fly back aboard, so the ship could head back to Yankee Station. Over the course of my watch, this is what happened. The buzz around the ship was electric! Everyone was aware that the rules of the game had just changed and that Nixon was letting the military do what Johnson hadn't during his tenure in office. Mining had been on the table any number of times previously, but Johnson was always afraid that this would be taken as a step too far by the Chinese and Soviets. Nixon didn't give a damn and frankly, we were all impressed he had the balls to do it.

What follows are the details of the operation and were taken from a webpage. There is also available documentation for Operation End Sweep (removal of the mines), which was initially a classified study contracted to Tensor Industries. But, they were allowed to publish the findings after the study was re-written in order to allow its general release. The *Connie's* following WestPac in 1973 was tasked with supporting the mine clearance effort, but I would depart only a couple months after arriving in WestPac, before this evolution was completed.

Operation Pocket Money, the mining campaign against principal North Vietnamese ports, was launched on 09 May 1972. Early that morning, an EC-121 aircraft took off from Danang airfield to provide support for the mining operation. A short time later, *Kitty Hawk* launched 17 ordnance-delivering sorties against the Nam Dinh railroad siding as a diversionary air tactic. Poor weather, however, forced the planes to divert to secondary targets at Thanh and Phu Qui, which were struck at 090840H and 090845H, Vietnam time, respectively. *Coral Sea* launched three A-6A and six A-7E aircraft loaded with mines and one EKA-3B in support of the mining operation directed against the outer approaches to Haiphong Harbor. The mining aircraft departed the vicinity of *Coral Sea* at 090840H in order to execute the mining at precisely 090900H to coincide with the President's public announcement in Washington that mines had been seeded. The A-6 flight led by the CAG, Commander Roger Sheets, was composed of USMC aircraft from VMA-224 and headed for the inner channel. The A-7Es, led by Commander Len Giuliani and made up of aircraft from VA-94 and VA-22, were designated to mine the outer segment of the channel. Each aircraft carried four MK 52-2 mines. Captain William Carr, USMC, the bombardier/navigator in the lead plane established the critical attack azimuth and timed the mine releases. The first mine was dropped at 090859H and the last of the field of 36 mines at 090901H. Twelve mines were placed in the inner segment and the remaining 24 in the outer segment.

All MK 52-2 mines were set with 72-hour arming delays, thus permitting merchant ships time for departure or a change in destination consistent with the President's public warning. It was the beginning of a mining campaign that planted over 11,000 MK 36 type destructor and 108 special MK 52-2 mines over the next eight months. It is considered to have played a significant role in bringing about an eventual peace arrangement, particularly since it so hampered the enemy's ability to continue receiving war supplies.

On 11 May Naval aircraft flying from *Coral Sea, Midway, Kitty Hawk* and *Constellation* laid additional mine fields in the remaining ports of significance in NVN— Thanh Hoa, Dong Hoi Vinh, Hon Gai, Quang Khe and Cam Pha as well as the Haiphong approaches. This early mining was not confined solely to the seven principal ports. Other locations, such as the Cua Sot, Cap Mui Ron, and the river mouths, Cua Day and Cua Lac Giang, south of Don Son and the Haiphong port complex, were also seeded early in the campaign.

The 72-hour delay arming time on the initial mines laid at Haiphong was up at 120900H Vietnam time on 12 May. Nine ships at Haiphong had taken advantage of the grace period to depart the port. Twenty-seven ships remained. Both Soviet and Soviet-bloc ships headed for Haiphong at the time had diverted to different destinations, thus avoiding a direct confrontation with the mine fields."

SUBIC BAY

19-23 May '72

After five weeks "on the line" delivering strikes in support of the growing United States response to the NVA "Easter Offensive," *Connie* was released to proceed to Subic, RP for our usual "working port" routine. However, we were told that from there we would proceed directly to Singapore! Finally!

LIBERTY CALL – SINGAPORE

26 May to 01 June

Singapore had originally been on our schedule as a port of call for this WestPac, but operational commitments nixed that. So, it took our being extended for three months to get Singapore offered up as a consolation prize for not going home as scheduled! You can guess what we would have preferred, of course.

Of course, none of us had ever been to Singapore, which meant that all we had to go by were generalized descriptions of what the city offered. The first night in, I left the ship with a group of division shipmates and while on the ferry from the ship to the landing we talked about what we wanted to do, namely find out where to go for a good meal and a good time! So, cramming all four or five of us into a taxi, we tried describing to the driver that we wanted to know where the hot clubs and hot girls were. He had his own idea of meeting that request and the next thing we know he's dropping us off at an "escort" joint. We were already there so we decided to go in and see what was "on the menu." The place was swank and the ladies were class and we knew this would be way too pricey for our pocketbooks. After being told what was what (price and services) we agreed that having one of these girls on our arm for an evening was all we were going to spring for as any other service would cut into our liberty funds way too much. We each picked a lady and as we all loaded up into two taxis we told them to have the cab driver take us to a restaurant that the ladies recommended. The food was great and once the ladies understood that we were only asking them to be "tour guides" for the evening, the mood lightened considerably and the conversation was lively. After dinner, they toured us around to three or four of the hot spots in town. Two of these I recall and were the "Dot Dot" on the fourth floor of the Hilton and a club called "The Mailbox," which had a U. S. (red, white and blue) mailbox at the entrance. We had a blast and the girls seemed to have fun too! A great time had by all! Because I had duty the following day, I made my way back to the ship shortly after midnight on the last ferry of the day.

Being a history buff, the day following my duty day, I talked Rudy into getting connecting rooms at the Raffles Hotel. This was an old British Colonial establishment and where the Brits had capitulated to the Japanese back in '42. Walking into the lobby, you glanced to your left and there was the bar, lazy fans overhead barely stirring the muggy air, waiters dressed in white jackets and a few stuffy old hands parked at the tables dressed in light tropical twill and sporting the quintessential Panama hat. Any film buff would have recognized it instantly as the spitting image of the interior of "Rick's Place!" The hotel grounds still consisted of some acreage, but the spread had been compressed from its former size by the cost of maintaining such an establishment in the midst of very expensive real estate. The rooms were still impressive and the service impeccable, but after one night we decided to move. You see, when I woke the next morning to tend to my morning routine, the first thing I spotted as I started towards the bathroom sink was a "water bug," otherwise known as a roach, the size of a mouse! I hollered to Rudy, who was also impressed with its size and then and there decided we needed to get rooms at a more modern hotel that hadn't been around long enough to grow such large insects. Or, so we hoped! Before we left, we made arrangements at the front desk to sign up for one of the tours the next day. We ended up getting rooms at the Hilton after I told Rudy about the "Dot Dot" upstairs and as we were checking in we noticed American stewardesses in line ahead of us. Things were looking up! That night was dinner at the restaurant in the Hilton and dancing in the club, but sadly the "stews" were a no-show.

The next day we made our way to the Raffles in time to board the tour bus. First stop was The House of Jade, which was the Ming Dynasty's collection of jade housed in the former Governor's Mansion. The collection had been sent out of China before the Communist takeover as a means of protecting it from being broken up or destroyed. The entire grounds were surrounded by a formidable array of barbed wire and armed guards and the bus pulled up to one of the gates manned by tough looking little Malay "hombres" armed with AK-47s. The bus driver stopped so close to the gate that when he opened the door, there was no way to go but straight through the gate, past the guards and follow our guide. The layout once inside the mansion doors was something like the "youngest" jade (shades of the green stones I was familiar with) lower down and as you ascended to the upper floors the jade displayed was older (red jade and black jade). With each color and each floor, the displays included numerous and large pieces of jewelry and small to larger statuary. It was all amazing and you had to wonder at the millions of dollars that you were looking at. This part of the tour lasted only about an hour and then it was back on the bus and on to our next stop. This was the famed "Tiger Balm Gardens" (although I'd never heard of them)! It had some of the oddest and most garish statuary displays I've ever seen. It struck me as though someone had created a visual display of their nightmares. Just plain weird! And, if it hadn't been on the tour itinerary, I doubt we would want to have put it on our list!

Our last stop was the Southeast Asian Cultural Show, which was very inform-ative and entertaining. One of the acts consisted of a leathery old Indian gent, appropriately in turban and loincloth, with his snake act. Just as in the movies, he placed a lidded wicker basket on the floor and seated himself cross-legged in front of it. Removing the lid, he commenced blowing his "snake charmer" tune on a "pungi" (Midwestern version of a flute?). What cracked us up though was his voice! When he was introducing his act, this little old Indian guy spoke with a decidedly thick English "brogue" accent. Totally out of character for what you would expect. Following his routine with the cobra, he also introduced various snakes, handling them and bringing them around and close to the audience. The last was a long, fat and huge python. He draped it across his shoulders and out across his arms, the tail almost dragging the floor. Then he called for a volunteer to come up and inspect the snake. After some shoving, I was able to push Rudy to the front. The snake charmer walked over to Rudy and after some persuasion from the audience, he let the guy place the snake in the same position across his shoulders and arms. I got a picture of that, but over the intervening years, have lost track of it. Too bad, as I would have loved to have shown it to his wife when he married!

The next evening, we decided to take a trip over to the British Naval Base at Sembawang and check it out. The taxi couldn't take us onto the base and it was too hot to do much walking, so we ducked into a nearby bar to discuss what to do next. As we entered the place, there was a long table we walked past on our way to the bar and seated around it were eight or ten guys knocking back some brews. We each glanced at the other, but Rudy and I took up seats at the bar and ordered a couple beers. When we did, the group at the table fell silent. One of the guys got up and came over to Rudy and me and asked "You're Yanks, aincha!" We chuckled and asked how he could tell. "By your bloody accents, mate," which cracked everyone up! We were invited to their table, which we accepted and for the rest of the night we were under escort by our new-found friends, a collection of limey's, kiwi's and aussies. A truly rowdy, profane and drunken night it was! The sport of choice was darts and I knew when I couldn't hit the dart board it was time to go. Warm brit and aussie beer thoroughly kicked us to the curb at which point we were placed into a cab and taken back across the island!

Upon departure from Singapore, all of us "pollywogs" watched the few "shellbacks" that were aboard gleefully making preparations for our anticipated "Crossing the Line" ceremony. With close to 4,500 men aboard ship and only a relative handful of shellbacks, they had their work cut out for them. The equator was approximately 60 miles below our direct route back to Vietnam, but the events that composed the ceremony meant that it would add more than the allowable time to our transit. So, at the last minute the event was canceled and we proceeded directly to our assigned operational area. It would be over 15 years later that the opportunity to become a "shellback" would present itself again!

BACK TO "DIXIE STATION" & THE BATTLE FOR AN LOC
3 - 13 JUNE 1972

Although the battle surrounding An Loc was winding down, *Connie* was ordered to proceed back to Dixie Station in support of the U. S. Navy effort to assist ARVN personnel on the ground through liaison with American military personnel attached to those units.

We departed Singapore 1 June '72 and *Connie's* aircraft "strike packages" from the southern coast of South Vietnam — as depicted in the map below — commenced on 3 June '72 in support of ARVN and U. S. advisors engaged in the battle for An Loc. We were finally released from the combat area on 14 June '72.

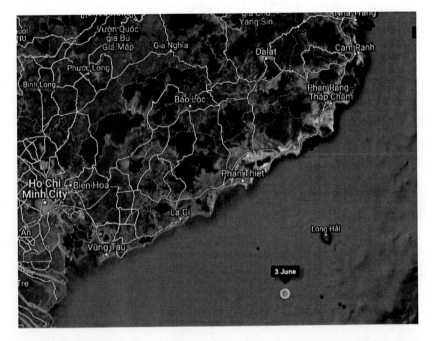

Once released from supporting combat operations over Vietnam, we laid in a course taking us to Subic Bay, for a brief stopover, before departing for CONUS and home!

CHAPTER 11
SAN DIEGO & SOCAL CARQUALS

MWR (MORALE, WELFARE & RECREATION) aboard ship had made arrangements for the crew to have the opportunity to purchase motorcycles, scooters and the like, directly from the manufacturers in Japan. What you did was set up an account with MWR, you selected the motorcycle make and model you wanted to purchase and then MWR calculated the expected number of paychecks between then and when the ship would load everyone's purchases aboard ship, for return to CONUS. Once those calculations had been made, they told you what the deduction amount from your paycheck would be, to accumulate the amount necessary to pay the balance when the motorcycle was taken aboard ship. During our expected last port call in Yokosuka, you reported to the forward mess decks where the Japanese companies had set up desks with each of their representatives and an MWR desk. You reported to the MWR desk to collect your accumulated cash, moved over to the line for the company you were purchasing from and paid the man. Because of our extended cruise, the bikes were loaded, off-loaded and re-loaded before sailing for the States.

A couple days after we arrived in San Diego, MWR had arranged for a trailer to be set up on the pier where representatives from three or four of the largest San Diego motorcycle dealers and repair shops were waiting. You went to the trailer, paperwork in hand, and selected the dealer of your choice (mine was out of Imperial Beach). For $35 the dealer would take delivery of your vehicle, take it to their shop, break open the crate, make any final assembly necessary and then ensure the bike was running and ready for the road. It was that easy!

My purchase was a Honda 350! It was a sweet looking ride and back then cost less than $1,000, factory direct!

A little more than a week after getting back from WestPac, a bunch of us "biker" sailors got together for a weekend ride out into the desert. It would be our first real chance at seeing what your bikes could do. Climbing up and down the mountains, we purred along at 65MPH, but once we got into the open flats west of El Centro, we opened them up. I know that when we were all screaming along with open throttles, I looked down to the speedometer, which read just a hair below 90! Soon, we turned south and drove into Mexico where we spent the afternoon eating, drinking a few cold *cervezas* and bragging to each other about our rides.

Later, when I took leave, I would ride the bike up to northern California and home and, with the return trip, pile up over 1,200 miles. Sadly, it would be all too soon before I would have to sell it on account of needing something that would seat more than two. But, she was a sweet little ride while I had her!

Buying the motorcycle also accomplished something else, something to look forward to during that impending nine-month WestPac: setting a goal and achieving it. I actually had more money than was necessary when I cleared the books with MWR. It was also something to show for all that time I'd spent on watch, slogging through the daily grind, the working parties and the duty days. With the payday withdrawals, it also meant I was on a budget and had to manage my funds more carefully. This wasn't too hard to do given all the at-sea time we had, but it kept me engaged and I tracked almost every dollar I spent. As a result, I was never in a position that made it necessary for me to borrow money from one of the many available "slush funds" (borrowing $20 for a return of $25 upon the next payday, etc.).

Anyway, once the ship had spent an all-too-short amount of time in port, we were going to sea again as an available deck for CarQuals. It was back to the daily grind with weekends spent in port.

RACE RIOTS AT SEA

1 -2 November 1972

Aboard some U.S. Navy ships during this era, racial tensions festered and, given the opportunity and impetus, sometimes broke out into shipboard rioting. Aboard *Connie* we first heard of this occurring aboard *USS Kitty Hawk* (CVA-63) and which is documented as happening on 12 October 1972. At the time of the riots aboard, her new CO was the *Connie's* previous XO during the '69 - '70 WestPac. In the fleet, she was referred to as the "Shitty Kitty" and although a sister ship to *Connie* a mere walk through the ship tipped you off to differences. Many of the main passageways had brown bulkheads, but the paint job was typical navy pea-green underneath the oily filth. The weather decks that I had to traverse when I had an occasion of "crossing over" were worn, chipped and showed evidence of rust. As a *Connie* sailor not used to such unkempt conditions, she gave the appearance of being a much older, much abused ship.

To be sure, some of these tensions aboard *Hawk* were not entirely "race" related, as evidenced by crew sabotage of shipboard equipment believed related to the Vietnam anti-war movement. *USS Ranger* (CV-61) and *USS Forrestal* (CV-59) in particular suffered equipment damage, but even aboard *Connie* there was some "lost" gear.

The version of events, as found at Wikipedia, states the following:

"While *Constellation* was conducting exercises off the California coast, a rumor started that the Captain was going to give 250 less-than-honorable discharges to black sailors. On 1 November 1972, black sailors waylaid a white mess cook in a passageway and broke his jaw. The Captain scheduled an open meeting for 21:00 3 November to clarify the 250 planned discharges. At noon 3 November a group of 50 black sailors began a sit-in on a portion of the mess deck. On the night of 3–4 November 60 black sailors took control of the scheduled meeting, refused to leave the mess deck, and threatened to "tear up the ship." *Constellation* returned to San Diego on 4 November to offload 130 men, including 12 white sailors, before returning to sea. *Con-*

stellation returned to San Diego on 7 November and the of-floaded sailors were transported back to the dock on 9 November, but only 8 boarded their ship. The remaining sailors sat down on the dock to be filmed by television crews and were ultimately transferred to shore stations for mast. Twelve received general discharges, 35 were honorably discharged but not recommended for re-enlistment, and 73 received punishments ranging from loss of pay and reduction in rate to warnings prior to being reassigned to sea duty."

A more comprehensive and in-depth study of the incident and a broader perspective of the racial environment in the Navy during this period, is to be found in John Darrell Sherwood's *Black Sailor, White Navy*. While he has delivered a comprehensive documentation of the events that transpired, I personally do not entirely agree with some of the conclusions that were made either by the author or by the various media outlets or government "fact finding" panels of the time.

Another relevant reference is *Troubled Water* about the "riots" aboard the *USS Kitty Hawk* in October 1972. However, I found myself sometimes questioning the author's understanding of some of the events and their supposed causes. In addition, the author states the change in the ship's deployment schedule and the "nearly unheard-of 274 days at sea" added to the list of tensions. First, the *Kitty Hawk* did *not* spend 274 days at sea. Her deployment was 274 days! Additionally, this was not "nearly unheard-of" either. The *Connie's* 1 Oct 71 to 1 July '72 deployment was 274 days and her following deployment (5 Jan to 11 Oct '73) was 279 days. Because the United States was withdrawing Army and Air Force personnel "in country" (Nixon's Vietnamization) the Air Force in Guam and Thailand and the Navy at sea were left to defend Vietnam in keeping with Nixon's promise to do so. Additionally, given the Easter Offensive by the NVA and continuous other "fires" to put out, the Navy was scrambling to fill the gap and deploy enough forces afloat to meet the demand. And that demand meant we sailors off the coast of Vietnam would spend more time on-station in a daily grind that would continue until national policy goals had been achieved (bring the POWs home and stabilize the military situation in Vietnam).

My own personal recollections of the *race riot aboard Connie* incident are detached because none of the personnel involved were from OI Division (the one African-American OS mentioned I do not recall, which is suspicious because there were only two or three in the division) and I was not personally involved in any of the events documented. But, these events did impact us directly. When assaults and beatings started (or were rumored to have happened) at random times and places aboard ship, the command decided to secure the CIC/CAATC spaces with the intent to prevent violence there. Guards were placed at the access points. We were allowed to bring mattresses into CIC from berthing, so we could "caulk off" when needed. Our meals were C Rations taken inside CIC. We were also "escorted" in groups to the heads. Keep in mind that the duration of this situation only lasted from dinner time of the first day until we pulled into port the following morning.

When we pulled into port, all hands were mustered at their normal topside locations and command personnel went through the ranks with a list of names. Those on the list were designated as part of a "beach detachment" and escorted to the aft inboard elevator and taken off the ship. The crew later learned that while we and the ship returned to sea to continue training in preparation for deployment, the "beach detachment" was allowed liberty ashore and faced no punishment or confinement until the powers that be could determine how best to proceed without creating any more of a media circus than was already in play. We were at sea, at work! They were ashore and on liberty! The shipmates I talked with were of the conviction that, at the very least, they should have been restricted to the base!

"PAPPY"

Every division aboard ship had a senior enlisted person assigned as LPO (Leading Petty Officer) and ours was "Pappy" Sarver. He was a Petty Officer 1st Class who had come out of a deck division as a striker. This meant he had completed the basic requirement to become a Radarman and then had to go before a review board and be approved for transfer from his division to OI (Operations Intelligence) and work in CIC. Pappy stood about 5'10 and was built like a block house — BIG and HARD! He was definitely what you would call today "Old Navy!" He was imposing, and this kept you respectful of him and his position. For sure, he was ALL Navy! His persona was tough and rough! But the first thing you learned was that he was also just and fair!

The first instance that I experienced that proved his character was when we were in port in San Diego for a pier-side upkeep period. During muster one morning Pappy asked for a volunteer to be in charge of required divisional upkeep on the ship's mast. OI Division was assigned the middle third of the mast as that is where some of the radar antenna platforms were located. I volunteered and asked if I could choose the rest of the crew that would do the work with me and he agreed. He told me we had 10 days to finish the work and I was allowed to select six others to make up the crew. Once I had done so, I pulled the guys aside and told them we could knock it out in a week and then "goldbrick" the remaining three days. They were all for it and "turned to" with a vengeance; we finished within the week. "Pappy" was up the mast twice to check on progress and told me that when we finished he wanted to meet with my crew. Well, we weren't happy about him monitoring our progress so closely, but we weren't about to try pulling the wool over his eyes now that he knew what our progress was. So, we finished the work and met with Pappy. He told us how pleased he was with the work and told us we all had 72 hours liberty as a result. So, instead of hanging around the mast "gold bricking" we were given three days off. All we had to do was make muster in the mornings and then we could leave the ship! Pappy made some loyal followers that day!

The second time Pappy "proved his salt" with me was when I was home one night with my current squeeze and came down with a fever of 102 and swollen tonsils. My girlfriend called the ship next morning and I had told her to talk to Pappy directly. That afternoon Pappy and his wife showed up at our door; they bundled me up and took me to the Naval Hospital and waited while I was looked at by a doctor. Thankfully, the practice then was not to yank the tonsils at first blush but to use antibiotics to combat the infection. So, with pills in hand, Pappy took me home and told me to stay in bed and he would be by in two days to check up on me. Which he did! A couple days later, he LET me return to duty! Later in my career, I came to realize how lucky the division was back then to have Pappy as our LPO and I still tell everyone he was my "sea daddy," proudly!

CHAPTER 12
WESTPAC '73
(5 JANUARY – 11 OCTOBER 1973)

USS CONSTELLATION (CVA-64)

Departed *Connie* via helicopter to *USS White Plains* (AFS-4) the latter part of the 20 March to 2 April Line Period

En route Subic and U.S. for separation from USN

Days Deployed: 279
Days At Sea/Underway:
Days In Port:
Days "On the Line": 98

ON LINE PERIODS:

31 January 1973; 27 February – 13 March 1973; 20 March - 2 April 1973; 12 – 25 April 1973; 5 -17 May 1973; 29 May – 12 June 1973; 28 June – 2 July 1973; 5 -15 July 1973; 6 -15 August 1973; remained on the line for two more periods after the cut-off date of 15 August 1973

OPERATION END SWEEP was a United States Navy and United States Marine Corps operation to remove naval mines from Haiphong harbor and other coastal and inland waterways in North Vietnam between February and July 1973. The operation fulfilled an American obligation under the Paris Peace Accord of January 1973, which ended direct American participation in the Vietnam War. It also was the first operational deployment of a U.S. Navy air mine countermeasures capability.[1]

Connie still flew strike missions up to the time of the Cease Fire on 21 Feb '72. After that and for the rest of her WestPac most aircraft missions were conducted ISO Operation End Sweep and the de-mining effort being accomplished along the Vietnamese coast.

Connie departed Yankee Station for an in-port period at Subic in late February/ early March with the usual five-day stay being expected. But this in-port period stretched into about 10 days. With most everyone broke by the end of the fifth day, there wasn't much liberty going on out in town and most of us spent much of the time aboard ship trying to find *anybody* with a few bucks to loan.

While the ship was at sea again, I departed the *Connie* on 18 March '73 via helo transfer to USS *White Plains* (AFS-4) (what is commonly referred to as a "reefer" because she carries frozen food stores) to the States, arriving at Treasure Island for separation on 3 April '73.

While aboard the *White Plains,* transit personnel (like me) were expected to work for our passage. So, that meant when the ship pulled up alongside another ship for UNREP, we were assigned to work in the refrigerated holds, transferring stores up to the main deck and over to the receiving ship. The way it worked was that you started the hour down at the bottom level of the refrigerated stores hold, which was at a temperature of around 20 degrees! You were given a parka and some cold weather gloves and spent about 40 minutes on that level. To avoid hypothermia or frostbite, you were then transferred up to the next level, which was at a temperature of around 60 degrees and we were able to shed the cold weather gear. After 40 minutes you were transferred to the main deck, exposed to the tropical sun and humidity. After the previous two decks you were only thankful to be topside until the heat began to take its toll. Then you started the whole rotation all over again. During my transit, I worked two of these evolutions and was very grateful when we headed for Subic and didn't have to experience another UNREP!

Arriving in Subic Bay, we were given transportation to Clark AFB to await a flight home. Checking in there, we were told it would be at least until the following morning before we could get manifested onto a flight. While sitting in the terminal talking to a couple of the others travelling with me, I was amazed to see across the terminal a bunch of *Connie* sailors. What the heck and how in hell did they get here? Among them was a Lieutenant I knew, so I walked up and we all exchanged our surprise at seeing one another. The LT then explained that less than a day after I helo'ed off the ship, their at-sea period had been curtailed due to the OpTempo being changed as a result of the agreements reached at the Paris Peace Talks. So, the ship promptly returned to Subic and arrived the same day as I did! Boy, was I pissed! Mostly because of those two UNREP's that I had to work!

Anyway, I spent the night on a nice comfortable terminal chair (NOT) and was on a flight the next morning, en route Travis AFB. Checking into Treasure Island for the discharge process was like old home week because I was familiar with the place from "A" school. It took three days of paperwork, medical and dental appointments, VA benefits counseling, etc. before I was handed my discharge papers and a USNR ID Card.

Upon discharge we were encouraged to change into civilian clothes because uniformed personnel were experiencing threats and harassment at the S.F. airport. Great to be back in the good 'ole US of A!!!! Welcome home, baby killer!

BETWIXT & BETWEEN

After mustering out and returning home, I still had two years of "Reserve time" left on my Navy contract and was required to check in with the local Reserve Detachment. So, I made the call and talked with the Det.'s CPO and he told me to meet him at his place of work the following night. That night I went down to the local bowling alley where he was working a shift as the bar tender. I ponied up to the bar and plopped my service jacket down for him to look over. While he did that and we talked, he offered me a brew and told me it was "on the house" and welcome home! He also told me there would be no drill time for me and that this was the only meeting I would be required to make for the remaining two years! So, I downed the beer, shook his hand and left!

I enrolled back into the JC I had left four years before, in time for the fall semester. I also submitted the paperwork to the VA so I could start getting my monthly checks for attending college. By the time I received the first one, I had already been attending classes for over three months, so I was seriously in the hole already! Working nights at a pizza joint and the VA checks – when they finally came – were still barely enough to subsist on and would never allow me to pay off the debt I had accumulated while waiting for the VA money! So, I dropped my class load down to 12 credits, hoping the fewer hours in school I could fill with another part-time job. Then a few months later, with no progress on my debt situation, I dropped down to eight credits. Now, keep in mind that anything below 12 credits meant that you no longer qualified for full time VA college funds and the amount of your checks dropped on account of your class load having dropped. So, it was a Catch-22 that I couldn't escape! Took the Postal Exam, but later learned that the opening was part-time for two years until the person on the route retired, so when they called me, I had to decline. I applied to the FAA, but was told "off the record" that my ethnicity and gender were not what they were hiring at that time! I wondered where MY Equal Opportunity came into play? Finally, I had to admit that I could not obtain gainful employment in my hometown area unless I went into the same field of work as most in the region, namely the lumber industry. Well, this was the same as my father had done, and which I grew up watching as what he had to go through to make a living. No Thanks! Then, I began to think of the Navy as a career path! My rating in the Navy was a technical field and there was always something new to learn. Also, there was advancement opportunity if you applied yourself, vacation, medical, dental and a good retirement package at the end of a career. The down side was that I would also be subjected to the whim of whoever was in a position over me and I had experienced the upside and downside of that reality. But, enduring that in the course of pursuing training, advancement and technical experience had possibilities that working in a lumber mill did not!

I arrived at the conclusion it would be my best course of action. Taking my service records down to the local recruiting office, I dropped them down on the recruiter's desk and told him I wanted to re-enlist. I was a week shy of the expiration of my reserve duty. When the recruiter took a look at my DD-214 and noted my re-enlistment code, he looked up, smiled and told me that wouldn't be a problem and asked what I had in mind. I told him I wanted a two-year contract so that when it expired I would be eligible for a re-enlistment cash bonus when I signed for the next one. Based on NEC & CREO (job codes and critical ratings) ratings such a bonus could amount to $12,000 to $16,000. A few days later, I found myself going back through the Induction Center in Oakland and a day later, in-processing continued at Treasure Island. I had to remain there for a couple extra days to await the expiration of my first (reserve portion) contract before they could sign me to a new one. While there, I was also given a voucher for a new seabag, which I had to buy from the Navy Exchange on base. In the course of this evolution, a Career Counselor was made available to us NavVets (there were more than just a few of us). When my turn came to talk with him, I was informed the Navy considered my two-year reserve stint as "shore duty" and that I would be assigned to a "sea duty" command. However, if I had a sea duty preference, the Navy would try to accommodate me. I asked where the *Connie* was and was told she had just started an overhaul at PSNSY Bremerton. Jack Pot! Both the command and the Puget Sound area were familiar stomping grounds and so I asked for and was assigned to duty back aboard my old command! I considered myself fortunate.

BACK ABOARD *CONNIE*

9 Apr '75 to 11 Apr '77

Back aboard the *Connie* and back at PSNSY Bremerton – familiar territory, crew and ship! Some of the guys from my previous tour were still aboard and in CIC and I got a pretty good ribbing for coming back in the Navy! But, because I was on good terms with most everyone, it was all good natured and I felt right at home. The ship hadn't preceded me into the shipyard by much and "ripout" was still in progress. Most everyone living aboard ship had either made the move out in town or was berthed aboard a barge moored alongside the pier across from the ship. After completing the check-in process, I was almost immediately assigned to work on the berthing barge in OI Division's designated berthing space and put in charge of about six compartment cleaners. The daily routine of sweeping, mopping, waxing and buffing the deck, collecting and distributing the laundry bags, etc. This didn't require six bodies, so by lunch the most difficult part of the assignment was to keep from getting "under foot" or caught "taking a nooner" or otherwise being someplace you weren't supposed to be or doing something you weren't supposed to be doing. This was not always an easy task to accomplish and we got caught once and reprimanded. But, I was told later by the person delivering the "ass chewing" that I was to tell my guys to "be more careful" next time and not to be so "obvious." Still, the days dragged by and we had to get creative with our time and with how to avoid getting in trouble!

Still at PSNSY and during a very cold winter spell, I came down with "strep" which led to tonsillitis and a fever around 102. At next Sick Call I checked in; the senior corpsman had a look, told me I had a cold and gave me a packet of APCs (all-purpose capsules), which is like giving a person aspirin! I was pissed and pointed out that my tonsils were obviously swollen and the APCs weren't going to do any good against the infection. He got testy with me (he being an E-6 and me being an E-4) and told me that was all he would do for now. I wasn't satisfied with that and demanded to see a doctor, which I believed was within my rights to do. He refused and told me to leave! Now, I was *really* pissed! I walked off the ship and across base to the PSNSY Naval Medical Clinic, close by the main gate to the shipyard. I signed into their Sick Call logbook and took a seat. Shortly, a CWO2 came out, took a look in the log book and called my name. In the space provided for "command" I had entered CVA-64 and he wanted to know why I hadn't gone there instead of coming to the clinic. So, after I explained the problem, he took me back to his office and checked my condition. Then he called the ship and asked for the four-striper (Captain) in charge of the Medical Department. Explaining the problem, he hung up shortly and told me to go back aboard ship and the medical officer would be waiting to see me. When I got back aboard ship and met the doctor, the first thing that happened was I got an ass-chewing for taking the problem outside the ship's "chain of command." The second thing that happened was that he apologized that I felt it was necessary to do so and that he had already chewed out his Sick Call corpsman! At that, he wrote a prescription for antibiotics and a three-day "no duty" chit; then he sent me home.

MASTER AT ARMS

Feb – July 1976

The division had a requirement to provide a body to the Master-At-Arms force aboard ship and I was selected to fill that billet (job). This was the shipboard police force. It was not very popular with certain parts of the crew and had the potential for being in harm's way if things went wrong. It was a six-month assignment, so for the remaining period in the shipyard and continuing into the first month's back in San Diego, I would be a "cop on the beat!" I wasn't enthusiastic about the idea, but it got me out of the boredom of running the division berthing. When reporting to the MAA Office, the master chief in charge sat me down for a little one-on-one, which was his way of sizing me up and giving his stamp of approval on newly assigned personnel. Across the P-way (passageway) from there was the working office, where MAA personnel checked in and out from their roving patrols and received assignments and were updated on any specific concerns during each shift. MAA shifts at PSNSY were 12 hours on, 24 off! This was an incentive approved by the command, because, as I said, it had its hazards and they recognized that! I spent the first day checking into the division and getting some U/I (Under Instruction) time with a couple of the guys who had been there a few months. In short order, I was given a clicker (one of those little hand-held counters that has three numbers on a rotating wheel with a button to push for advancing the number by one with each click) and taken down to the after brow (where the enlisted crew and shipyard workers boarded the ship). There I was given a randomly assigned and daily changing number that determined which person boarding the ship you were to stop and search. The tacit understanding within the MAA Force was that if your gut told you someone needed to be checked out, that was the number he was when boarding! I hadn't been doing this very long when this "space cadet" came aboard and I pulled him aside for a "random" search. He had been carrying a large brown paper bag which I placed on a podium that was stored in the after brow's entryway. After patting him down and checking his pockets, I reached for the bag and opened it up to discover it was half full of raw marijuana! Holy shit! The MAA Office was located the next deck up from the after brow and I leaned into the ladder well and yelled up to the office to have someone get down here and take this guy into custody!

When a couple of the guys hustled down they couldn't believe what they saw. They gave the guy the bum's rush getting back up to the office and that was the last I saw of him. It made us all wonder how many of those types had made those trips before and not been caught! Why did I single out the "space cadet"? He had nervous, shifty eyes!

When we didn't have duty on the after brow, we were assigned in pairs to the roving patrol. The patrol, at times, was assigned a specific portion of the ship (aft, amid-ships or forward) and other times you just randomly patrolled. You were looking for dopers, high-stakes gambling, theft, fights or any other situation which violated the UCMJ and the CO's directives. While in the shipyard, many of the spaces were torn apart and in the process of being upgraded. This left many spaces unmanned as to their normal function, but also places where illegal activity presented an opportunity. These were spaces that we looked for and frequently checked out. Case in point: My partner and I had entered a space that had been used as a berthing area, but the bunks were all stacked up around the edges of the space and the ducting had been torn out of the overhead to prep for an upgraded installation. On closer inspection we saw that between the stacked bunks and the bulkhead, someone had been using the space to sneak a quick "toke"–we found evidence in the form of "roaches," that is, left over butts of marijuana "cigarettes." We made note of that and a couple days later we came back and caught two people engaged in that activity and took them into custody. Unfortunately, one of the guys I knew from OI Division.

From time to time, the MAA Office would get a tip about a big poker game or tournament going on and were told to bust it up. When we did, no one was taken into custody and no charges were filed, so it was just an attempt to discourage the activity. These were mostly targeted because some disgruntled player had lost more than he felt was fair or because the stakes in the game were so high that the command wanted to dissuade players from participating. Card games were everywhere and for the most part were nickel and dime affairs. To try stopping more of them or all of them would have been a hopeless task. Odd though, that on the two ships I served on as MAA, the location of choice for the big games ended up being the Barber Shop. Go figure!

Late one night, my partner and I were sitting in the MAA office on one of our breaks when a call came in asking for MAAs in one of the aft berthing spaces.

When we got there, one of the guys living there took us over to an aisle of racks where two guys were kneeling down with the curtain pulled back on one of the lower berths. They told us they had tried to wake their buddy up and he wasn't responding. Evidently, one of them had called the corpsman because moments later they arrived and started checking out the "patient." The corpsman asked us to get a "stokes stretcher" and then made a call to sick bay for assistance. We found a stretcher and when we got it to back to the area, another corpsman had showed up. As we watched, they pulled the patient out of the rack and placed him in the stretcher. We asked what the problem was and were told the man was dead and had drowned in his own vomit. Too intoxicated to help himself! After it was all over and we made our report, those of us in the office wondered what the Navy would tell his folks. Died in the line of duty? That would be difficult to explain!

Another incident that sticks out in my mind was on a cold winter's night and a couple of us had been called out to the pier to assist the Shore Patrol with unloading prisoners from their van and getting them aboard ship. Everything was going pretty smoothly at first, but one of the last prisoners bolted from the SP's grasp and started running up the pier. One of the SPs and I ran after him, but when he saw he was losing ground in the chase, he stopped and hopped up on top of one of the pier pilings. As I got closer, I recognized him as someone I had casually known and had been in a group of shipmates that I went out on liberty with. He started yelling at me and the SP that he was going to jump into the water if we came any closer. That water had to have been in the mid-40s and if he jumped he'd be hypothermic in minutes. Fortunately, I recognized that and looking at him, I knew he knew too! So, I called his bluff! I told him he was coming back to the ship with me, but if he jumped, no one would be going in after him and risk dying in that freezing water. After a few moments of silence, he resigned himself, climbed down off the piling and we escorted him aboard ship.

I hadn't been on the MAA Force long when they informed me that I would be attending a training course for MAA in San Diego. So, from 14 to 19 March '76 I was on TAD (Temporary Assigned Duty) to the MAA Afloat, Course of Instruction at NAVSTA San Diego. The course consisted of a few days classroom instruction which dealt mainly with the legal processes and procedures for establishing evidentiary "chain of custody." The third day was devoted to "Riot Control" and self-defense. Riot control training took place in a gymnasium and entailed the trainees being provided with "rioters," who were TAD personnel from the base. We were placed in formation, armed with batons and instructed on how to manage unruly crowds. But most of us agreed that you can't learn that in a couple hours and expect to be able to handle such episodes.

The latter part of the day was training in self-defense. We were taken onto a roof-top, outfitted with chest-protectors and given three-foot long bamboo batons. The batons consisted of strips of bamboo encased in canvas, so there was some "give" in a blow when struck. We were formed up and told that the exercise would consist of half of the class as the "aggressor" and the other half as the "defender." The aggressor would try to land blows to the defender's chest protector and the defender was to parry the blows. After a few minutes of this, the aggressor and defender positions would be reversed. Well, I was paired up with a chief and I was initially the defender. The whistle blew and the chief came at me with his baton! I was able to parry some of the blows with my baton, but he did manage a couple on my chest protector. He didn't seem too happy with the results, so he stepped up the pace and on one blow he came in from the side and struck me in the ribs, outside the area covered by my body armor. I immediately groaned and fell to my knees, actually seeing red from the pain. The instructor came over and asked if I was okay, but I was already starting to stand up, glaring at the chief. I saw no remorse in his eyes and he offered no apology. I was pissed off !! Shortly, the instructor called a halt and told us to reverse rolls. Now it was MY turn! I didn't waste time and waded right into the chief with quick, sharp blows to his armor. I wasn't going to do the same to him by striking outside his chest protector, but I was in "vent" mode and wanted to make him sweat. I kept up the pace, the chief giving ground until we neared the edge of the roof. A couple more steps back and he would be at risk of going over the edge. Realizing this, he yelled out to the instructor. I stopped attacking and looked into his face, recognizing that I had definitely let him know that he'd messed with the wrong guy. The next day, before class, I checked in at the base clinic for "Sick Call." When I reported to school late, I showed the instructor my sick call slip stating I had a cracked rib and two with contusions and assigned "Light Duty" status. Of course, I didn't need such status because the course was over and all that remained was for me to check out and get back to the ship

Upon returning to *Connie* I was in for a surprise. The Master Chief called me into the NCIS Office and told me I had been selected to be the MAA's "Brig Chaser." He explained what that entailed and that I would be assigned a vehicle, driver and expense account. When called upon, I was to transport a prisoner from the ship's brig to Sand Point Naval Station in Seattle for JAG Courts-Martial. Upon completion of the trial, I was to transport the prisoner to the Sand Point medical clinic for a physical and then remand him to custody at the Navy Brig in Seattle. This duty happened once a week or when JAG was "in session" at Sand Point and one of our prisoners was on the "docket" for trial that day. A typical day spent as "Brig Chaser" entailed me arriving at the XO's office around 6:30AM to pick up the orders allowing me to transport the prisoner. I would then make my way to the CO's cabin for his signature to those orders and then proceed to the brig where the Marine on duty would sign the prisoner over to me. My vehicle and driver were on the pier waiting when I brought the prisoner off the ship and once in the van I would secure the prisoner's handcuffs to the seat frame. Then, we would proceed to the Washington State Ferry dock and catch the next ferry to Seattle. While aboard the ferry the driver and I would take turns going to the cafeteria for a cup of coffee and a Danish. The ferry crossing took about 50 minutes. When arriving at Sand Point, the three of us would sit in the waiting room outside court until our prisoner was called for trial. While the trial was going on I did double duty and functioned as bailiff. By the time the Court-Martial was over, it was lunch time and the three of us would go to the cafeteria on base for a burger or whatever was appealing on the menu. But we were under a pretty tight schedule from here on out and didn't spend much time dawdling. Once the prisoner had been adjudicated, we had to get him through the required physical, which was necessary to ensure he was fit to be incarcerated (which I found rather amusing, as he'd already been in the brig aboard ship). Once that was done, we had to go across town to the Navy Brig and get him checked in there before my tasking was complete. By the time I had finished the process, it was mid-afternoon and we still had to get back across town, onto the ferry and back to Bremerton. By the time I returned aboard ship it was usually around 5:30PM. My day was over and I could go home!

During my tenure as the ship's designated "Brig Chaser" I was ordered to pick up a particularly notorious scumbag! The ship had charged him on 26 counts, a half-dozen being arson. And not just setting fires in spaces aboard ship, but also setting fires to bunks with people sleeping in them! When I came aboard ship the day I was to transport this guy, the Master Chief buttonholed me and made sure I knew that this person deserved "special attention" and that in the course of his being in my custody I was to interpret that status to the utmost intent of the UCMJ. I didn't know exactly what his interpretation of the applicable UCMJ articles was, but his demeanor told me all I needed to know. The way I understood the conversation, the prisoner was to be afforded no leniency, courtesy or kindness while in my custody! So be it! And, do you know, that while on the ferry over to Seattle, the creep had the temerity to ask for a cigarette and a light? What an ass!

Well, when the Court-Martial started and I was sitting as bailiff, I was appalled that the JAG judge started dismissing one charge after another until he was down to seven or eight out of the original 26. I was ticked off and under the impression that our fire starter was going to be let off easy! Then, when the Judge started reading the charges that would be upheld, I realized that he had dropped most of the other charges because of the difficulty proving them, duplication of charges or other mitigating issues. When the trial was over, the prisoner was proved guilty on all remaining counts and the sentence was the most extreme I had ever heard handed out while I was chasing prisoners! I truly believed that he got what he deserved!

My duties as Brig Chaser ended shortly before the ship departed Bremerton for San Diego. It was back to regular duties as MAA, patrolling and manning the after bow for search and seizures. As was a habit of mine, I enjoyed taking breaks from the daily routine (either while in my parent division or assigned elsewhere) by taking my breaks and relaxing out on the fantail. The fantail on a carrier in fairly protected and out of the weather due to the flight deck overhang and deck structures on both sides. While underway, it's quite idyllic to take a seat on a bollard and watch the wake and feel the throb of the screws. One such night, while underway in SOCAL during normal ops, I and my partner had been patrolling spaces in the aft portion of the ship and as a break, I led us back to the fantail for a smoke. We had been sitting there for only a few minutes when my nose told me that somewhere in the near vicinity someone was smoking marijuana! Where the hell was *that* coming from? Shortly, we figured the smell had to be coming from the starboard side and there was only one hatch opening there. That was to the Aerographer's Loft, where they stored, prepped and launched the weather balloons. Climbing the ladder one deck up to the hatch, we could tell the odor got stronger. I put my face close to the hatch and the smell got stronger still. There was no longer any doubt, and we whispered about what to do next: call for back-up or bust into the space. But, we weren't allowed to make that decision because just then the "dogs" on the hatch started to be opened. We waited until the person inside had all the dogs opened and, as the hatch swung open, we faced five or six surprised faces. With batons at the ready, we told them to move back from the door and against the bulkhead on the far side of the room. The whole place reeked heavily of marijuana. I immediately reached for the phone and called the MAA Office, told people there where we were and to send back-up! While waiting, my partner broke out some "chain of custody" evidence bags and started picking up the roach butts still in the ashtrays on the table in the middle of the room, while I kept an eye on the "suspects." While doing that, I noticed one of the guys glancing up to the bulkhead behind me, with nervous, furtive looks. Once our back-up arrived, I checked out the area he had been nervously eyeing. The bulkhead had angled cross pieces to support the wall, which would be a convenient place to hide a stash. While the rest of the MAA's had taken the guys in hand, I started climbing the angle irons and looking down them left and right. Two or three rows up, I spotted the stash. There were at least five or six big baggies of marijuana. I called to my partner, who came over and I started tossing the bags down to him. I actually heard a couple of the suspects groan. We would spend most of our remaining shift writing up our reports and ensuring the paperwork was completed for the "chain of custody" evidence we had gathered.

The ship never pursued a Court-Martial for this bust! Instead, NCIS was able to "turn" one or two of them and get them to give up their suppliers' names. However, to protect the identity of the informer(s), all of them were transferred off the ship. That way, no one would know who snitched. A few days later, while talking about the incident with one of the other MAA, I came to the realization that, with half-dozen of them and only two of us MAAs, they could have easily over-powered us and tossed us off the fantail. Because no one knew where we were, no one would have known we were missing for at least a couple hours. And, there would have been no witnesses or rationale to establish the pot smokers and us being in the same place around the time of our disappearance! The thought caused a cold chill down my back. I could only believe that the sole reason that hadn't done so was because they were in such a "mellow" state. Possibly!

Just before I was due to rotate back to OI Division, a televised event was going to occur aboard ship! **The Great American Celebration** in recognition of the country's 200th anniversary was to take place on designated navy aircraft carriers on both the east and west coasts on 3 July 1976! *Connie* was selected! There were to be television crews and Hollywood stars and all the traffic control and security were to be provided by the ship's MAAs. There were no off duty MAAs for that day – we all worked until it was over! I have never seen a ship so crammed full of civilians; network TV types, movie actors, singers, comedians and then all the audience. I don't recall what the numbers totaled, but it had to be a couple thousand at least. My assignment in this madhouse was on the flight deck, wearing a helmet with a comms link inside. Through the comms link I was given direction from the officer in charge of our management and placement; he ran it from Pri-Fly, a couple decks above us in the ship's island.

As reward for this duty, I was given tickets for my family to attend. Of course, I would be busy, and once I got them aboard and seated, for the most part they were left to fend for themselves. I spent the next six hours delivering messages, escorting guests and informing some of the Hollywood types when they would be expected on stage. Burl Ives, the Lennon Sisters and Anson Williams (from *Happy Days*) were the acts that I was assigned to escort to the stage directly. By the time I left the ship that night I'd been on my feet for six hours and on duty for fourteen! My two daughters were most impressed by the fact that I had escorted "Potsie Weber" to the stage!

USS CONSTELLATION CV-64
BOARDING PASS
"The Great American Celebration"
July 3rd 1976

Admit: _____

(Not Transferable)

Guest of: Allen E. Kirkpatrick

ADMIT ONE

BACK TO OI DIVISION; SOCAL "WORK-UPS"

When I returned from the stint as MAA to OI Division and CIC the LPO asked for a meeting with him in his office. During the meeting, he asked if I would take a position as Watch Supervisor in the Surface module of CIC because he didn't like his choices of the more senior personnel assigned there. I mentioned that this wouldn't make me popular with some of the E-5s and E-6s because that position was normally filled by personnel of that rank and I was only an E-4. He laughed and said if someone had a problem with that, he would take care of it. He had also "pinched" another E-4 for that position (my watch relief in the eight-on eight-off rotation), who was a buddy of mine. Here we were, two E-4 second-hitch OSs standing watch as supervisors aboard a carrier. Now all I had to do was live up to the LPO's expectations! The ship had been operating in SOCAL waters for a couple months after returning to San Diego. Operations included drilling for Refresher Training (RefTra), a qualification requirement necessary to advance the ship in her readiness status prior to deployment. Also, she was tasked with conducting carrier qualifications (CarQuals) for navy pilots needing that "box" checked off before being deemed proficient in landing an aircraft (day or night) aboard a pitching, rolling, moving postage-stamp of a flight deck. Most of these were to qualify or re-qualify pilots assigned to the air wing that would embark aboard *Connie* for our upcoming deployment.

This time period (mid to late '70s) was pretty dismal for the armed forces in general and the navy, in particular. Post-Vietnam defense budgets were shrinking faster than the navy could decommission ships and discharge "dead wood." This left funding available to operate the ships that would remain in commission, but with little "wiggle room" in the operational budget. So, the navy came up with ways to save money! One was "Deferred Maintenance," a term which we all were dumbfounded by because it implied that maintenance was required but would be accomplished at a later time! How brilliant was that! Some bean counter had sold it to some desk pushing admirals in the Pentagon and everyone in the fleet was expected to salute and say "Roger that!"

Another means of cutting costs was less operating time at sea to save on fuel, wear and tear on the engines and other equipment necessary in the operation of ships while at sea. So we would spend the day at sea doing what was necessary, then make for Coronado Rhodes, "drop the hook" a half-mile off shore, remain overnight before getting underway in the morning and go back out into the SOCAL operating areas again. Well, obviously this didn't sit well with the crew. I mean, there you sat at anchor, less than a mile from port! Someone got the bright idea of giving his wife a walkie-talkie and telling her where to stand on the beach and what time to be there so that he could use the other walkie-talkie handset to communicate with her. Well, that was *really* popular and before you knew it there was a crowd of wives and girlfriends standing on the beach talking to their husbands and boyfriends clustered on the flight deck or hangar deck. If you didn't have a walkie-talkie, you could make arrangements before leaving port for your wife or girlfriend to tag along with a buddy's wife or girlfriend and then you would pair up with your buddy on the ship. It was less preferred than being in port, but better than just sitting there staring at the beach!

While working in the Surface Module of CIC during these SOCAL operations, we had a chief that stood in rotation as Surface Watch Officer. A big block of a person, he liked to throw his authority around and was loud and frequent with it. He did know his rate, though, and most of us just let the bluster slide. Well, one period when he and I were on watch at the same time, he was on his soap box, talking about the coming football games during the weekend. As he droned on, it got to the point that I was really getting fed up with the BS! One of the games he was talking about was a St. Louis Cardinals game, but I don't recall who they were playing against. He didn't like the team and was yakking away about if he were to bet on the game, he would take the other team. That was it! I told him I'd bet my paycheck against $100 of his, on the Cards! Silence settled over the space! The challenge surprised him and for longer than normal, he didn't say anything. Finally, in an effort to save face, he said he'd take that bet. Jim Hart and the "Cardiac Cards" pulled a win out of thin air and the chief paid up! That still didn't shut him up, but he did avoid talking about betting on sports games whenever I was around.

The schedule, during our work-up period, consisted of a full day of flight ops and for the rest of the crew, GQ in the morning shortly after breakfast and another GQ after lunch. With few variations, this was consistent for the duration of our at sea periods. It wasn't stressful, but very tedious and repetitive.

As part of the recent overhaul, *Connie's* designation was changed from CVA to CVS (later dropped to CV), reflecting her "conversion" to an anti-submarine platform. Many of the training evolutions performed during our SOCAL work-ups reflected this and implemented those technical capabilities that had been installed aboard ship or added to the air wing's configuration. Specifically, this was the S-3A "Viking" and its primary ASW function. In support of these aircraft, the forward port side of CIC had been gutted and replaced with what amounted to a Tactical Operations Center (TOC) that would directly manage the S-3s during any coordinated ASW tactical problem. As a culmination of all the ASW training that had been conducted during work-ups, a large portion of the ship's transit from San Diego to Hawaii during RIMPAC that year was put into play. The ship and its assigned task group were to consider the transit to be under a "hostile" ASW environment and as such all ASW assets were engaged. This included voluminous use of sonobuoys employed in "roads" preceding and encompassing the carrier's intended path of transit. What was amusing to us in CIC was that whenever the decision makers were not sure of where the "hostile" submarine(s) were or if they had been unable to maintain "contact" on the "hostile" force, they had an ace-in-the-hole. Aboard ship, assigned in support of the ship's ASW effort, was a Commander with previous experience as a submarine skipper. When the situation warranted and when his opinion was requested, he would be called to CIC and the ASW Officer and he would stand over the chart table. The Commander would talk the ASW Officer through the problem and "lead" him to the correct decision for ongoing prosecution of the "enemy" without actually pointing and saying "here he is!" We watched this evolution play out a half-dozen times during the course of the exercise. I'm sure the former sub skipper thought he was being punished for some unknown sin he'd committed, to be assigned such odious duty aboard a "target!" (As any submariner will tell you, he works on a "boat" and all surface craft are referred to as "targets.")

CHAPTER 13
MAKING ENDS MEET

I WOULDN'T CHARACTERIZE MYSELF AS A HUSTLER, but rather an opportunist. If a situation presented itself where it would be advantageous for me to act, I would. And, occasionally, if I knew of a way to "expand my paycheck" I certainly took advantage! When you were trying to feed a family in the '70s and early '80s, it was practically a necessity! As it was, my family qualified for welfare assistance. This usually meant that when surplus staples were available, we could pick up our share; rice, cheese, flour, etc. However, it didn't sit well with me and so I took every opportunity to work my own "deals" and add income to the family budget.

An easy and accepted means of doing this while in port was to take someone else's duty for him, for which you would be paid by that person. If the duty consisted of just being aboard and available for the duty section, the fee would be around $20. If duty also consisted of standing a watch, the fee rose commensurate with the qualification level required of the watch. If you just had to man a desk in the division or work a four-hour period on the ship's telephone switchboard, that was an extra $10 or $15. If you had to stand watch on the quarterdeck as POOW (Petty Officer of the Watch) or had to stand a roving patrol, the fee rose higher. You couldn't do this too often because you also had to stand your own duty day as well and didn't want to end up working a regular five-day week as well as adding duty days and nights to your days away from the family.

Then there were the card games. I really enjoyed playing spades or Backgammon now and then. But, aboard the *Connie* during '76 I found a partner that was pretty good at spades and he and I really started taking it serious. A game "payout" was agreed upon by you and your opponents such that the winning team would collect a penny a point, 5c per "set" and 25c per game for starters. When the losing team tried to win their money back, the stakes rose: 5c per point, 50c a "set" and $5 per game. Eventually, this could and did lead to some serious bucks. I ended up having to keep a log book (in code) for my team's winnings. I was the accountant, my partner was the collector and with his higher rank and more imposing physique, well suited to that purpose.

Another means of income was to run "anchor pools." This was done by taking two sheets of paper with a carbon in the middle. The bottom sheet had the numbers (in random order) 1 through 60 written in gridded squares (one for each minute in the hour). The top sheet also had sixty squares, but they were blank. You could run multiple "anchor pools" with varying "pay outs," each square you "bought" varying depending on the "pay out." You bought your square, paid your fee and initialed the square(s) you wanted. For example, one pool could be a dollar a square with a payout of $30 for the winner – whose square showed numbers corresponded to the exact minute the ship's log recorded the anchor being dropped or line being tied to the pier) and consolation prizes to the two squares the minute before and the minute after (winning $5 each). This meant the person running the pool pocketed $20. Multiple pools meant multiple pay outs and thus higher profits. The opportunity to work this angle didn't occur until I was aboard the *Hood* in '77, but during that time it was a very good source of revenue. My partner in this scheme was a Yeoman 2nd in the Personnel Office and his position helped guarantee no one would mess with us or rat us out to the command. The last anchor pool that we ran was while en route back to the States at the end of our '77 WestPac. We put together multiple pool sheets with varying payouts, all the way up to a $500 sheet. The day before entering port at Concord, California I was attending the Navigation Brief in the Wardroom as part of the CIC Radar Navigation Detail. During the course of the briefing, the CO was chatting with the Navigator when he asked if he knew of any good anchor pools floating around. I instantly looked up from my briefing material and fixed on the Navigator. He chuckled in response and told the CO that there were a few floating around and that one was actually pretty large for such a small ship. As he finished his remarks to the CO he looked right at me and grinned! As soon as we were finished with the brief, I hurried down to the Personnel Office and told my partner about what happened and we discussed whether to kill all the pools or not. But, as most of them were already "sold out," we opted to take the risk and we ended up "reaping the rewards." A *very nice* payday supplement!

During most of 1976, '77 and '78 my paycheck was $25! The rest I sent by allotment, to my wife and my check was used as "seed" money for whatever angle I was working to make more money.

While aboard *The Big E* in the shipyard at Bremerton a couple opportunities arose that proved financially rewarding. While assigned to HAB-6 (Vents & Voids Division of SFOMS Department) an opportunity arose that would put some food in the family freezer. This occurred when I was given the job of putting together all the arrangements for a division party. In addition to coming up with a "theme" (picnic, baseball, bowling tournament) it was also necessary to provide the chow! By navy regulation, each person assigned to a division represented 50c allotted for a quarterly "welfare & recreation" expenditure by the division. So, 80 men assigned meant $40 (not much) or you could collect that amount in ship's stores (burger patties, hot dogs, buns, etc.) which back then, amounted to a sizeable lot of food. However, you still needed to have each person pitch in a "ticket price" to cover the expenses if you wanted to have a decent party. Ticket prices were usually around $1 to $1.50 and kids were free.

So, while casting around for something that the guys would want to pay for and come to, I found that as an "official" navy function, I could reserve a waterfront park at what is now referred to as NUWC (Naval Undersea Warfare Center) Keyport, which was a few miles outside of Bremerton on Puget Sound. The location included picnic tables, barbeque pits, a covered pavilion, and the use of the items in the boat house (canoes, kayaks and paddle boats). After committing to that location, now all I needed was some more victuals to add to the standard burger/hot dog fare. One weekend I was sitting home (Jackson Park Navy Housing) browsing through the local "Penny Saver" when I noticed someone advertising to sell salmon fresh off the boat in Poulsbo, Washington about 15 miles up the road from me. So, I immediately called him. After discussing his advertised price, I asked him how much I had to buy for his rock-bottom price and he told me 500 pounds for $1.25 per pound. I jumped at the offer and committed to buy the 500 pounds and told him we'd work out the particulars for delivery in a few days. I had some work to do! The following week I told the division officer and chief what I wanted them to know and cut them in on being able to buy some of the salmon! So, they allowed me to use our division "artist" to make up a banner, which we were allowed to post up on the SFOMS Trailer down in the hangar bay. Fresh, whole salmon $1.50 per pound, call ext. xxx and ask for OS1 Kirkpatrick. Well, by the close of that day, I had sold out that part of the 500 pounds not necessary for the division party (and were not reserved for myself, the chief or the DIVO), which allowed me to pocket enough money so I could pay for a share of the salmon for my family, with some "coin" left over. The remainder was 150 pounds and was earmarked for the party. What wasn't consumed there, which wasn't much, was given away to the attending personnel who had families. The party was a big hit! So much so that I ended up being tasked as the "official" division "Party Coordinator," something I would have rather been assigned to someone else! So, I did this again, but this time with Australian style ribs and my family ate free ribs for a few months.

One of my most opportune endeavors was while I was stationed at NAS Whidbey Island. One day, I got a call from a P-3 Orion aircraft commander out of Brunswick, Maine. He was looking for help to make arrangements for his plane and crew during their upcoming assignment, flying out of NAS Whidbey. He asked if I could make arrangements for a parking place for the aircraft, car rentals and hotel accommodations for his crew. I asked a few questions (about what type of cars and what his per diem allowance was for hotel rooms per night, etc.) and told him to call back in a couple days. I was able to secure a tie-down spot for the aircraft just off to the side of the WINGSPAC building the tower was located in, plus hotel room reservations and car rentals. I would provide a ride for him and a few of his crew to the car rental office and a map showing where their hotel was located. The pilot called back a couple days before they were due to leave Brunswick and I let him know what had been arranged and if there was anything else he required. He told me no and then said how much he appreciated the effort and was there anything he could do for me! Well, there was the opening I was hoping for! Everyone knows what Maine is famous for and I was not going to miss this opportunity. Quickly, I asked if he could bring some lobster. "How much?" he asked! "Five hundred pounds," I said; it sounded like a hopeful request. But without missing a beat, he said "No problem!" Whoa! My immediate thought was about how much more I could have asked for. I told him when he arrived to let tower know to contact me and I would meet him out on the tarmac with my station wagon! That night I put up a couple posters around the base (the PX and the EM Club) stating that personnel wanting to reserve fresh Maine lobster should call ext xxx and ask for OS1 Kirkpatrick! I was sold out the next day! The 500 pounds cost me $1.35 pp and I sold them for $1.65 pp. The difference I pocketed to pay for my share of the lobster! Three months later, I was still getting calls asking when the next lobster sale would be!

The most frequent and easiest means of augmenting our food supply were my frequent fishing outings. Most productive was while we were stationed in Bremerton and Whidbey Island because Puget Sound provided endless choices. While stationed there, you always had a current license and you *always* carried the current "tide tables" in your back pocket. Extreme low tides provided the best possibilities and you did your best to ensure that on that day you were *available* to take advantage. There were even a couple days my fishing buddy and I maneuvered our work schedule around so we could catch the tide. One spot in particular offered a smorgasbord of seafood when one of these low tides occurred, because the entire estuary would empty out and in the course of the day you could fish, dip net for crab, shuck oysters and dig for clams. I don't recall ever having a freezer that wasn't full of seafood while we were stationed up there!

DUTY DAYS

Duty rotation aboard a carrier back in the '70s was dictated for the most part by where the ship was. If she was in port and overseas, the ship would normally be in a three-section rotation, meaning that every third day in port, you would "have the duty." Duty days began at 0800 and the next section in rotation assumed the duty at 0800 the following day. Ideally, if you stood a duty watch during that day's working hours, all you had to do for the remainder of your duty day was be aboard ship and make any duty section musters. After working hours that day, you would muster with the duty section leader for any work assignments he might have and tell you when the next duty section muster would be. Other than that, you stayed aboard and your time was your own, unless you were assigned a "watch" that was scheduled to occur after normal working hours. In that case, you would not only complete a normal working day routine, but you could also stand a watch during the evening or early morning hours of your duty day. That makes for a long day!

Depending on your level of qualification, a watch assignment could be standing guard or manning the telephone switchboard. The more qualified duty personnel could also be assigned to stand watch at one of the positions on the forward or aft Quarterdecks as Petty Officer of the Watch (POOW) or messenger. When the ship returned stateside, in San Diego normally, the duty rotation would be modified to allow more days between rotations. At times this was changed to either a four- or five-section rotation. The upside was more liberty time between duty days, but the downside was that, with fewer personnel in each duty section, the likelihood of your standing a watch increased exponentially – not an altogether desirous result! While aboard *Connie* in the early '70s you could swap duty days with someone by simply having the two people swapping sign a division log book specifying the two days being swapped. But both had to be qualified to stand any watches to which the other was likely to be assigned. However, this didn't last long and by my last WestPac aboard *Connie,* this process had reverted to the necessity of having to formally submit a request chit up the divisional chain-of-command to swap duty. Needless to say, duty swaps fell off considerably after that.

As previously mentioned, while in port and on my designated duty days, one of my earliest assignments was as a telephone switchboard operator in aft IC aboard *Connie.* Because I wasn't trained for much else, other duty assignments were of the "warm body" type, such as while overseas guard duty on one of the many sponsons or the fantail – a sponson was an open projection from the hull used to help stabilize the ship and also affixed with bollards for securing mooring lines. Because this area was open access to the ship from the water, personnel were stationed on-watch at these locations for security purposes while the ship was moored in a foreign port. I hadn't been aboard long when I was assigned one of these watches on the fantail while in port at Subic. There was no training and just a vague description from the guy I relieved on what my duties were. Well, I was walking my beat, when a PO2 came out carrying a wrapped package and stood watching an approaching small craft. When it closed on the fantail and he noticed my concern, he assured me it was okay because he was working with the people on board. He handed down the package to one of the guys in the boat and then left as the boat pulled away. Just minutes later, a whole gaggle of officers showed up and watched as the small craft motored away. They quickly asked why I hadn't reported the boat and I explained about the PO2. They weren't happy, but after a few more pointed questions (how long had I been aboard ship, etc.) they left. I'm assuming I narrowly missed Captain's Mast and being busted for dereliction of duty!

As I made rank and qualified for other duty assignments, I moved on to positions of higher visibility and level of difficulty when qualifying for them. But that didn't mean they would be any less boring that standing a sponson or fantail watch.

One of these positions was as JOOD (Junior Officer of the Deck) while aboard CGN-9 and when the ship was at PSNSY, Bremerton. This position was manned at the after-brow, a gangway rigged on the fantail and which was used as access for enlisted personnel and shipyard workers. The forward brow, or Quarterdeck, was for officers only. Because you were in a colder climate, a small shack had been placed just off the gangway and a heater had been rigged inside to ward off the cold during winter months. Sometimes, the shack had a door and other times not. And, even if it did have a door, some of the CDOs (Command Duty Officer) or OODs (Officer of the Deck) would dictate that you wouldn't be allowed to close it while they were on duty. Without a door or with an open door, the only thing the heater could do was warm your feet. During the day though, you spent so much time outside the shack checking security badges, rendering salutes and such, that no matter how cold or wet it was, you spent most of your time outside the shack. Of course, during periods of rain, you had your slicker over your uniform in an effort to keep dry, but that didn't change how cold and miserable you would get. At night, after normal working hours, when foot traffic fell off, you could retreat to the relative warmth of the shack, but you were expected not to spend too much time there regardless of the weather. So, many of these watches were an exercise in tedium. Cold and sometimes wet, they proved to be numbing, both physically and mentally. Needless to say, it wasn't something to look forward to other than to get it over with!

While the *Long Beach* was in San Diego and as an OS working in CIC, if my duty day fell on a day the ship was getting underway, I would stand whatever watch I had been assigned and then also fulfill any requirements in preparing CIC for getting underway. This could mean spending the early morning hours before breakfast ensuring R/T circuits had been properly patched into CIC, laying out navigation charts for radar-assisted piloting/navigation, ensuring all the necessary TDS consoles were on-line and the CDS program properly loaded, plus a host of other tasks that were necessary before getting underway.

CHAPTER 14
WESTPAC '77

USS MOUNT HOOD (AE-29)

(17 FEBRUARY – 5 OCTOBER 1977)

Days Deployed: 230

Tons of Cargo Transferred: 13,000

Ships Alongside for Underway Replenishment: 99

Advanced to OS2 (E-5) Jun '77

USS Mount Hood AE-29

WHEN CONSIDERING WHERE TO GO for my next duty station I was aware I would have control of that decision by using the "Guard II" program. This was a navy program that allowed the sailor to select where he would like to be stationed as a means for ensuring his or her retention in the service. If a request were made, the detailer was obligated to work within his constraints to ensure that the duty assignment request was met. I wanted a ship stationed in the San Francisco Bay Area, which would put me closer to my home town and make it possible to visit the folks over weekends without spending 12 hours driving each way, as was the case from San Diego! The detailer told me there was a billet aboard AE-29 and she was homeported out of Concord, California but currently deployed overseas. I agreed to take it. I had two weeks leave, travel and proceed time to get everything and everyone up to the Bay Area and into whatever quarters I could arrange during that time. This would be a navy move and that meant the movers would be contracted by the navy, load up my belongings and take it to the Bay Area for storage until I told them what residence to deliver it to. I had been in contact with Base Housing in Concord and the lady working there told me that housing didn't have a waiting list, that when I arrived to give her a call. After spending some time in my hometown, I gave housing a call again to check in. The same lady told me the place wouldn't be ready for a few days and to take a room at the Navy Lodge on NAS Alameda and she would contact me when it was ready. After three days and no call, I called her! She apologized and said we could move in two days from then. I asked her about our household goods and she said they were in storage two buildings down from where we were staying, so I walked over to the storage facility and made the arrangements. Navy Housing for the Weapons Station was a couple miles east of downtown Concord and about a 20-minute trip to the Weapons Station piers on the Sacramento River. Housing was a three-bedroom Korean War era duplex. Roomy, a good-sized yard and carport. No frills or luxuries, just very utilitarian!

Now, transferring to a ship overseas is never simple and, as was the case with the *Connie* back in '69, it involves a lot of "hurry up and wait!" This time was no exception. Leaving out of Travis AFB, with a stop in Hawaii for fuel and personnel changes, it was on to Japan. We landed at Yokota Air Base outside Tokyo and spent five or six hours waiting for a connecting flight south. The next leg of the journey took me on a flight from Yokota to Fukuoka on the island of Kyushu.

Shortly after arriving, U.S. service personnel destined for Sasebo were loaded onto a "haze gray" standard issue Navy bus for the trip. Now, this is back before Japan had created the network of super-highways that it has today, which are four lane (two each way) and cut right through the mountains with enormous tunnels and breathtaking bridges. Back in 1977, it was a narrow, two lane (one each way) "highway" that followed the terrain features – without much engineering involved. On the flats it followed the dikes between the rice paddies and in the mountains, it was a virtual snake, twisting and turning at the slightest change in terrain. What would now take less than two hours, back then turned into a four-hour plus marathon! Arriving at the Naval Station in Sasebo late that evening, we checked into the Transit Barracks and reported next morning to have someone tell us when we could expect to board the ship. At muster that morning, we were told the ship wouldn't be arriving for a few more days and that we would be assigned duties every day, by our mustering PO, until the ship pulled in. So, I was put in charge of a few guys and told to go out and paint the white lines in the parking lot! Uh huh! Having been around the block already, I made sure the guys understood that this job would last until the ship arrived. They understood! No use getting done too quickly only to be assigned something worse, right?

When the ship pulled into Sasebo, we checked out of the Transit Barracks and reported aboard. It was 21 May 1977. Checking into the Personnel Office, I was given the standard "Routing Sheet," only in this case, there was a block marked "CO" (Commanding Officer), which wouldn't be there on a ship with a bigger crew, but in the case of the *Hood*, there it was. It was the next day before I made it to the CO's stateroom to get that block on the sheet checked off. Standing in front of the CO as he looked through my service jacket, I noticed a series of five still photos, taken in sequence, behind him on the bulkhead! Just then the CO looked up and noticed where my attention had been drawn and said, "That's the *Hood*'s namesake (AE-11)," he said, "taken when she blew up in Seeadler Harbor, Manus, Admiralty Islands on 10 November 1944. Of those aboard ship, there were no survivors!" *THAT* is when I recognized the full import of being assigned aboard an "ammo boat!"

The ship would be in port Sasebo for a three-week SRA (Ship's Restricted Availability). Most of the shipyard work involved upgrades to the Mess Hall, but the crew were assigned various maintenance duties that couldn't be accomplished underway and during normal, limited port calls. OI Division was assigned the task of stripping and re-painting an exterior deck of approximately 600 square feet, port and aft of the stack! This meant chipping and painting for the next couple weeks! *Welcome aboard!*

On the positive side, with the Mess Hall secured for its planned upgrades, the crew would be bussed back and forth to the base chow hall for meals. Sasebo at that time was staffed with a skeleton crew of navy personnel, tenant commands and Japanese nationals in support positions. The chow hall seated approximately 250 personnel, but there weren't even that many navy personnel left aboard the entire base. So, when we showed up for meals, we were about the only ones there. Let me tell you, with all those Japanese nationals lined up behind the serving line taking our "requests," we were in hog heaven! Breakfast was steak and eggs, to order. Or, ham and eggs, or pork chops, whatever! For lunch and dinner, a salad bar that the ship couldn't compete with and an entire "turnstile" area for desserts! Boy, did we ever take advantage of that!

While the chow hall was a big hit, I still made a few trips into town to sample the local fare. Just across the canal and outside the fence to the navy's recreation park, I found a very small yakitori restaurant that only seated 18 or 20 people and as I was passing its entrance, the smell drew me in. That was when I discovered how delicious aged, marinated and grilled kobe beef could be. The stuff practically melts in your mouth. Well, I made several trips back to the same joint and usually ordered the same thing; beef yakitori, with breaded, deep fried vegetable "sticks," a small scoop of sticky rice and a small shredded-cucumber salad. While you waited, the owner/cook served up dried seaweed rolled in roasted sesame seeds as snack food. When he noticed how much I liked them, he slowed down re-loading my dish because I was downing them as soon as he set them in front of me.

Another perk to the SRA was that the ship was tied up to the quay wall and directly across from the base gym! So, my daily routine was chip & paint during working hours, knock off and get cleaned up for dinner. Next I'd return aboard ship, change into gym clothes and spend the next couple hours playing volleyball, basketball, indoor soccer or whatever sport that teams were made up for that day. There wasn't much point in going out in town as the "sailor bars" had mostly closed up with the draw-down in base personnel. And, you weren't welcome in the "local" bars – you'd usually be politely asked to leave because these were "not for American sailors." Such are the customs of our allies! Fortunately there was still one club on base open to all enlisted ranks, so there was no point in going into town for a brew!

During the course of the SRA and while familiarizing myself with the CIC personnel and organization, I had a few discussions with the leading OS1. He had had a couple tours "in country" during Vietnam and after being wounded badly, was shipped back to the States for advanced medical care, including a few plates and pins to hold him together. He told me he had read my service record and was surprised to find that I had qualified for and had functioned as a Watch Supervisor (Surface Module) as an E-4 on a carrier. He got a lopsided grin and told me when he read the orders for me to report to the *Hood* and saw where I was coming from, he expected to get an E-4 that was proficient at writing backward on a status board. So from the start, he gave me a lot of leeway and we got along great. The OS1's relief was already aboard, but he wasn't happy with what he got, namely a shore duty rotation "body" who had no interest in acting the part of "Leading Petty Officer" for the division and who was more than content to hang out in the First Class Lounge whenever he was not on watch. Thus, much of the day-to-day divisional admin duties fell to me, a newly minted E-5. I was quickly learning that a person in my position, on a small ship and with only a handful of personnel in the division, could rise to the occasion and make a difference or coast along like the newly arrived OS1. With the support of the other OSs, I felt I was able make a positive contribution during my tenure aboard!

Upon completion of the ship's SRA and after nearly a month in Sasebo, we would finally get underway for our next port of call, Yokosuka, Japan in Tokyo Wan (Bay). The Navigation Brief held in the wardroom the previous evening revealed that we would not be taking the outside, easterly route but rather the western route. This would take us south from Sasebo then west and northwest to the Shimoniseki Straits, a navigable waterway separating Kyushu Island (where Sasebo is located) from Honshu Island. The strait then debouches into the Inland Sea. We would then exit the Inland Sea between Shikoku and Kyushu into the Pacific and north to Tokyo Wan and Yokosuka Naval Station. Looking at the charts for the passage, it was obvious this was going to be a very long and busy transit. Due to the narrow channels and extremely busy shipping we were expected to encounter, we would remain at a modified "Navigation Detail" throughout the transit until exiting the Inland Sea. This was expected to last all day. Bridge and CIC watch personnel would only be spelled for chow (which never entirely happened) and were to remain fully manned for the entire trip. In CIC, this was necessary because of our limited manpower and the manning requirements for the Navigation Detail. I would be manning the navigation chart station, swinging arcs from the points called out by the radar operator.

Our approach to the straits was easy enough, but once we closed to the southern entrance, navigation by radar became problematic owing to the narrowness of the strait and the dominating high bluffs. So, the radar scope operator and I would compare notes with what I was looking at on the chart and what we could match up with the display on the radar screen and selecting the most prominent features we could. Although we were supposed to be "in sync" with the same points the Bridge was using, this was not always possible due to the geography and how it was displayed on the radar. The shipping we experienced wasn't a problem for much of the transit through the strait because there were ships anchored in mid-channel that served to separate the north bound and south bound traffic. Once we got to the northern end of the strait, made the turn in the channel under the bridge and exited into the Inland Sea, was when things started getting hectic!

Shimoniseki Straits

Now, unidentified surface contacts, as previously mentioned, are designated "skunks" and assigned an alphabetic designation starting with "Alpha" for "A" and proceeding through the alphabet. We were somewhere in the middle of the alphabet when we entered the Inland Sea and looking at the radar display it seemed to us that every other son, daughter, aunt and uncle of Nippon had a boat and they were out on the water and in our way. The plot looked like it had a very bad case of measles! As we were supposed to plot and report everything within a 10-mile range, I quickly requested from the Bridge that CIC be required only to plot, track and report any contacts forward of the beam, because that would eliminate half the requirement and I was still in doubt as to if we could handle contacts forward of the beam. We "turned over" the alphabet reporting in short order and were now reporting the second succession, which began with "Alpha Bravo" and proceeded through the alphabet as "Alpha Bravo, Alpha Charlie, Alpha Delta" and so on. This wasn't working. Plotting on the radar repeater, DRT and maneuvering board was outstripping our limited capability! No matter how good you were at it! So, CIC requested from the Bridge permission to be required only to report contacts that were CBDR (constant bearing, decreasing range) or within 30 degrees of the bow. If a contact remained CBDR, this obviously indicated a collision would occur unless we or the contact changed course or speed. Bridge was just as overwhelmed as we were and quickly agreed. Still, we proceeded through the alphabet at a very brisk clip! When I was finally able to leave CIC, it was after 8PM that night. This would prove to be the longest and most exhausting Navigation Detail that I ever stood in my entire career! We may have saved a few hundred miles by taking this route, but I sure wouldn't want to do *that* again!

There were a number of tasks to be performed in this CIC that were not within the assignment of OSs while I was aboard the *Connie*. These included taking custody of the crypto for IFF, breaking it open and loading the codes into the male portion of the device and then "plugging it in" to the female part. Another unfamiliar task was to act as part of the ship's intel gathering activities regarding surface ships we encountered along our way. When within visual range, designated Bridge personnel would stand out on whichever Bridge wing was closest and take pictures with one of the ship's cameras used for that purpose. Designated CIC personnel would fill out a formatted message blank with specific information about the profile of the ship, course and speed, latitude and longitude, etc. This was referred to as "rigging a ship" and noting characteristics from bow to stern, such as Bow, Kingpost, Mast, Bridge Funnel/Stack and Stern. Upon filling in all the required fields on the form, it was then released in a Naval message. The pictures and the Naval message were all parts of the Ocean Surveillance Information System (OSIS). Depending on whether the ship was a NATO nation ship, a "non-aligned" ship or a "Soviet-bloc" ship, the type of message generated was classed as OSIS White or OSIS Red. Technically, if you were employed in this effort, you were to have attended the "Shipboard Duty Intel Officers" COI (course of instruction). I hadn't completed that course, but once back stateside, the ship made sure that box was checked and during 3 to 5 May '78, I completed this requirement.

SRA RIVERA PIER, NAVSTA SUBIC, R.P.

Our stay in Yokosuka was short and in less than a week we were underway again, en route Subic Bay, R.P. Arriving the last few days of June, we tied up at the Weapons Station to off-load ammo in preparation for our move across the bay to Rivera Pier and another three week SRA. This one was dedicated to work in the Engineering spaces. Fortunately, OI Division wasn't tasked with much topside maintenance because working topside in P.I. in the tropical heat and humidity is absolutely *miserable!* With another three-week SRA and no appreciable work package assigned us, the CIC gang found itself with a lot of time on its hands, and that's not a good thing! While in Sasebo, putting together the navigation charts necessary for our transit to Yokosuka, I had noticed how disorganized and outdated our chart portfolio was. At the time and being so new aboard ship, I didn't feel comfortable with calling anyone's attention to the problem, but by the time the SRA in Subic started, I knew how I could best make use of the time available. So on my own initiative I began pulling charts out of the drawers and going through them, checking for editions, updates completed and updates outstanding. After doing this for a few days, some of the other guys started taking an interest and helping out. Because there was a DMA in Subic, when newer edition charts were needed, we could acquire from them. Any changes needed to be made to the current chart in use could be accomplished using the latest Notice to Mariners, which detailed every change to that specific chart. However, the volume of charts and the hundreds of updates necessary to bring us current would end up keeping a couple of us busy for weeks. Soon I found that walking into CIC each morning, someone would almost invariably be at the chart table, making necessary changes and updates without me having to do it or asking for help. I believe the real reason it hadn't been kept current was because no one had shown them what that entailed or how it could be accomplished. Even when we returned stateside, it became a task that was folded into the daily routine as part of the normal work day.

Before starting the SRA, the ship made a "Dependents Cruise" to Manila for the Philippine Republic Day Parade (also called Filipino-American Friendship Day), held on the 4th of July. We moved from the Weapons Station to the Naval Station side, to onload our passengers and get underway for the trip around the Bataan Peninsula and up into Manila Bay. Arriving about mid-day, we were berthed there at what was referred to as the "Glamour Pier" due to its central location to downtown. It was only a few blocks from Rizal Park, the Cultural Center and the waterfront route for the parade to take place the following day. That afternoon, I did not get ashore because it was my duty day as MAA. I had been walking the spaces as usual when I came up to the Bridge to get a look around the waterfront and check the QM's chart markings for updates (to compare with ours in CIC). When I got there, there were civilians on a ship's tour and asking their designated "tour guide" a lot of "what's this for" questions. Then I noticed a blond "round-eye" female in her early to mid-twenties asking question of one of the junior QMs about the equipment on the forward deck. When he said he didn't know, she must have noticed me and turned and asked me if I knew! I said yes, and started to walk away. I heard her ask "Where do you work?" and turned and told her. She asked if I would show her, so I led her back to the door to CIC (all of 6 feet behind the Bridge door) and invited her in. After explaining what CIC did and answering some questions she had about different equipment, she plopped down in the XO's chair and conversation turned more personal. As there was no one else in CIC and would most likely not be anytime soon, I figured I'd better get her out of there before one or both of us made a mistake! No easy thing to do as she was easy on the eyes!

The next day and the day of the parade, a buddy and I were able to get a good curbside location to observe the parade, but after an hour we were soaked in sweat from the afternoon heat. Right across from us, on the corner was a Beer Garden and we retreated there for some much-needed rehydration! When the waitress asked our order we told her two pitchers of San Miguel Dark, my favorite! She brought the two pitchers, with two glasses. We were so parched that we downed the pitchers without having need of the glasses. It was *"Mississippi Hot"* out there! We left Manila two days later, returning to Subic to begin our SRA.

Being at Rivera Pier for the SRA put us close to many of the base facilities, which was unusual for us on account of being an ammo boat – most of our port berths were remote from centrally populated parts of the places we pulled into! The reason for that should be obvious. Just up the street from Rivera Pier was "Spanish Gate" and the cafeteria there. Then there's the PX Electronics Annex with all its stereo, recording equipment and camera gear. Close by and a couple blocks over was the EM Club, too.

Because we were going to be in port for so long, one of my guys decided to "shack up" with his "squeeze." He told us he had a three-story place right off the main drag on Gordon Street, with kitchen, TV, maid and cook. So, that was our OI Division hang-out for our time in port, which stretched out further than we had anticipated and ended up being close to two months. The group would pitch in money for food and drinks and the cook at the house would use that to buy "groceries" and whenever we were over, we ate whatever was being served, grabbed a cool one from the 'fridge and hung out on the second floor balcony making "honeyco" calls to the passing girls below. Had a great time! Cutting short by a few days the completion of our SRA and due to an oncoming typhoon, we were moved over to Boton Pier, which was classed as a "protected anchorage" from heavy weather. All other units present were ordered to sortie as is standard procedure when it is anticipated that a storm will impact the port facility. We remained in port due to the remaining work required and also because we were not "in ballast" because we had off-loaded before going into the SRA. Going out the gate into town that evening was eerie with no other sailors on the streets and many of the storefronts and bars closed due to lack of customers and the approaching storm. That night the wind howled, the rain poured down in sheets and most of us spent the night aboard ship, sound and dry. The following afternoon the rest of the fleet began straggling back into port. As it 'twas the season, this wouldn't be our last bout with typhoons this trip.

Our next liberty port was Hong Kong and we were in port there the first week of August. I spent some time in Kowloon again and bought some more tailor-mades in Wanchai. What was notably changed for was the difference between pulling in aboard a carrier versus an ammo boat. First, we were anchored out a few more miles (in recognition of our status as a floating bomb) and the offered choice of transportation to and from the British Navy Pier. When I was there aboard *Connie* we had a floating pier tied off alongside the ship and regularly scheduled double-deck ferries would pull up to the floater for sailors making the trip, with the capacity to carry a couple hundred personnel per run. The *Hood* was not offered (and could not afford to pay) for such luxuries. We lowered our accommodation ladder and a "walla walla" pulled up to the platform and could manage to take a couple dozen at a time. Given the added distance from our anchorage, a trip was usually around 40 minutes! And, the "walla walla" was not what you would call a *stable* craft. It pitched and rolled like a canoe or kayak as a result of even the slightest of wakes or chop on the water. Riding back to the ship with the usual number of drunks proved to be an exercise in fortitude. Sometimes you managed and other times you surrendered to the contagious urge!

THE AGI TWO-STEP
(OR, TWO MOONS OVER MIDWAY)

En route from Hong Kong back to Subic, we were tasked to rendezvous *with USS Midway* (CV-41) south of the Ryukyu Island chain early on the morning of 11 August in the Okinawa OpArea for a weapons transfer UnRep/VertRep. We made the scheduled meeting only to find out that also attending this event was a Russian AGI. And, every maneuver that was made to displace him from observing our activities was met with his own maneuvers to keep him in place as an observer. We all (the AGI, *Midway* and *Hood*) realized two truths about the situation: 1) the

Hood was slower than the *Midway* and could not outrun the AGI, and 2) the AGI only needed to keep station on the *Hood* if it was to observe any weapons transfer. (Recall the old woodsman's axiom: You and a buddy are in the woods being chased by a bear – you don't need to outrun the bear; you only need to be faster than your buddy!) Well, *Hood* wasn't faster than our buddy (*Midway*)! So, a rethink of the problem by the powers that be was going to require a delay in the evolution. We were released to proceed to Subic and tied up to Camayan Pier, Naval Weapons Station, Subic on 14 August.

11 Aug '77 Deck Log entries en route Hong Kong to Subic Bay

The Weapons Station was a good eight miles from the Naval Station through the jungle and along the bayshore. Trips to and from the Naval Station were usually by navy bus during the day, but after the bus stopped running around 6PM the only way to get out on liberty was if someone was driving the ship's Welfare & Rec van. As duty MAA, I had the keys to the van and would make runs every hour or so back and forth to the gate. Although this was done as a favor and not as a requirement, whoever drove the van could pick up some spare dollars from tips. A "tip box" was set up on the console next to the driver and the passengers would all pitch in with no request or requirement on the part of the driver. Any funds put in the box were just a "thank you" from the passengers! On the runs to the main gate, you could pick up anywhere from $5 to $10, but on the return runs most of the guys only had pesos left and would throw those in the box instead. So, before leaving port I would have to make a trip to the Philippine National Bank, located by the main gate, to change the pesos to dollars. You wouldn't get rich providing this service. It was just another means of picking up some added "walkin' around" money.

As we finished on-oading ammo, we were told that we would be getting underway for Keelung, Taiwan with some scheduled UnReps along the way. So, early on the afternoon of 17 August we left Subic. Our first scheduled transfer was with the *Connie* on the morning of the 18th. Completing that evolution, we prepared to rendezvous again with USS *Midway* for an UnRep/VertRep transfer. Again, the AGI was in attendance and we spent most of the day sending "dummy pallets" back and forth between us and *Midway*, while the AGI kept close watch on our efforts. I should explain here that the *Midway*, which was coming out of Yokosuka after completion of an SRA, needed to be "back-loaded" with ammo, which would include some "special weapons." This likely accounted for the keen interest of the AGI, which also knew what a carrier coming out of upkeep required. Obviously, the U.S. Navy didn't want the Soviets monitoring that process, photos included. Giving up that effort for the day, the *Hood* made a scheduled VertRep with USS *White Plains* (AFS-4), on 19 August. The following day, we were back in company with *Midway*, bringing our AGI "shadow" along with us. It was painfully obvious that "the plan" wasn't working and so we were detached from *Midway* and proceeded back into Subic, tying up to Nabasan Pier, Naval Weapons Station, Subic at 9PM, 23 August.

The following morning, the crew was informed that we were going to be allowed liberty, but that everyone had to be back aboard NLT midnight, in case an opportunity arose to run out and finish the *Midway* backload should the AGI displace out of position and be unable to observe. ***Cinderella Liberty!***

Thankfully, this wasn't necessary for very long, because mid-day on the 25th, we got the word that the AGI had fallen for the apparent cancellation of the "special weapons" transfer, with the *Hood* in port and the *Midway* feinting a transit through the San Bernardino Straits for exit into the Pacific east of the Philippines. Most likely, reporting what had happened, the AGI received instructions that they were to proceed north along the west coast of Luzon. Our navy, noting this, waited until the AGI had reached a latitude north enough to make it impossible for it to return in time to observe. The *Midway* reversed course from its approach to the "San Berdoo" straits while we slipped out of port. We rendezvoused with the carrier and completed the weapons transfer.

Here is where I would be obligated to insert that absurd and hackneyed navy phrase "I can neither confirm nor deny" that what we had transferred were nukes!

As we were preparing to "break away" from the carrier and proceed back to port, a couple of my guys left CIC for a short period, unknown to me. When they came back laughing, I should have suspected something was up. About then, the XO came storming into CIC, mad as heck! Well, the two OSs had decided they would take the opportunity to get back at *Midway* for making us go through this extended "dog-and-pony" show, Cinderella Liberty included. And so, they went out to the aft portion of the Bridge Wing, dropped trou and shot the "bird farm" a couple "Moons Over Midway" as a parting gesture. There was a lot of cussing and ranting by the XO, but nothing else came of the incident and the matter was dropped. Hey, everyone else thought it was funny as hell! And, in his stateroom that night, I'm sure the XO did too!

KEELUNG, TAIWAN

After the Midway job, we spent a couple more days in Subic before we got underway for Keelung, Taiwan.........again! This was during typhoon season and because we were approaching the north end of Luzon, the Bridge personnel were tracking two storms to the north and east of us, which were moving southeast to northwest through the Luzon Strait. The ship kept a large plot on the Bridge of the storm centers and their movement in relation to ours, and CIC watchstanders made many trips out to the Bridge to keep an eye on the current plots of the typhoons so they could be compared with the weather fronts we were seeing on radar. It was obvious the first typhoon would move across the southern tip of Taiwan and the other would pass south of there and cross our route. The ship altered course and speed to allow the later to pass ahead of us, which slowed our approach to Taiwan. We took some rolls from the outer area of the typhoon, but nothing serious as we continued up the east coast of Taiwan, on our approach to Keelung.

A buddy of mine on the ship told me he knew a guy stationed at the AFRTS (Armed Forces Radio & Television Station) facility on Grass Mountain, just outside of Taipei, which was only about 20 miles from Keelung. So, he sent a "Class Easy" naval message (think telegram) informing him that we would be in port at Keelung. Details had to be worked out because there would be four of us and some would have duty the first day in port and some would have duty the second day. So, it was agreed that he would be on the pier waiting for us the morning of the third day, which still left us two days of liberty in Taipei.

Entering port at Keelung was a unique experience because the Nationalist Chinese used the port for their navy and it was accordingly protected. The bluffs bristled with anti-aircraft emplacements and we had to be cleared through the anti-submarine net strung across the harbor entrance. The morning of our second day in port, the ship was host to a "herd" of over 50 Nationalist Chinese sailors who came aboard ship for a tour. Arriving in CIC in groups of 10 or 12, they weren't too interested in us showing them around; rather it seemed they were only there trying to procure *Playboy* and *Penthouse* magazines and left abruptly when we couldn't produce any for them.

Meeting up with our DJ buddy on the landing the next morning, we were off to see the sights of Taipei! Of course, the first thing he wanted to do was show us where he worked and took us up to the station atop Grass Mountain, overlooking Taipei. I don't think we did a good job of pretending to be interested in what he did as a disc jockey and thankfully, after an hour or so, we climbed back into the car and drove down into the city.

All the US military facilities were in "compounds" located fairly close together in the heart of the city. So, we ate lunch at the Army compound, watched *The Pink Panther Strikes Again* (Peter Sellers, 1976) at the Navy compound and shopped at the PX. One of the things I wanted to do while in Taipei was to pick up a two-volume set of *Jane's Fighting Ships* because the ship was required to have them aboard, but didn't – and one of the functions of CIC was to assist in identifying ships. It would be half the cost of buying them here rather than through the supply system because these were illegal reproductions and without copyright, something that occurred quite freely in both Taiwan and Hong Kong. But, they would help us immensely in our requirement to "rig" ships and that was all that counted. The Ops Boss was a happy camper when I brought them back aboard ship! The Navigator was green with envy!

Speaking of the Ops Boss, he had a habit of coming into CIC during Sea & Anchor Detail, and kibitzing around the chart table. He was aware that we kept our stash of "munchies" in the top right-hand chart table drawer and would use this opportunity to help himself to whatever was there. This was usually a three-pound navy issue tin of "Mixed Nuts" donated by a ship's cook who liked to hang out in CIC, or it might be a package of cookies stashed by one of the CIC gang for the watch to munch on. It didn't matter which and he didn't ask; he just helped himself! We referred to him as Cookie Monster, a reference to the Sesame Street character and because he resembled the character so well. Well, sorta! But, as a nod to his capacity to perform his duties aboard ship, I would also mention that he was a "ship-handler extraordinaire" and whether pulling into port or coming alongside for UnRep, Lt. Odell would most often "have the conn"!

One of the nights in Taipei, after dinner at a local Mongolian bbq place, our host took us over to the huge China Fleet Club. After parking the car and making our way toward the entrance I noticed a long line of girls queuing up at a kiosk standing outside the door to the club. I asked our host what the deal was and he explained that they weren't allowed inside unless they were "signed in" with a U.S. Armed Forces member. Well, one of our guys decided to check out the local talent while the rest of us proceeded inside. About an hour later, our talent scout found us and took a seat at our table. We asked if he hadn't found what he was looking for and he told us he had and that he'd signed in a real hot number. Not more than five minutes after they'd entered the club she'd ditched him to find her girlfriends or her boyfriend. In either case, our shipmate was not happy.

Our last night in Taipei, our host took us out on the town and we hit a few of the classier clubs. Around midnight, we piled into two cabs and he provided directions to the driver, the other cab "in trail." Across town and down an alley, we stopped next to a closed roll-up storefront. Our host got out, banged on the roll-up and shouted a few words in Chinese. Shortly the roll-up opened with a bleary-eyed little old lady on the other side. She waved us in and we found the space inside dominated by one large round table where we were directed to sit. Our host had a girl with him and one of our guys did also, so we now were seven. We spent the next couple hours in the middle of the night down an alley in Taipei eating some "local cuisine." Most dishes I was able to recognize and some were pretty strange looking, but what I ate was great! It sticks out in my memory as the end to a perfect day – one of those rare occurrences in life and even rarer in my profession.

The following morning our host dropped us off at the boat landing in Keelung where there was a crowd of 25 to 30 shipmates waiting for the last launch to take us back to the ship. But, the launch never showed at the scheduled time; it didn't show up until much later. We all piled in and made the ride back to the ship, not suspecting anything was amiss other than the boat being late. Well, when we climbed the gangway to the Quarterdeck we found the Chief MAA confiscating everyone's Liberty Cards, by order of the XO. We were dumbfounded, to say the least and pissed off to put it mildly! Less than an hour later, upon direction from the CO (after what I am sure had been a pointed and rather one-sided conversation with the XO) our Liberty Cards were returned and the matter dropped. But, we all cast a gimlet eye on the XO after that!

I might mention here one of the characters I encountered aboard the *Hood*. He was a CWO2 from the Weapons Department. I had seen him around the ship for the first few weeks I was aboard, but we were never in a position to interact until we started out of port en route to Yokosuka. I was out on the Bridge talking with the QMs about the upcoming transit through the Inland Sea and the CWO2 was also there. After I finished my conversation with the QMs the CWO2 walked over to me and struck up a conversation, asking about how I found duty aboard ship compared to being on a carrier. All while his nose was about four inches from mine! I maintained the distance and we continued to talk. As our conversation wound down, his grin got bigger and he asked if I was uncomfortable. I told him I was and he asked why. I smiled back and asked him if he couldn't guess. He laughed as we both took a step back. He told me he had been stationed in Turkey for a tour and found the Middle Eastern idea of personal space to be one of the most difficult to get accustomed to during his tour. He used this as a "teaching moment" with newly reported personnel aboard the *Hood* and explained the difference between eastern and western customs and how they impacted personal relationships between the two cultures. During my remaining time aboard ship, I saw him go through this same routine three or four times and was always amused at his targets' reaction. Most everyone quickly moved back away from him to gain space and he would then move toward them again, closing that space. You get some really smart – and *really unique* personalities in the Navy! Some were one or two clicks left or right of center; others required a few more clicks. We were underway and en route back to Subic the morning of 6 September, but not without obligations. On our way south, we rendezvoused with two U. S. ships for UnRep, pulling into Nabasan Pier, NWS Subic the morning of 9 September.

One more task, prior to departing for home, was the usual U. S. Customs Inspection. As part of preparations for completing this requirement and as one of the ship's duty MAAs, I had been directed to attend a Military Customs Training Course given by the base Provost Marshal, in company with the other duty MAAs. This was done so the ship's MAA personnel could augment the U. S. Customs personnel when they came aboard for our "welcome home" inspection. So, the day that occurred, I had to tag along with a customs inspector and his dog while they inspected personnel bunks and lockers. They made a few seizures of "contraband," but I don't recall any big "busts" and the dogs never did "alert!"

CHAPTER 15

HOMEWARD BOUND

FINALLY, ON THE MORNING OF 17 SEPTEMBER we got underway for the first leg of our journey home. Our first stop on the way was the naval station at Agana, Guam. I had never been there before, but it didn't matter because we were only expected to be there 48 hours and I felt no need to get ashore. Our berth was at the end of the jetty, just inside the bay. Even relatively lightly loaded ammo boats aren't welcome parked too close to the rest of the naval station. Hell! It had to be a good four or five miles up that jetty! It turned out that it didn't matter though. The CO was requested to depart the next day! Turns out there was a little brawl in a bar in town involving our sailors and some locals. The story I heard was that some ass-hat made a derogatory comment about one of our corpsman (we had three, an HM1 and two HM3s) being a little light in the pants and that's all it took! When you don't have a doctor aboard ship and all you have are corpsman, *nobody* talks trash about your "doc!" So, off we went and glad to be headed east!

We briefly pulled into Hawaii, tying up to NavMag, Lau Lau Lei on the 28ᵗʰ of September for some final transfers of weapons; on the following day we moved to West Loch for refueling. The Deck Log recorded our departure for Concord NWS, California the morning of 30 September.

A couple of days east of Hawaii we were informed another navy ship headed for the West Coast had experienced an engine room casualty and was dead in the water. *Hood* was being redirected to her location and expected to take her in tow! It didn't take a genius to know that towing at 3 or 4 knots would not allow us to make our expected arrival in Concord. We could also calculate an arrival time should we be relieved of towing duty by another navy ship. The math didn't leave us much time. We had been towing for a little more than a day when we heard that a tug out of Pearl was en route to take up the tow. We all wondered if the tug would arrive before our "drop dead" time for making the West Coast on schedule. Well, we were allowed to stop towing a few hours before the tug showed up and immediately the CO put the ship in hyper-drive, which for an AE was all of 18 knots with favorable winds and sea (or, downhill with a tailwind). We had less than four hours remaining before our "drop dead" time! As we departed the cause of our delay, the outboard speakers blared our "break-away" song, something we always did, with various selections being played. Today's selection was *most* appropriate: *Wasted Days & Wasted Nights!*

Arriving at the Golden Gate Bridge early on the morning of 17 October 1977, we passed underneath, dog-legged to the left and made up the channel to Concord. We had a Coast Guard escort going up-river in front of us, but the CO wasn't happy with the speed. So, he rode the "coasties" butt until they got the idea and made better progress. What speed limit?

The ship tied up to the pier at NWS Concord for a short period before moving up river to Vallejo for an upkeep period. Repairs, maintenance and the attendant chipping and scraping of paint went on for a few weeks before we were back at the Concord piers. Because I hadn't been able to spend any time familiarizing myself with the location before flying overseas to catch the ship, this was my first experience aboard a ship in the Bay Area. And, I do mean "area." It was soon made clear to me that any given day or week, we could be tied up at any number of locations and your commute had to conform to the new location — time and traffic added! Most of our time for the remaining part of the year and into the spring of '78 was spent in Concord. But, once we came into our work-up schedule we made a couple transits down to San Diego and back. Completing our pre-deployment schedule, we moved around a lot. After Vallejo and Concord, we moved down to NSC Oakland to take on stores. After spending a couple days there, we moved over to the pier at NAS Alameda. Then, on Halloween night of '78 we got bumped to an anchorage off Hunter's Point. The move had been fairly early in the afternoon and I had been able to call the wife before we moved so that she knew where to come pick me up. Well, things went south from there and it was after 10PM that night that I was finally able to get a spot on the MWB (motor whale boat) for the ride across the bay to Alameda where she was waiting. When I arrived, I found one pissed off wife and three very unhappy kids. I would spend the next couple weeks trying to come up with a way to make it up to them!

From my place in Navy Housing to the pier at NWS Concord was only about 20 minutes and there was never any traffic to deal with, so it was always nice for me when the ship was tied up there. The weapons station was part of the larger and encompassing Port Chicago Naval Weapons Magazine, which covered a large chunk of territory on that portion of the south shore of Suisun Bay. The admin building (personnel office, PX, barracks, etc.) was located on the south side of the hill from NWS and the piers and I only recall ever going aboard that part of the base two or three times. Driving north from Concord to NWS every morning, just as you neared the river the road turned east toward the piers. At that point, I had noticed off to my left a series of concrete streets and bare foundations and was curious about why they had been left there. Asking around, I was told that those were all that remained from an event that occurred during WWII. Sailors and workman were loading ammo stores onto a navy ship when there was a cataclysmic explosion that wiped out the pier area and damaged or collapsed the houses and commercial buildings in what was then the town of Port Chicago. Casualties were 320 dead and over 390 injured. This was another sobering reminder of the potential hazards of working aboard an AE!

Port Chicago NavMag & NWS Concord: 1940s & Now

SUMMER "MIDDIE" CRUISE

1978

The annual summer Midshipmen's Cruise was the first opportunity I experienced one-on-one basis with any of the Naval Academy midshipmen, but not my last. As a PO2 aboard a ship with a rather small crew, it was expected that I would be assigned to act as mentor to a midshipman. The "middie" assigned to me was a likable enough lad and of course enamored with the idea of life aboard ship. That didn't change while aboard *Mount Hood*, but I'm sure at some point in his naval experience that outlook would be sorely tested and tempered over time.

A summer aboard a ship with no operational commitments, going from port to port is drastically different than that of a WestPac deployment! As mentor to a middie, I was expected to ensure he was schooled in the duties and responsibilities of watchstanders in CIC: radio-telephone circuits and procedures, radar navigation, maneuvering board solutions, message traffic, maintenance of navigational charts, radar tracking, etc. After a week in CIC, the middie was sent to his next assignment aboard our ship. By the completion of the cruise he had experienced assignments in engineering, Bridge watch & navigation, deck handling during underway replenishment, flight ops, the comm center and gunnery to the point that he had been exposed to each department's duties aboard ship.

Anyway, our "summer cruise" consisted of port calls to Seattle, Ketchikan AK, Pearl Harbor and then back home to Concord, California. Seattle was great and because I had spent two extended periods while aboard the *Connie* at PSNSY, Bremerton I was on very familiar turf. I spent one day at the Space Needle and the venues around there — Pike Street Market and the chowder houses down at the State Ferry Wharf. I had duty the day before we left, so didn't get time to ride over to Bremerton and look up some of my friends.

Next up was Ketchikan, Alaska where we were scheduled to be in port over the 4th of July holiday. Traveling up the "Inside Passage" we found ourselves about 20 odd miles south of town when the CO "dropped the hook" and we anchored there for the night. It soon became apparent what was up. Over the 1MC, word was passed that "fish call" was open on the fantail. After securing from Navigation Detail, I headed aft to see if the guys were "fishing" or "catching." Fish call had only been going on for less than an hour and already the fantail was a mess of flopping, slimy fish of all descriptions. I watched as a buddy of mine hauled up something that you would only expect to see in a SiFi movie — big head, spines down the back, bright orange with huge yellow eyes! And, it wasn't just a dozen or so guys fishing, it seemed like everyone off duty was back there and they all had fishing poles. I must have missed the memo! Shortly after dropping anchor we'd noticed the CO's Gig had been lowered into the water and watched as he boarded; they soon took off toward the northeast and into the darkness. Some of the cooks who were fishing made sure everyone knew that if you scaled and cleaned your catch, you could store it in the ship's cold storage until we returned home. The following day, scuttlebutt had it that the CO's fishing trip was a bust. Huh! Must not have been using the right bait!

The first day in port, I had duty. My collateral responsibility aboard ship and duty assignment while in port was as MAA, to which I had been selected because of my previous experience aboard the *Connie*. That first night, while making my required rounds of the ship I happened to be up on the Bridge at 2200 (10PM) when Taps was played. It then occurred to me that, as it was still not sunset in this northern latitude, colors had not been passed and the ensign was still on the truck. A truly Alaskan experience!

The next day, my buddy Bob (who was also an MAA) and I headed off the ship together to check out the town. Our duty day had been 3 July 1978, so Bob & I were sure to have some fun on our first liberty ashore in Alaska and the 4th of July to boot! We spent the morning walking the town, which isn't much of an effort because most of the town is located to the south on the only flat area and where the fishing fleet and cruise ships docked. The northern part of town, with the exception of two blocks along the water, is nearly vertical, the mountains rising almost directly out of the sound. We rode the lift car up to a restaurant at the top of the hill back of town for lunch and took a look around. After lunch, we decided to check out a couple of the "watering holes." Spotting an interesting joint we slipped inside. What was most surprising to us, coming from the "lower 48," was the fact that in Alaskan bars, you could check your hat and coat at the door AND your gun! You had to leave it at the counter while killing some brain cells! Yep, we sure weren't in the "lower 48" anymore!

After passing some time in a couple more of these "venues" we were ready for dinner! We were told by one of the barkeeps about where to get some good grub and headed straight there. The dining room was also a lounge and we settled right in after ordering. As we were finishing dinner the couple seated next to us introduced themselves as Jim and Ali and struck up a conversation; they asked if we were off "that navy ship." The conversation rolled on and some time passed before they told us they had a hotel room where they were supposed to meet up with friends and would we like to come along. It didn't take long for us to decide to go with them. Back at their hotel and up on the third floor, there were about eight of us crammed into a fairly small room, shooting the breeze and quaffing a few brews. One of the crew had opened the window and was looking around outside when someone else decided to light and throw a small firecracker out the window. We peeked around him to see where the bang had gone off and immediately pulled our heads back inside. Across the street we had spied two Shore Patrol eyeballing our window and heading for the door of the hotel. As the only navy ship in port, our crew was tasked with providing the manpower for the SPs, so we knew they had to be from *Mt. Hood*, which didn't bode well for us! We sure didn't want to be hauled back to the ship just because we were in the same room the firecracker happened to come from. Sure enough, there was a loud knock on the door and a loud voice announcing "this is Shore Patrol; Open up!" One of the ladies grabbed me and Bob and quickly pushed us into the bathroom and followed us in, closing the door behind. We could hear the conversation, asking about who threw the firecracker and "was there anyone in the bathroom." The girl with us responded to a rap on the door and one of the SPs apologized and they both left. After waiting a couple minutes and hearing one of the people in the room saying he could see them back on the street, the three of us came out of the bathroom and everyone had a good laugh! Whew! That was close!

It was getting late so Bob and I begged off to head back to the ship! As we were saying goodbye, Jim and Ali invited us to meet them the next morning at the hotel and they would take us to their house to continue the visit. Sounded good to us! The next morning we met them in front of the hotel and they took us the two blocks down to the water and onto one of the pontoon docks where the sea planes tied up! Bob and I both looked at each other and then asked Jim what was up? He then told us that they were waiting to load some freight into one of the planes and would be ready to leave! "And where is that?" we asked. He explained that their house was about 15 miles south of Ketchikan at Metlakatla on Annette Island. He also told us he'd already paid for our fare! What could we do? Refuse? Well, just go with it, right? The freight loaded, we climbed into the plane followed by Jim and Ali. This was a first for Bob and me, a ride in a float plane! Yeah! Airborne we got a bird's eye view of the entire sound and the surrounding landscape. It was awesome! It only took a short time before we were coming in for a water landing at Annette Island. A station wagon was waiting for us and, after introductions, we helped load the freight into the car and we were off! A couple miles later we arrived at Metlakatla, a very small village whose primary industry was a fish processing plant. We were the guests of the Tsimshian native people, who made up the majority of the approximately 1,200 inhabitants at that time.

Word quickly spread around town that two of the sailors off the Navy ship in Ketchikan had arrived on the island and were staying at Jim and Ali's house. For the next two days, it seemed like the entire community came through the house to visit and made sure we were VERY well fed and cared for. It was one of the best experiences Bob and I had ever had and so impressed Bob that when he rotated off the *Mount Hood* a couple years later, he managed to get stationed aboard the Coast Guard cutter out of Ketchikan and later at Adak!

The evening of the second day on the island, we had planned to fly back to Ketchikan, but the fog was so thick that nothing was flying. We began to worry about getting back on time because the ship was leaving the next morning. Early the next day, walking outside, the fog was thick as ever and now we were in trouble! If the ship got underway without us, we would definitely be punished at Captain's Mast for "missing ship's movement." Jim told us to get down to a specific house by the water and one of the locals took us there. The owner had a short-wave radio and was able to call the Coast Guard in Ketchikan to relay a message to our ship of our predicament and our efforts to find a way back. After the radio message was sent, we started walking back to Jim's house when a station wagon coming down the road stopped and the driver asked if we were the two navy guys trying to get a ride back to Ketchikan. Excitedly, we replied "Yes" and he told us to hop in because he had a plane ready to leave from the old Coast Guard airstrip on the backside of the island. We were in business!

We arrived at the old CG airstrip and climbed into the plane, anxious to be off. As the pilot warmed up the engine, he leaned over and tapped one of the gauges. The needle on the gas gauge bounced slightly and he announced that that should be enough! Bob and I didn't share his confidence, but off we went. The fog that had delayed us, was still thick, but once airborne, it occurred in patches at altitude, with the terrain still obscured in the lower fog "blanket." The pilot was using a beacon of some sort to "ride the radial" into town and shortly he descended through the fog layer and at about 300 feet we broke through as he banked the plane. Below, we could see our ship still riding at anchor! Boy, were we relieved! After landing and taxiing up to a pier we noticed the ship's motor whale boat headed for the CG pier. The plane had hardly been tied off when we jumped out and started running down the pier, headed for the ship's boat. Out of breath as we jumped into the boat we asked if they were making a last-minute mail run. The answer was not what we wanted to hear. "Nope, this boat's just for you two," one of the line-handlers said grinning. Uh Oh! We knew we were in trouble! Reaching the side of the ship, we tied off to the boat fall and were hoisted into the davits. During the ride up we looked up to the Bridge wing and saw the XO glaring down at us! Now, we knew we were **REALLY** in trouble! They already had us for missing quarters and not being on our assigned stations for Sea & Anchor/Navigation Detail. But, at least it wasn't for being AWOL!

We were underway for Hawaii and three days en route there was still no mention of what our fate would be. They were keeping us in suspense! Finally, on the fourth day and just two days out of port the Chief Master at Arms told us we were to conduct our own investigations into the events. Irony piled on irony! The following day we were summoned to XOI (Executive Officers Investigation). Standing at attention in front of the XO's desk, we had no idea how things would pan out and even if we had, we couldn't have expected what ended up happening. After reading our investigation reports and relating to us what the ship had known of our travails, the XO looked up at us and with his best poker face asked if it had been worth it. Looking at each other, we both smiled and told him it was! And, come what may, it had been a great experience. The XO leaned back in his chair and told us what the command would exact in punishment so that the crew would know that we weren't exempt. First, we would submit to voluntary restriction aboard ship while in port Hawaii. We would also stand port and starboard MAA duty while in port. Each of us relieving the other at the end of a 24 hour duty. That was it and we readily agreed! We later learned that the ship hadn't, in fact, waited on us as much as they were waiting for the fog to lift! We had made it back minutes before they were preparing to pull up anchor and get underway! Sometimes you get the breaks, sometimes the shaft!

During our stay in Pearl Harbor, the ship put the word out that they had made arrangements for a specific number of seats on one of the MAC (Military Airlift Command) flights flying out of Hickam AFB to Travis AFB located very close to our homeport in Concord, California. Crewmembers desiring a seat on the plane were to submit request chits up their COC (Chain of Command). Bob and I talked it over and figured we had nothing to lose so we both submitted the required chit. To our amazement, both were approved. We ended up flying home five days before the ship would arrive. Who would have guessed!

While en route Hawaii, I had to "escort" two shipmates to Captain's Mast (a form of non-judicial punishment), but wasn't aware of all the charges as I had been involved with my own self-investigation and the chief had done the investigation for this case. Once CO's Mast began, I was flabbergasted to hear the entire story. In an obviously alcohol-fueled moment of inspiration, while on liberty in Ketchikan one night, the two young sailors had decided they didn't want to go to Hawaii before going home – to Concord, California! So, they "commandeered" one of the local fishing boats for the trip. Enough brain cells were still functioning for them to realize that a trip of this distance would require a full tank of gas, so they took the boat over to the fueling pier, topped off the tanks, and off they went. The next morning, after the Coast Guard had been alerted to the theft and had commenced looking for the boat, they quickly located the culprits and took matters in hand, returning the two to the ship and towing the boat back to town.

During mast was when I learned the rest of the story. When the two decided to top off the gas tank before starting their trip home, they failed to notice their boat engine was diesel and put marine gas into the tank instead, thus ensuring the engine wouldn't last long before seizing up! The funniest part of the whole escapade was that when the Coast Guard found the boat, it was NORTH of town! How they were going to get to California by heading north from Alaska, is anyone's guess!

While we're on the subject of CO's Mast, previously and while the *Hood* was still overseas, I was charged with attending another mast for some minor infraction that I can't recall. However, after the Captain had passed sentence, the sailor was dismissed and as he turned to exit the Bridge, he reached for the handset to the 1MC (the ship-wide announcing circuit) speaker and without taking the time to activate it, pretended to speak into the microphone, "Beam me up Scotty, there's no intelligent life down here!" Damn, the kid had balls! The CO immediately re-convened mast and additional punishment was awarded for that little act of defiance!

After our return from the Middie cruise in the later part of that summer, I submitted a one-week leave chit to take the family up to the summer cabin at Willow Creek. In passing conversation aboard ship, I had mentioned this to a few shipmates and two of them seemed very interested. So, I asked if they would like to go with us, to which they eagerly agreed. But, as neither of them had time to submit leave requests by then, it was agreed that they would drive up for the weekend and return Sunday night. What we had planned for their stay there was to rent a two-man canoe from Special Services on base, tie it down on top of my Volkswagen Bus and bring it with us for some white-water runs down the river. The first day on the river, the four of us (me, my two shipmates and my oldest son) loaded into the VW and drove about eight or nine miles upstream, past the North/South Fork split of the Trinity River to Salyers Bar and put in. As we loaded up, we tied everything off so it wouldn't be lost if we capsized, which proved to be fortunate. I also strapped my boy into a life vest because he wasn't the greatest of swimmers. I knew both of my shipmates didn't have much stick-time in a canoe, so I was in the back steering while they were forward paddling, with some direction from me. The first rapids we came to were a mild Class Two, but with a bend at the end. At the bend, they weren't able to bring the bow in the right direction and we capsized. Three heads popped up! Uh Oh! I ducked back under and took a look. No one at the bottom, but out of the corner of my eye I saw legs kicking. It was my son, *under* the canoe! I ducked under and came up in the air pocket facing him and told him to hold his breath. Then, I yanked him from under the canoe, sputtering a bit of water, but otherwise no worse for wear. We pulled the canoe to shore, righted it and piled back in as I explained to them what had caused us to go over and for the next hour we ran two more sets of Class Two rapids with no problem.

The following day, we put in below the cabin and rode downstream to our planned take-out location, where we had staged the VW. My son was with us again and this time he had wanted to ride an inner-tube tied off to the back of the canoe. He had his life vest on again and so I told him OK. We hit some fast water, but nothing worth being concerned about until we approached our take-out point. Just before that, there was a wide set of Class Two rapids with a portion in the middle that had a few Class Three waves. Staying in the middle, to avoid the rocks on either side, we hit the big ones and as the canoe passed over the last large one I took a quick look over my shoulder to see how my boy was doing. At that moment, he was on top of the last big wave and holding on for dear life. The look on his face told me all I needed to know and when we pulled the canoe ashore a few minutes later, I was surprised to find out he didn't require a new set of skivvies! He made "tall story" of the ride when we got back to the cabin and I didn't mention how scared-shitless he looked! Well, not right away.

While aboard the *Hood* and after our return stateside, the ship was one of those selected to be a test-command for some new uniform items that were being considered for the rest of the navy. We all got a look at what items were being changed and no one I spoke with gave them much of a rave review. A funky style ball cap with a high forehead piece, straight-legged work pants with a crease and a new style material for the work shirt. After the trial period, *Navy Times* reported that the proposed changes had been well received by the trial command personnel. I don't know where they got that impression because it sure wasn't the mood prevailing aboard *my* ship! Unfortunately, these changes were incorporated into our seabag requirements and stayed with us for a number of years. This all began in the mid-70s when the navy was having budget problems to begin with and somehow had arrived at the conclusion that spending money to change clothing styles was more important than fuel or weapons or everything else that required attention than trying to make us look spiffy! I swear, if they'd tried to add a clip-on tie to the outfit, I would have been sorely tempted to bail!

As fall rolled around, it was time to start our preparations for RefTra, which would begin in just a few months. For an AE homeported out of Concord, that meant we had to transit to San Diego for many of the RefTra preps and the events themselves. In the meantime we were occupied with getting our paperwork in order (charts, certifications, Watch-Quarter & Station Bill, etc.) and conducting practice drills to emulate those we would be required to perform during RefTra.

Finally in San Diego and after completing preps and practice, by the third week in SOCAL we were ready for the RefTra finale. The only events remaining were the "Emergency Sortie" and the "Final Battle Problem," which would be an all-day event. The requisite Navigation Briefing was held in the Wardroom and shortly after the ship got underway. First, we had to stop and pick up the RefTra "observers" about mid-way down the channel and then proceeded to conduct our "Emergency Sortie." During this evolution (and for every ship undergoing this portion of RefTra) it was simulated that your sortie was being conducted during a war-time environment and as you exited the harbor you would be transiting a simulated "mine field," which had been superimposed over your navigation chart. As usual, our job in CIC was to provide radar navigation input to the visual data gathered and applied on the Bridge chart by the QMs. Well, just after passing Ballast Point, the narrowest part of the transit, our track in CIC showed us being "set" (being pushed by the current) to starboard and into the "minefield." As I was swinging the arcs from the radar "cuts" being called out, I reported over sound-powered phone to the Bridge, where CIC held the ship, our set and drift, and CIC's recommendation to regain our track. Standing next to me was the CIC RefTra observer, watching, listening and taking notes. After repeated fixes and notifications to the Bridge but without any corrective courses or speeds to take us out of the "minefield," the observer called out "Stop the Problem, Stop the Clock" and quickly exited CIC for the Bridge. The ship came to a stop! In CIC, through the cable transits from Bridge to CIC, we could hear a heated exchange occurring, and shortly the Bridge RefTra observer came into CIC and took a look at our chart, comparing it to what he had seen on the chart on the Bridge. The bottom line was that the Bridge had still held us in the channel and as is usual on navy ships, the command tended to follow the Navigator's recommendations. In this case, they were not correct and the command failed to resolve the conflicting Bridge and CIC solutions during the evolution. Bridge did not get a good review from RefTra, but CIC ended up with a final grade of 86%. The added benefit was that, from then on, CIC navigation data received a lot more attention than previously! Our CIC gang were pretty smug there for a while after that.

Back in Concord, I was looking at a rapidly approaching deployment date because the ship was scheduled to head back to WestPac in the first few months of the new year. We had made a trip to NSC Oakland and then moved over to

Alameda in late November. While there, we were tied up across the pier from *USS Enterprise* (CVN-65) and I got a visit from a former shipmate and buddy of mine from the *Connie* who was now stationed aboard *the Big E*. He had heard from another shipmate that I was aboard the *Hood*. We got to talking and both of us found that we wanted what the other was getting! Namely, Rich wanted to get back overseas and I wanted to stay stateside. *The Big E* would be departing for the shipyard in Bremerton at the beginning of the year, which is what I wanted. We both agreed that we should submit request chits to exchange ships. Which is what we did! After some lobbying by each of us up our respective command chains, both chits were approved. So, shortly after Christmas, we each grabbed our seabags and walked across the pier to our new commands. We had successfully "swapped decks" as was the term applied for this timely maneuver!

Now, the tricky part would be getting the family moved up there, because I was going to attempt doing that without taking any leave. I mean, you don't transfer aboard ship and then immediately turn around and ask for leave, right? Anyway, once we arrived in Bremerton, I did ask for a Friday off so I would at least have 72 hours to make the move. Tight, but better than nothing! The weekend planned for the move arrived and the Thursday night after work, I boarded a plane at SeaTac and flew down to Oakland, where the wife picked me up. The following day, I called the *Mount Hood* and told my former shipmates that there was free beer and food for anyone who showed up to help load the rental van on Saturday morning. We had also sold our car to help with the cost of the move and make the process simpler (not having to tow a vehicle). Because the wife and I had already started downsizing and packing prior to me leaving for Bremerton, things were well in hand and ready for loading. Four or five of the guys off the Hood showed up Saturday morning and by mid-afternoon everything we owned was crammed into the van, the wife, kids and dog included. Well, not exactly crammed as we didn't have all that many belongings, because we'd only been in Concord for a year-and-a-half and we hadn't time to accumulate stuff in the interim. But, by crammed, I mean loaded quickly and haphazardly because of the rush we were in to get going. This "fire drill" was what the navy termed a "self-move" meaning that it was not being scheduled through the navy and that you had to make all the arrangements and carry it out. With a self-move, you were provided with a portion of the expenses up-front and then reimbursed the difference (up to a set limit based on mileage) after the fact. As we got set to leave, I thanked my former shipmates and with bear-hugs and handshakes all around, I said my good-byes, climbed into the truck and drove off.

Our move taking place in January, we would be at the mercy of the weather going through the mountains on Interstate 5. By the time we got to Redding, California we knew the road conditions were not looking good. By then it was around 10PM as we drove through Shasta City, on the flanks of Mount Shasta; the snow was coming down sideways and starting to build up along the roadway. Enough traffic was still moving to keep the road fairly clear, though. With the snow coming down so hard, our speed had dropped down to 35 or 40 miles an hour. Soon, we were approaching the California-Oregon border and it wasn't getting any better. And, up ahead, there it was! The roadblock I had been dreading. CHP and CAL-TRANS were stopping all traffic and requiring all vehicles to "chain up" before being allowed to proceed. When my turn in the line came, I shoved my Navy ID card in front of the officers' face and told him if I wasn't aboard ship by Monday morning, I would be UA (AWOL in the more recognized acronym). He looked over his shoulder and turning to me he said, "Follow that truck!" A semi was just pulling back onto the roadway after putting his chains on and I thanked the officer then quickly fell in behind the truck. All the way up the mountain and down the other side, at 15 to 20 miles an hour, I stayed tucked in behind our big-rig buddy. By the time we reached Ashland, Oregon it was after 1AM and I was exhausted. We pulled off at one of the exits, got a hotel room for the night and I was quickly out-like-a-light! Ashland was just below the snowline then, so the rest of the trip was routine and we pulled into Bremerton late the next day. I later heard they had completely stopped all traffic on that stretch of the highway shortly after we got through that night and didn't open it again until the following morning.

There would be another trip along Interstate 5 that would prove to be just as troublesome. No mere snowstorms, either. That trip would involve a volcano!

CHAPTER 16
USS ENTERPRISE (CVN-65)
4 JANUARY 1979 – 25 JUNE 1980

USS Enterprise (CVN-65) after "Snow Cone" Removal

CVN-65 SLEP OVERHAUL, PSNSY
January 1979 to February 1982

The Big E was in the shipyard for what is termed a SLEP (Service Life Extension Program) Overhaul, which in many cases meant a complete gutting of

.those spaces in which obsolete equipment was being replaced by an entirely new, state of the art suite. This was the case in CIC and the Computer Room where the processors that supported the NTDS Consoles, were located. In just a few weeks, you could walk into either space and they were completely barren — not a single piece of equipment remaining! With deck prep, supporting elements (air, water and electricity) needing to be re-routed, it would be more than a year before any of the new equipment was "landed" and months later before connections were made and yet more months before individual and integrated systems testing could begin. So, there being no CIC to work in, so to speak, we were all "farmed out" into the SFOMS Department for assignment to various divisions. This was all too familiar to me having been through the same process aboard *Connie*.

During the ship's overhaul and while assigned to SFOMS Department and HAB-6 (Vents & Voids) Division, I had managed to work my way up from being assigned as crew leader, to being in charge of three work crews; then I became the division's administrative assistant and assistant crew coordinator. This was mainly due to our division chief having noticed my knack for writing personnel evaluations, something that he didn't like to do. With over 80 personnel assigned to the division, he was able to task me to take "inputs" from the various crew leaders, make the necessary changes and then put them on his desk for review and signature, which cut his work load considerably. It also got me a desk in the division office. This was a considerable upgrade from working on a crew changing out ventilation ducting and all the dust, noise and sweat it involved. To justify my continued position when between evaluation cycles, I was also assigned the job of "man-hour accounting" and the weekly reports that were required.

I was also to oversee the management of the "tool issue" room for the division and to assign personnel and tasking to the "Asbestos Removal Team" that the division had been required to provide. In anticipation of the difficulty recruiting division personnel to willingly work in this field, I pointed out to the division Officer and the chief that some kind of "carrot" should be offered to sway enough people to volunteer for the duty. So, when the word went out for recruiting team members, the ranks were quickly filled – we had announced that the work-week for the asbestos team would be four days and not five! Working on or managing the Asbestos Removal Team meant that I and the team members had to attend a one-day class on the subject. The training was provided by the shipyard and pointed out the hazards of the work as well as the required protective measures, such as paper suits, booties, gloves, masks and re-breather LP air provided while working in the space. Part of the training also included a medical screening during which you had to exhale into a device for a certain period so your efforts could be recorded as a benchmark, should the issue of "asbestosis" arise in your medical record later.

Some of the division's work demanded tools that were not in sufficient supply (enough to outfit all the division's teams) or specialized tools, rigging and safety garb. Even though we had been assigned tasks requiring this gear, we couldn't stay within projected expenditures unless we were able to "procure" some outside of regular channels. The common term in the navy was "cumshaw" a slang term that I understand originated during the navy's experience in China before WWII. If the item you wanted was being used by someone else who it was being issued to, you could "barter" for the item with something you had that they wanted. On the *Big E* in Hab 6, what we had a lot of was *coffee!* Coffee was issued aboard ship by division and the number of men assigned to the division. Problem was, with all our work crews spread throughout the ship, a person just didn't take his break, walk half the length of the ship to get a cup and then return to work. So the only people using coffee in the division were the four of us in the admin office and a couple guys in the tool issue room. The rest of our issue sat accumulating in the office. I had learned that our tool-issue guy was a real "wheeler & dealer," and if asked if he could get something outside channels he only had two questions; How many do you need and when do you need it? So I also put him in charge of procuring what was needed. When I informed the chief and division officer that our guy would be stopping by from time to time to pick up some cans of coffee, they said they didn't want to know!

Ex-*USNS General Hugh J. Gaffey* (T-AP-121) was tied up across the pier from the *Enterprise*, to provide berthing for the crew while the ship was laid up. ADM Hyman Rickover visited CGN-65 and berthed in a stateroom aboard *Gaffey*. Standing orders from the CDO (Command Duty Officer) aboard CVN-65 stated that, should Mr. Rickover depart *Gaffey*, the QD and CDO were to be informed ASAP – the admiral had a habit of sneaking aboard and raising havoc! He tried that when I had the Quarterdeck watch aboard *Gaffey* one morning and I asked if he was going aboard ship. He turned, gave me that infamous Rickover scowl and said, "Go ahead and make your call"! Brilliant man, but what a "tool!"

The ship being in Bremerton, we endured many rainy days during our stay, but there was one notable stretch where it rained every weekend for over a month. Sure, there were clear days during the week, but having your weekends spent dodging rain or cooped up at home started to wear on morale. So, the division officer and chief decided the division would have a picnic the middle of a selected week, in an effort to outsmart mother nature. Sure enough, the planned day of the picnic dawned clear and relatively warm. The picnic involved a baseball game and lots of grilled hot dogs and hamburgers. It was a big hit with the crew and everyone appreciating that the effort had been made in an attempt to ease the drudgery!

I had always been an avid outdoor enthusiast, fishing, hiking and camping were activities I was continuously involved in from the time I was old enough to fish and strap a back pack onto my back. Growing up across the road from a Redwood forest, I was "in the woods" almost daily. There were forts to build and a nearby stream afforded good trout fishing if you were aware enough to learn how to read the stream. At around 12 or 13, my best friend and I would come home from school on Friday and strap on our packs and disappear into the woods, not to come out until Sunday afternoon. As I grew older, this was followed by more organized trips into the Shasta-Trinity Wilderness Area, the Trinity Alps and the Marble Mountain Wilderness Area, spending a few days or up to a week in the mountains.

After the previous overhauls aboard *Connie* at Bremerton and while aboard *the Big E,* I started mulling over a trip to the Olympic National Park, just across the Hood Canal. It soon became obvious that if I were going to make the effort to spend some time over in the park, I may as well go "whole hog" and hike the trail from east to west! If that was going to be the goal, it was obviously going to entail more than just my family to pull it off. I would need at least two other hikers because two vehicles would have to leave the eastern entrance so that one could be dropped off at the western exit and the driver ferried back to the eastern entry point. So, I started talking it up with some of the guys in the division and very quickly had candidates for the trip. After further planning got underway, the number settled out to four other men, me, my wife and all four of our kids, the youngest son being six! Due to work schedules and each of us having to submit a leave chit for the specific dates we anticipated for the trip, we could not get going any sooner than the last few days of August and the first couple days of September. Anything after that would be too late in the season, given the altitudes we would be hiking over. Before we departed, of course, there was a lot of planning to do. Aboard ship, during lunch or after hours, we would gather in the tool issue room or the division office, spread out the map and discuss the route. At other meetings we would discuss equipment and provisions. In East Bremerton, there was a small camping and outdoor store, but after picking up the few items we needed out of their limited offerings we started asking around and found that the place to go was in Seattle at the REI store. So, setting a Saturday aside to make the ferry trip across the sound, we made the trip and were very surprised. For the time, it was a huge store and carried anything and everything an outdoor enthusiast would want. One of the best surprises was that they rented "lightly used" equipment and sold second-hand hiking boots at very low prices. This meant that if I could find the right sizes for the kids, I wouldn't have to buy brand new boots or backpacks. Also, they had a large variety of dehydrated trail foods from which to choose and we stocked up on those. The last week before leaving for the mountains, we spent the nights packing and repacking our backpacks. – Where we could we trimmed or shifted weight from one person to the other, depending on what we felt each could bear. Even the six-year old had a daypack, into which we put three pairs of socks and skivvies, three shirts, one change of pants, rain gear for protection from the expected rain, and one small frying pan. My pack ended up being around 34 pounds! Ugh! To save weight, we wouldn't be tent camping and only brought two tarps for use in constructing lean-to shelters each night. Because we weren't allowed an open fire within the park, I bought a very small, Swiss made single-burner camp stove and brought four small fuel canisters. Because it would be cold, much of our weight was dedicated to clothing, including "slickers" for each of us.

The day of departure arrived and all 9 of us convoyed in three vehicles to the entry point, Dosewallips Ranger Station, on the eastern edge of the park. Arriving around 10AM, as soon as we off-loaded all the gear (except for that of the two guys ferrying the vehicle) our two drivers departed with the two vehicles, for Graves Creek trailhead, to stage the one vehicle and return in the other. While they were doing that, we filled out the paperwork the park required: number in party, nightly campsites and expected exit location and date. After that we loaded up and took off up the trail. Our two ferry drivers would catch up to us that evening at our first campsite. The first night's stop was a place called Honeymoon Meadows. We set up camp at the edge of the meadow and had just started dinner when our two ferry drivers showed up. Everything was clicking! The next day's hike took us to our next stop, a few miles below Anderson Pass. We hadn't made a lot of miles the first two days, but we had gained over three thousand feet in elevation. The next day we left camp and were just below the Anderson Pass summit when the rain hit and hit hard. Fortunately, we soon found a trail shelter for just such conditions and we all piled in there. As we waited, lunch was a couple hours over-due, so we set up the stove and started building a mulligan stew. Everyone pitching in ingredients until the pot was full. It sure was good going down and helped keep off the cold. As we were finishing up, two other hikers came up the trail and squeezed into the shelter with us. We still had a little mulligan left and offered it to them. They were duly grateful and we had a nice chat with them until the rain stopped and we packed up and left.

We were through the pass in short order and came down off the mountain into Enchanted Valley, on the Quinalt River. A half-mile further and we arrived at that night's lodging. That's right, I said lodging. We would be staying in the shelter side of the chalet that had been built in the '30s. One third of the chalet was being used as a park ranger station and the other two-thirds we would share with other hikers. These included, two Japanese who had also hiked the Cascades that summer, and a couple of Germans who had just come off hiking in the Andes. The interior of our portion of the chalet consisted of rough-hewn lumber used to build bunks, tables and benches. Big enough for all of us to fit comfortably.

The next morning at breakfast was when we realized that our "plan" wasn't "clicking" as well as we thought. We were short on rations! The climb up to the pass burned a lot more calories than we anticipated and our portions at meals were larger than we thought they would be. We had also consumed most of our bags of trail-mix that we each carried for munching along the way. And, then there was our shelter stop and the extra ingredients we had all thrown into the mulligan stew. We had enough for breakfast that morning, but whatever was left over in our packs for dinner was about it. We still had one more night and day left before reaching the exit to the park. So it was up to us to catch some food! The Quinalt River was right outside and in the valley had spread out into a half-dozen small rivulets. The water was barely above freezing, coming out of the mountains we had just traveled and much of it directly from Anderson Glacier. You could tell it was snow melt and glacier water because it was still a lightly diluted milky color. But it was full of Dolly-Varden trout and we got our share! Now, before we had begun this trip, one of the safety concerns I had was that one of the kids would get separated and lost from the main group. So, I had spent some time talking to them about that and what they were to do if they found themselves alone. I bought each of them whistles and hung them around their necks and explained that if they did find themselves separated from the group, they were to stop right where they were and start blowing those whistles for all they were worth. Well, while out fishing with my oldest boy that morning, he got separated from me and he did just what I had told the kids to do. He blew that whistle until he was red in the face! I heard it and did some quick back-tracking and came around a bend in the river to find him honking on that whistle, as hard and loud as he could make it. We had fish and rice for dinner!

The next day, our second night in the chalet, we had agreed that two of the fittest of our group would set out ahead of the rest of us, setting a brisk pace, getting to the car, driving to town and bringing back lunch to the rest of us who should be showing up about then at trail's end. We had a *very* light breakfast, though!

We had thirteen miles to go and that didn't seem to be unachievable. But, as the miles passed, I grew more concerned with the youngest boy! He was holding up, but it wasn't fun anymore and I could tell. Looking at the picture below, it's obvious that he had regained his pluck! It may have been as a result of those burgers and fries that he knew would be arriving soon! I was damn proud of all of them, though! It had been a 34-mile hike and a 3,869 foot elevation change.

One of the crew (L) and my son, Sean

As *the Big E's* overhaul rolled on and HAB-6 worked through its assigned tasking schedule, it became evident we would meet our requirements before the scheduled completion date. At the beginning of the overhaul, the work package consisted of approximately eight miles of ventilation ducting that would need to be taken down, cleaned, flange gaskets replaced and everything re-installed. Based on planning estimates, the division had been assigned over 80 men to accomplish the task. But, there were bumps in the road and all too many times we came to realize that the planners, when looking at the blueprints of a ducting system, were not aware of other co-located equipment or ducting runs that would require removal before we could proceed with work on the assigned run. So, one week, we would be rolling along making good progress and then come up against a situation that would require more man-hours because we had to expend time and effort to re-move these obstructions and then replace them when we were done with that specific ducting run. Naturally, a definite completion date was somewhat elusive. With that in mind, when man-hours scheduled were exceeded, the division officer was reluctant to report that because this was used as a benchmark for the draw-down of personnel as the completion of the overhaul drew near. How do you plan for what you don't know will happen? Murphy was a player and we had to allow for that! So before submitting the man-hour report each week, the LT, chief and I would sit down and go over the numbers and try to arrive at a figure that would allow us to keep a larger number of personnel for a longer period. Even though we still lost bodies to draw-down with our adjusted totals, it was at a much more sustainable rate than would have been required otherwise. Creative man-hour accounting would continue for the remainder of the overhaul and, yes, we did have occasion to use that advantage!

Toward the end of my tour aboard *Big E*, I made a few trips to CIC and while structural work had been completed and a few pieces of new equipment had been brought aboard, light-off (connections made and support systems available) had not occurred and systems testing was still a long way off!

I was fast approaching my rotation date to shore duty and had started inquiring of the ships' Career Counselors about the positions that might be available. As this would be my first rotation ashore, I took the matter seriously and began researching the possibilities. While I did so I discovered there were OS billets at locations called OPCON's (Operational Control) facilities located on the West Coast at NAS Moffett Field and NAS Whidbey Island. Because Whidbey Island was only about 80 miles from Bremerton, I was keenly interested on account of having enjoyed the times aboard the *Connie* and *The Big E* while they were in the Puget Sound area. The problem was that the person whose billet I was qualified to fill at Whidbey was not due to rotate out of that billet until six months after my rotation date off *the Big E*. So, I worked a deal with the Career Counselor that I would extend my term onboard the *Enterprise* for six months, which would place me in the right time period to fill that Whidbey billet. Before the paperwork was signed, the Career Counselor called the detailer, in my presence, and pitched the plan. The detailer had no problem with that, so the necessary paperwork was generated and submitted up the chain of command. I would get confirmation from the Detailer as the rotation date approached.

About a month before I was due to rotate, I got a phone call in CIC on the outside line that could have really upset the apple cart. The guy on the other end was all excited because he had learned from his detailer that I would be his replacement at OPCON NAS Moffett Field! Whoa! I told him he was mistaken because I was due to take the billet at OPCON NAS Whidbey Island. He said that he had just spoken to the detailer and that's how he got my name and phone number, so I apologized and told him someone had their wires crossed. I told him before I hung up that I would be talking with my Career Counselor and the detailer within the hour to straighten everything out. After hanging up, I hurried up to the Career Counselor's office and we had a short conversation because it was necessary to get the detailer on the phone back on the East Coast before he left for the day. When all was said and done, the detailer agreed that he had gotten the billets and names mixed up and promised to make it right as soon as possible. We (the CC and I) asked him to send confirmation when that was done, in the form of official orders because those were soon expected to be "cut" anyway. He agreed and I had orders in hand before the week was out! Whew! Close call!

The day finally arrived for our departure from Bremerton and *The Big E*. This move would not be a self-move and the Mayflower van had already loaded our household goods for delivery to Whidbey Island and in storage until we called for it. But we were heading in the opposite direction. I had over a month between leaving the ship and reporting to Whidbey Island. Cumulative Leave and Proceed & Travel time meant that from 26 June to 28 July I was en route.

The first stop on our drive south would be for a one-day visit with my parents, who were managing an apartment complex in Beaverton, Oregon, a suburb of Portland. But our route and timing were not very opportune. On the morning of 18 May 1980, Mount Saint Helens blew up! The explosion and subsequent debris flow would impact southern Washington and northern Oregon for months — and we would be driving toward that mess. Certainly, we had been monitoring the situation. The bridges on the interstate in that area were still up and traffic was still flowing, but that could change at any moment. Initially, the ash cloud was being blown east southeast and had not yet been an issue to the west and south. But, shortly before our departure and on the morning of 12 June, the mountain experienced another explosion (the second of five) and this time the prevailing winds blew the cloud over Portland, our first destination. The cloud dissipated quickly but it left a mess in its wake. When we arrived at the Cowlitz River and the southbound bridge on I-5, the traffic slowed to a crawl. We could see the work crews and cranes in place next to the two bridges; they were there to stave off anything large enough coming down the river that could damage the north and southbound bridge structures. Flagmen were also positioned at the bridge approaches in the event they were given the signal to stop all traffic. We also noticed the mountains of wet, gray mud that had been bulldozed away from the bridge approaches, remnants of earlier flows. As we inched across the bridge, looking below to the river, what we saw was unrecognizable as water. It was not blue or blue green as normal, but a thick slurry of grayish brown mixed with brush and trees and moving slowly downstream. And there were only a scant few feet between it and the bottom of the highway bridges. Later, it was estimated that from the entry of the Cowlitz River into the Columbia River and downstream, the depth of the Columbia River was lowered by over 10 feet, due to the entry of all the mud and ash from the volcano. What a mess!

Arriving in Beaverton, we pulled into the parking lot of the apartment complex where my parents worked to find my dad on the roof of one of the complexes, sweeping and shoveling off the volcanic ash from the event on the 12th. His first words were, "Where were you when I was hosing all the ash out of the parking lot?" With four acres of parking that was no small project, which was why he was still working on clearing it from the roofs. His inducement was the Portland mayor's threat of a fine for businesses that didn't remove the volcanic ash from their parking lots.

Our visit was short and the next day we proceeded south to the family's summer home in Willow Creek, California. For the next few weeks, fishing, swimming and inner-tubing down the river, was the order of the day! When we made the return trip almost a month later, crossing over the Cowlitz River bridge, we could see that the water level had dropped back to near normal and that the river was again its normal blue-green color. But, the mess left behind was strewn along the banks and would be a constant reminder for years, of the cataclysmic power of Mother Nature!

CHAPTER 17

NAS W*HIDBEY* I*SLAND*
28 J*ULY* 1980 – 16 J*ULY* 1982

As IN MOST TRANSFERS WITH FAMILY you went through more than one move! By that, I mean, you traveled to the location of your new duty station, by car or by moving van. Once there, you had to put the family up somewhere (hotel or some other interim housing) until you could move into Navy Housing, because these always had a waiting list. The move to Whidbey was no exception and I'll use this example to demonstrate the level of difficulty a family typically can end up going through.

Driving into Oak Harbor a week before the end of my leave-and-travel time, we arrived early enough to still have some daylight left and I managed to get us checked into a hotel for the time being. The following day, I drove around town until I found a realtor's office with a sign in the window saying they placed navy personnel in rental units. So parking the car and walking inside I asked the lady behind the desk what they had available and she showed me a few of the places that would take navy families. I wasn't impressed. They were either too small or above the Basic Allowance for Quarters (BAQ). She asked that I leave my phone and room number at the hotel and someone would contact me if anything else popped up. Well, a couple days later a person from the office did call and as it turned out he was a retired WO (Warrant Officer) who had "homesteaded" on

Whidbey for years, as many of the air station personnel did as part of their retirement planning. He mentioned that he might have something for me if I would keep an open mind, so we set up a meeting for the following day. When he showed up at the hotel, we followed him to the place he was to show us and were we surprised. Turns out that the old Catholic Rectory in town had been evacuated by the church for newer facilities and they were renting/leasing the old one. We pulled up to an enormous building that covered the entire corner of the block. Three stories and about 26 rooms! We had the kids with us and when we got inside they all took off to check the place out. The wife and I roamed around and after almost an hour we had managed to look at most of the rooms. I told the WO that I thought it was too big and would obviously be way outside BAQ limits. But, he said it wasn't! I told him we needed to talk it over and could I call him the next day. So, we talked it over that night and agreed that we'd move in there until something better and more our size showed up as the cumulative daily hotel rates would soon eat up a month's BAQ if we didn't move out of soon. So, for about six months we lived in the old Catholic Rectory, rattling around in that huge space soon settled into the norm and the kids had a blast!

Our WO realtor called about six months later and said he had a three-bedroom mobile available for under BAQ, located up the hill and right outside the gate to the base. This would cut my travel time back and forth to work down to seven or eight minutes each way! And, a very opportune time, too. With winter beginning, the heating bill was rising fast in that big old rectory. A few more months of it would break the bank. Obviously, we moved into the mobile as soon as we could! Being right up the hill from the base, when the Blue Angels used Whidbey as their practice field prior to their air-show over Seattle during SeaFair Days, we just set up lawn chairs out front and watched them run through their routine every day before they left. Most everyone in the neighborhood did the same!

One of the first things I did when I went through the "check in" process aboard the air station was to get my name on the waiting list for Navy Housing. Two moves and almost a year elapsed before they called us up and told us they had a unit available for us and asked if we wanted to take it. Hell yes! So, finally, with my two-year tour at Whidbey half over, we made the move into housing. Counting our move when we departed Whidbey we made four moves in a little over two years!

The place I worked in while stationed at NAS Whidbey was called OPCON (Operations Control). I spent the first couple months learning and becoming familiar enough with the duties of the person I was relieving to take them up. Actually, he left before I really got to that point, but with the help of the other two guys working that billet, the transition went pretty smoothly. OPCON was located in the basement of the building that housed the airfield's control tower. Above us, on the top floor, was the tower control for the airfield, with the floor below occupied by the COMMATVAQWINGSPAC's admiral and staff. Your entered OPCON from a back door that had a cypher lock; you entered the set code, the door buzzed and you pushed the door open. There were no windows and your shift was 10 to 12 hours unless you had duty. Duty days were only a couple times a month, but you started that duty shift by manning the office at 3PM and bunked in the back room overnight until relieved the following morning at 8AM. From 3PM to 8AM, you spent most of your time bored out of your gourd! There were very few calls to answer, no scheduling was done after 5PM, and the TV we had back then sure as heck wasn't cable! So, I did a lot of reading!

During normal working hours, our tasking included taking calls from the various air squadrons stationed there and assisting their scheduling officer who would request entry and exit times for the various air routes and operating areas that we managed. These included the Bomb Range at Boardman, Oregon; the ACM (air combat maneuvering) ranges; torpedo drop areas off the southwestern coast of the island and designated ship's operating areas off the coast. The most demanding of these tasks was scheduling the entry/egress of aircraft for use of the IR/VFR (Instrument Rules/Visual Flight Rules) air routes we controlled. Because some of the routes crossed other routes, entry had to be carefully managed so that aircraft using different routes wouldn't collide over one of these intersecting points. So if we had someone entering a route that crossed over another route, we would "block" that time on both routes to prevent such an occurrence from being possible. All this was done on paper, by hand, and formatted with entry routes and entry times displayed across the page. I imagine that now it's all done using a computer "app," but we had no such luxury back then! Scheduling of the Boardman Bomb Range was comparatively simple because once the aircraft arrived in the range's vicinity, their tower personnel took control. The same held with most other OpAreas in that you scheduled a start time and stop time and if required you restricted the unit requesting the area to a "slice" of the area and or designated minimum and maximum altitudes, as necessary.

NAS Whidbey and OPCON in particular was the POC for all things related to military aircraft within our sphere of operational oversight and thus designated as the command to contact when civilians had issues or complaints regarding those aircraft. This included Air Force aircraft and a Navy four-striper (Captain) was assigned as liaison at McChord AFB outside Tacoma. If a call came in complaining about an Air Force asset, I would contact our Captain there and he would relate the problem to the Air Force. My favorite story related to this function came when a little old lady called one day complaining that her chickens had stopped laying eggs because "my" planes were flying too low. After having her describe the aircraft in question and where she lived, it was obvious that they were B-52's flying "nap of the earth" ingress training up the Columbia River gorge. Our Navy liaison got a chuckle out of that.

Another function that OPCON was tasked with was fielding complaints from civilians living near OLF Coupeville, located 18 miles south. The problem there was that, after the landing field was built in 1943, civilian housing gradually encroached around the field and noise complaints naturally ensued. Of particular concern was a housing complex south of the field and under the approach pattern of landing aircraft. When this group of houses were built, it was required of the realtor to include in his paperwork and sales pitch that he explain to the prospective buyer the noise zone his house was in, the impact of that issue and his rights as the homeowner, should damage occur that could be attributed to excessive noise. For the most part, everyone understood their rights and responsibilities and OPCON would only receive complaints when the pattern at OLF got "sloppy" or the wind impacted the pattern. But, from time to time we would receive complaints from a homeowner outside OLF. On the wall at OPCON, there was a huge chart of the area, with expanding noise zones displayed in red, pink and yellow. If the callers house was inside a red zone and complained of the noise, but there was no physical damage, he was reminded that he knew the problem existed when he bought the place and the Navy was under no obligation. If he lived in the pink or yellow zone and a window had been broken, the Navy would be obligated to pay for the repair and OPCON would immediately contact OLF to have the pattern "tightened up" or shut down. As of 2013, there is ongoing litigation pending results of an Environmental Impact Statement. When I was stationed there, as you drove down the highway approaching NAS Whidbey, there was a huge billboard displaying a flight of Navy aircraft with the logo "Pardon Our Noise, It's the Sound of Freedom". I would think that would apply to OLF, as well!

One of OPCON's collateral duties was to serve as the initial contact for squadron personnel casualty reporting. If called upon, we had a set of index cards with names and phone numbers of personnel to call should we be notified of a casualty. One of those was for the base or squadron Chaplain, who would set in motion the "Bereavement Team" to notify next of kin. Sadly, I had to use those index cards!

During my tour at Whidbey, the Falkland Island War between Britain and Argentina broke out. Being inside the basement of the building behind thick steel cypher-locked doors and two- foot thick concrete walls meant that throughout the conflict, WINGSPAC staff conducted their daily Intel Briefs covering events in the Falklands and were given in the room out front of our office. The office being closed off from the rest of the room by glass walls meant that we could crack the door open and listen to the entire brief, maps, graphics and narrative included. Each day the chief of staff, the intel officer, the admiral and a couple of staff "weenies" would show up around 8AM and brief the admiral on events transpiring since the previous day's briefing. We were all impressed with the Argie flyboys and if they'd had an army their equal the Brits would have been in more considerable trouble than they were. As it was, after a steep learning curve, the Brits got their act together. But, it wasn't cheap or easy!

During our second summer on Whidbey, we debated on how to keep the kids engaged, because with the wife working part-time there were too many hours of the day when the kids wouldn't be under adult supervision. That's when we found out what many of the other navy parents did with their kids! Make them work for their new school clothes! As June rolled around, the rural community surrounding Oak Harbor was engaged with harvesting all the various crops on the island and in the flat lands to the west of neighboring Mount Vernon. The farms would send buses out to the surrounding communities and collect workers at prearranged pick-up/drop-off stops. Any child over 12 could work half day shifts. Three of ours met that age limit. So we told them that if they wanted new school clothes, they would have to pitch in their share. For every $50 they earned, we would match it! The more you earned, the larger the match, the more money you would have for clothes. The older daughter wasn't too enthused, but the other two were already counting the money they could earn. Three mornings a week they would catch a bus out to whichever farm and crop was on the day's agenda and harvest whatever crop was there. Corn, beans, cucumbers, strawberries. The youngest came back one day with strawberry juice all over and quite a bit of it was around her mouth! Don't think she made much on that crop. In the end, the oldest boy and the youngest girl did very well. But it was the youngest daughter who outdid her much older brother for the season! She didn't like the work, but she did like the money. And, wouldn't you know it, she's been in the banking business most of her adult life!

A good buddy of mine from when I was stationed on *The Big E* called me up one day and told me he'd finished his flight training and got his pilot's license. That being accomplished, he had also put in for the flight-training program the Navy offered at Pensacola, Florida. Ultimately, his goal was to "get jets!" He was having a party and wanted to know if I could make it down to San Diego for the bash. Wild horses! So, I put a chit in for a couple days off on either end of the weekend of the party to give myself some extra leeway for travel. Then I checked the NALCO (Navy Airlift Command) flights leaving Whidbey for points south. The Friday I was to fly, I checked in at the terminal counter as "Space-A" hoping for a flight out on a small 12-seater that was flying to NAS El Centro, which would put me in close proximity to San Diego from which I hoped to catch a hop over to NAS North Island. Well, the flight was full and the loadmaster told me there was no more room. At that, he boarded the plane and I was left pondering what my next move should be. A couple minutes later the loadmaster returned and said I was to board the plane. What? He asked if I knew the pilot and I asked who that was. When he told me I broke into a smile and trotted out to board the plane. When I stepped inside I heard a familiar voice from the cockpit asking what kept me! Looking forward I saw the pilot grinning back at me! He happened to be one of the staff duty officers that rotated through OPCON and he and I had spent many boring hours chatting during our watches there. Taking the one remaining seat (the loadmaster had off-loaded some weight out of the cargo hold to off-set mine in the seat) I quickly noticed that my neighboring passenger was a four-striper (Captain). As we waited for the plane to take off, we chatted to pass the time. He asked where I was going and when I told him he said he was too. Hoping to catch a ride from El Centro to San Diego with him, I asked if I could tag along. Then he told me that when we got to El Centro he intended to have tower reroute the terminus of our flight to San Diego, so there would be no connecting flight or other means of transportation necessary.

On our flight over southern Oregon, we passed over Mount St. Helens, which had exploded the previous May. The pilot dipped his wings left and right for a bit so we could all get a look at the devastation wrought by such a cataclysmic event. Other than mile after mile of trees laid flat by the eruption on ridgeline slopes exposed to the blast and on the opposite slopes , there was little evidence of the blast. The IR air route we were flying down, managed by OPCON Whidbey, had only been reopened with authorization from the navy and by our office a few weeks since it had been closed the day of the eruption.

Landing at El Centro we debarked and I waited in the terminal for the four-striper to return from his efforts to reroute the flight. Sure enough, he soon appeared and motioned me along with him as we walked out to the aircraft and boarded. Next stop, North Island. Sweet! My buddy graduated flight training from Pensacola, but was heartbroken when he was told he'd got helicopters and not jets! He asked if I could make it to the graduation and give him his silver dollar and first salute. But, by then, I was aboard CGN-9 and my schedule was too busy to make that possible. Much to my regret!

My final six months at OPCON Whidbey was spent number-crunching. Somewhere up the food chain, the navy had decided a survey needed to be compiled, reflecting usages of all the OpAreas and air routes we managed. That meant going back through two years of paper documentation and gathering that data into a report. As by now I was the person with the longest tenure in the billets for OPCON, it fell to me to put the requisite information together. So I spent hundreds of hours going back through our archived documentation and retrieving those numbers for inclusion in the report. It was tedious and boring! But, the end result was illuminating because there, in one document, were all the statistics reflecting our tasking for the previous two years. And even before it was put into the official navy format, word had got around and a number of collateral commands, including the RAG Squadron, wanted a "raw" copy.

It was while I was stationed at Whidbey that the CNO announced the "Zero Tolerance" policy on drugs. This had never been an issue for me. But here I was, an E-6 at that point in my career, when I had already made up my mind to carry it through to retirement. What the CNO's new policy made me realize was that, while I wouldn't be forced to make a choice like some of my peers, it would change my perception of the navy. It was no longer "the Navy," I realized! It was *"my Navy."* The policy change would merely serve as the catalyst that sparked that change of mind-set. That was when it struck me! I was a "lifer"?

CHAPTER 18
USS LONG BEACH (CGN - 9)
16 JULY 1982 – 16 AUGUST 1987

I HAD BEEN TALKING WITH MY DETAILER trying to determine where I would be going once my stint was up at Whidbey. Evidently, those discussions had come to the attention of OSCM Jess Mahon, with whom I had served previously aboard *Connie*. I received a phone call from him while on duty at OPCON and he "sold" me on transferring to *USS Long Beach*. The pitch was that she was currently undergoing a complete overhaul classed as a "Mid-Life Conversion Phase II" at PSNSY Bremerton and would remain there until 23 March 1983! The extent of the overhaul was so complex and complete that just about everything aboard ship would be upgraded, reconditioned or replaced. The draw for me was two-fold! First, the move from Whidbey back to PSNSY Bremerton was familiar and short. Second, the Combat System being installed would be a one-off suite specifically designed for *Long Beach* and a compromise between current configurations and the newer AEGIS system. State of the art had always appealed to the "geek" in me and learning a new system was right up my alley!

During our conversation, OSCM had also asked if I could make it down to the shipyard prior to transfer because courses were being given by the contracted techreps to familiarize CIC personnel with the new CDS (Combat Direction System) being installed; taking the courses would give me a jump start on the learning process. I told him I'd see what I could do and went off to do just that! Very shortly, I was talking with a buddy of mine on the WingsPac staff who worked in personnel and she told me that if the two-week trip was "no cost to the government" it shouldn't be a problem. She told me to submit a request chit through my chain-of-command and she would make sure the proper authorizing signatures were acquired. In just a few days, the deal was done and I told OSCM I would be there for the courses.

A couple weeks later, I found myself walking down the pier towards the ship. When I first laid eyes on her she was disguised in the usual shipyard camouflage of scaffolding, welding leads, air and water hoses and other assorted and sundry work-a-day equipment. Even with all that, her sleek hull, missile launchers and gun mounts announced her power and purpose! And, then there was that huge, incongruous aluminum box superstructure! The "box" was originally built to accommodate the mounting of one of the first prototype "fixed, phased array" radars. The phased arrays had already been removed during this yard period because they no longer worked. So, now its only function would be as an aiming point for incoming missiles (as far as I was concerned). The two weeks in Bremerton passed quickly. I attended classes on the berthing barge tied up across the pier from the ship. I was able to have an EW1 take me aboard ship and show me around, being primarily interested in CIC and the OI Division spaces. Walking into CIC, located two decks below the chow hall, I was really surprised. There was nothing there but a deck, an overhead and four bulkheads. Every bit of equipment had been torn out in preparation for installation of the new equipment we were to receive when that stage of the overhaul arrived. And, that time was still a long way off!

After officially transferring from NAS Whidbey Island to CGN-9 on 16 July 1982, I berthed aboard the barge until I could locate a house for the family in town while they waited in Oak Harbor. The daily divisional work schedule did not leave much time for me to pursue a house search and it would be over two months before I could bring the family down to Bremerton. The wife was not very happy about that, but at least we were able to complete the move before school started in the fall so the kids didn't have to jump from one school to another during the school year. And, this wasn't out of the ordinary — we'd had to endure delays such as this before and would do so again when moving from Bremerton back down to San Diego when "*the Beach*" returned there.

While the ship was being put back together, as already mentioned, training for the CIC "gang" had already begun. OSCM was back in Dam Neck, Virginia at the Combat Direction Systems Facility shepherding a group of approximately 26 boots through a "mock up" specifically designed and configured to replicate the CIC they would be working in aboard CGN-9 when CIC was put back together. This group was fresh out of Boot Camp and as incentive to undergo this program, participants were given accelerated promotions to OS3 (commonly and derogatorily referred to as a "push-button 3rd). That was the carrot! The stick was that if you washed out or dropped out of the program, there was no deal! The other CIC personnel reporting to the ship, such as me, were going through the courses provided by the tech reps aboard the berthing barge across the pier from the ship. Additionally, any necessary NECs (job codes) that needed to be filled were either provided by sending personnel to the appropriate navy schools, having personnel en route report to the school first, or having personnel transfer in who already had the required NEC.

As the equipment was installed in CIC, power, water and air were hooked up. Once these services went on line, single equipment and element testing could begin. Once those basics were accomplished the next step was systems testing. For CGN-9, this meant that for the first time, the CIC crew would sit at their stations and perform their designated functions. During each of these evolutions, the crew was assisted and mentored by tech reps from the support facility at Dam Neck. The tech reps were also there to work out the bugs. And there were many! But because they were on site, the turn-around time from observation, write-up and solution was minimized considerably. Systems testing was conducted most afternoons and after dinner, finishing up around 6PM or 7PM depending on the level of difficulty, equipment glitches and post-testing debriefings.

As much as training had focused on station requirements, on NECs and on filling the Watch, Quarter & Station Bill (WQSB) billets, there was still the problem of being qualified aboard a ship and for a CIC that were both one-of-a-kind. You may have been qualified as Radar Piloting Officer aboard your previous command, but that didn't qualify you to stand that position aboard CGN-9. So, to overcome the problem as much as possible, the senior enlisted personnel had to build a CGN-9 Personal Qualification Standard (PQS). This meant building a systems-specific standard using cross-over requirements where they were common with other ships' stations or, where they were not, using CGN-9's Combat Systems Technical Manuals. It took almost six months to get it put together, publish a first-draft and get it approved by the command.

When *the Beach* got underway the first time for sea trials, there were 68 personnel assigned to CIC. Of these, 26 had never been to sea before and of the remainder, only 11 of us had been able to qualify for the stations required to get underway! Training and qualification continued even as we sailed down Sinclair Inlet, moved out into Puget Sound and made our way north and west for the open sea.

"TIGER CRUISE" (BREMERTON TO SAN DIEGO)

Before we departed Bremerton, the command announced it would sponsor a "Tiger Cruise" for male crew dependents. So fathers, sons and brothers were allowed to make the trip when requested by the sponsor, a member of the crew. I talked with my father about this rare opportunity and we made the arrangements for him to come along. At the time, my parents were living in Beaverton, Oregon so the train trip up to Seattle wouldn't be all that far and I met him at the station for the ferry ride back over to Bremerton. Getting him into the shipyard and aboard ship took most of the remaining day before our departure the next morning. Before I had to go on watch in CIC for Navigation Detail, I took him to breakfast and brought him down to CIC with me. He'd been in CIC on the *Connie* once while we were in port, but never before been in CIC with the lights out, radars turning and people manning their stations. And, he'd never seen the CDS system with all the data entries, vehicular tracks and navigation lines. So for the next couple hours, he sat at one of the consoles on the other side of CIC from me and watched the radar scope as we transited Puget Sound. Navigation Detail having been secured as we started west in the Juan de Fuca Strait and after lunch, I took dad up to the Flag Bridge to see the sights. When we had first got underway, I had asked if he would need anything for sea sickness (Dramamine or one of those patches you stick behind your ear) and he declined. But now, seeing the horizon rise and fall, he got a bit queasy and asked if I could get one of those patches. So, I dialed a corpsman buddy of mine and explained what the problem was. He asked where we were and when I told him, he said he'd be right up. Minutes later, dad got his patch and we headed back down below. After dinner I told him I needed to get some sleep on account of having the mid-watch, but before that I helped him get his rack made up and made sure he knew where the head was. So, I'm down in CIC and it's probably two or three in the morning when I get a call from one of the guys in OI Division berthing saying he had my dad there and he couldn't locate his rack. He'd gotten up to use the head and couldn't find his way back to bed. So, I told the watch officer the problem and excused myself to go take care of it. When I collected dad and took him around the corner to his bunk, he was pretty embarrassed. From the bunk to the head was about 30 feet. We got to spend some time together the remainder of the trip down south and it was good to have him along. Having arrived in San Diego, I took him to the airport and put him onto a plane back to Portland. Then, I called my mom and told her he was on his way! He'd been gone five days and I believe that was the longest they had been separated........ever!

USS Long Beach CGN-9

SOCAL WORK-UPS

Some officers, as with some enlisted personnel, were better or worse than others! *Long Beach* had her share. While steaming in SOCAL, I had been standing watch with a TAO(Tactical Action Officer) who could best be described as one of the latter. And, everyone interacted with him based on that conclusion. I was manning the AAWC console, when he asked me why he couldn't "hook" a piece of video on his console. I looked at him and was distressed to see that he was serious. You can't "hook" (take into local control) raw video; you can only "hook" a TDS track associated with that video, if one existed. There was no track associated with this piece of video. To humor him, I told him I would get a console tech to take a look and see if the "problem" could be fixed. So, I had a DS2 I was on good terms with come out and, before he got to the TAO, I explained to him what the problem was (the TAO, not the console). The DS2 smiled and nodded his head. Going over to the TAO, he listened to him relate what was wrong. The DS2 "tinkered around" for a bit and then told the TAO that he would have to take the console "down" and schedule a period when it could be worked on. Problem solved! Well, at least for the time being!

Another time, we were steaming south from Alaska when one of the watch officers asked me why there was no track on a piece of video he had been watching and tracking with grease marks on the "scope" face. I took a look at the video he was referring to and told him it was most likely an island, as there were many of them along the southern panhandle of Alaska, which we were passing. He gave me a peeved look and said, "No it isn't, I've been tracking it here with grease pencil and it's moving!" I asked him if he had compared the radar video with the navigation chart to confirm it wasn't an island and got another peeved look. So, after taking a range and bearing on the video in question, I walked over to the chart table and checked. Sure enough, there it was, his "moving" island! He and I didn't speak the rest of the watch! In all fairness to the officers, though, it was difficult enough for the enlisted personnel that worked in the CIC to grasp all the technical aspects of the various consoles, displays, control panels and peripheral equipment associated with our Combat Direction System. It was even more so for the officers because CIC was for the most part a "ticket" that needed to be "punched" on their career path. They would rotate into CIC from another department, stay for six months and then rotate to their next assigned "slot!" How can you become proficient doing that?

Three tours on two "bird farms" had not prepared me for the scope and depth of the training that would be necessary to fulfill all the requirements to master CIC's tasking aboard an AAW platform that also entailed being proficient in ASW, ASUW and NGFS (Anti-Submarine Warfare, Anti-SUrface Warfare, and Naval Gunfire Support). You don't fire guns, torpedoes (long range), anti-air or anti-surface missiles from a carrier. During the course of our SOCAL training I would be brought up to speed, but the learning curve was again a fast-paced and steep one to overcome in just six months' time. The schedule entailed classes at facilities ashore, local exercises in SOCAL at designated OpArea Ranges, and "in-house" training aboard ship using both our own experts as instructors and brought-aboard MTT (Mobile Training Team) personnel as instructors and ob-servers. We conducted countless "synthetic" exercises generated in-house as well as exercises with ships that would be sailing with us in the Battle Group. Some of these exercises were demonstrations held for the benefit of command and staff personnel in "mock-up" modules at FAAWTC on Point Loma, because they represented command and staffs first integration into the training. ASW training ashore was held in mock-up modules at the ASW Training Center and NGFS training was held in modules aboard the Amphibious Base on the strand, by Coro-nado. In the designated OpAreas in SOCAL, ASW TorpExs were held on the range to the west of San Clemente and NGFS was held off-shore San Clemente, firing at pre-arranged "targets" within the range on the island. Usually, there was more than one ship going through training and so other modules were manned by teams from other ships. When your event was done, your team was taken into an auditorium that had a huge scale sand table replica of the actual NGFS range on San Clemente. There, you could watch the efforts of the team currently work-ing their problem, with simulated rounds down range, spot, correction and fire-for-effect.

NAOPA (Naval Air Operating Area), between the California coast and San Clemente and the AOR's (Air Operating Ranges) to the south and west of the is-land was for helo and fixed wing ops within their limited boundaries. All of this required detailed planning and coordination, much of which had to allow for the crowded nature of SOCAL itself. Air corridors, sea lanes, fishing trawlers, and other private craft all had to be contended with and allowed for, within the construct of standing rules and agreements. There were numerous times where exercises would have to be canceled, interrupted or placed in a holding status to allow for areas to be cleared of interlopers.

Anti-Surface Warfare (ASUW) training not only required NGFS training, but on account of the addition of Harpoon box launchers added to the ship during our overhaul, it now also required that we go through the training required for the employment of that system. Classroom instruction was held aboard ship with tech-reps providing the instruction. After classroom work, we moved to CIC to incorporate the use of the HWS weapons control panel and our CDS system into the training. When ashore facilities could be scheduled, more training was conducted in the use of Harpoon at modules aboard the ASW Training Center. All of this culminated in a "live fire" exercise in SOCAL using as a "target" a decommissioned U.S. Navy ship. With range time, chase planes and our target, this was a *very* expensive demonstration!

ASW training and the preferred method to prosecute an underwater target was with the use of aircraft and at extended range. However, CGN-9 did have a sonar suite and both CIC and sonar trained in scenarios demonstrating the ship's capability in that field. But we also spent a considerable amount of time and manpower practicing the "art" of TMA (Target Motion Analysis). TMA uses passive (preferred) or active (not preferred) lines-of-sound (LOS), fed from sonar to CIC and plotted on the NC-2. This would show you what LOS the target was on and by maneuvering the ship at sharp angles to the LOS, you could calculate range, course and speed using established formulas (T-Hat & T-Squared; Ekelund) and applying "speed strips" across the minimum/maximum range LOSs. As stated, and as we learned during training, this was more "art" than science. With continual practice and talented personnel, your results could improve to the point of acceptable accuracy. Most times!

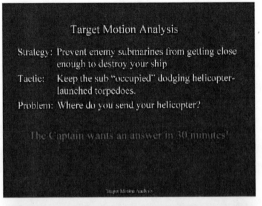

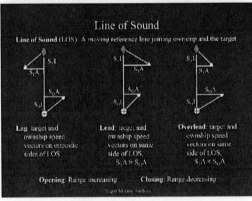

So, are we clear on this?

Note: CGN-9 was equipped with the NC-2 in lieu of a DRT. Canadian manu-factured, "The Anti- Submarine Warfare (ASW) plotting system NC2 was used in the ship's Combat Information Center (CIC) or similar shipboard areas for dead reckoning plotting of ship's position and moving or stationary underwater, surface, or airborne targets. The systems are used extensively for ASW operations and related tactical situations, as well as an aid to navigation." The NC-2 brought added capa-bilities over the DRT, but also brought its own set of problems. First, was the fact that if some of the inputs were tracing contacts, as well as own ship, it would take more than one person to operate because there were always more contacts in addition to these. Second, was maintenance! All too frequently, input data, drive gears or com-pass roses' would fail and without resident expertise and parts support, these features were not always available.

Another proficiency practiced weekly in port and applied daily at sea was the establishment and maintenance of the Link-11 tactical data link between your own unit and those of ships operating together and ships within the operational range of the configured data link. In port, this was done as a training tool, both for your own ship and other ships in port. Message traffic was generated for each weekly exercise, providing transmitting frequencies, track-block assignments, designation of the NCS (Net Control Station) and other necessary information. Bringing up "the net" required coordination between those personnel in Radio assigned to support the drill and those personnel in CIC to man the required stations and TDS consoles. With all the hours spent at sea maintaining a tactical net 24/7, it would seem this function would be more on the order of a routine, seamless effort. But, in port, it all too often required more effort than it should! Although most everyone above a certain grade was expected to know how to bring up and configure a Link-11 network, such was not the case. Getting underway and proceeding out to sea was a different story because there were no in-port distractions and the "resident experts" were available to overcome any difficulties. By the time the ship cleared the harbor, Link-11 was up and "ping pong" (data exchange) with the other PU's (Participating Units) was good!

And then, there was RefTra! RefTra included the emergency sortie through the simulated minefield, the repeated GQs, and the simulated "hits" and efforts by the repair parties to overcome the (simulated) damage. Hits were simulated in CIC and (simulated) casualties were given first aid by OSs applying dressings, splints, tourniquets or whatever was necessary. (Simulated) shoring was applied to breached bulkheads. During one simulated "hit" one of the outer bulkheads was "breached" and one of the RefTra observers told one of our young OSs that the breach needed to be shored. As there was no shoring immediately available, the young lad was at a loss as to how to shore the simulated hole in the bulkhead. The observer pointed out that when no shoring was immediately available, there were (simulated) dead bodies available to stuff the hole and stanch the flow of seawater into the ship until shoring could be applied. You could see the abhorrent realization of what was being asked cross the young man's face. And, I'm sure it was also the thought that his dead body could be used to do the same.

The threat of CBR (Chemical, Biological, Radiation) was also injected into the scenarios and the crew had to react accordingly. Coming out of the shipyard, the ship had been issued the latest CBR suits and we actually donned these for familiarization — the only time I ever fully suited up during my career! Once Ref-Tra was over, it was on to more complex tactical training involving other ships at the same stage of training as we were and those that would also deploy with us. COMPTUEX, READIEX & FLEETEX were all required leading up to our scheduled deployment.

"Shipping Over" 1984: L to R OSCM (SW) Mahon, OI DIVO & author

CHAPTER 19
WESTPAC '84 USS LONG BEACH
13 JANUARY - 1 AUGUST 1984

Deployed: 201 days
In port: 45 days
At Sea/Underway: 156 days

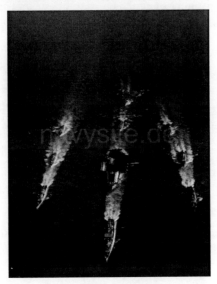

Battle Group Bravo

USS Kitty Hawk (CV-63); USS Long Beach (CGN-9); USS Chandler (FFG-996); USS Lewis B. Puller (FFG-23); USS Stein (FF-106); USS Harold E. Holt (FF-1079); USS O'Brien (DD-975); USS Berkley (DDG-15) & USS Wabash (AOR-5)

THE "BEAR BOX"

We had been assigned to the *USS Kitty Hawk* (CV-63) Battle Group for this WestPac deployment and departed CONUS 13 January 1984. We had a few days in port at Pearl Harbor before departing with the rest of the BG headed west. We were a day or two out of Pearl when the ship experienced a reduction gear failure which required us to drop out of the Battle Group and return to Pearl for repairs.

The ship pulled into Pearl Harbor a couple days later and then moved to the dry dock at Hospital Point, because the repair work would require us to be out of the water. As we had all spent liberty in Honolulu just a few days previously, most of us had spent our funds accordingly and were broke. Our CO, aware of the problem, told the Disbursing Officer to commence holding paydays every other day, for our remainder of time in port. Our esteem for our skipper immediately soared to record heights. We all realized he'd used a command prerogative in consideration of his crew and we wouldn't forget this gesture any time soon!

Repairs were completed and we departed Hawaii 18 Feb. En route to rejoin our Battle Group, our transit would take us through the "Bear Box" and an encounter with the Russians. The "Bear Box" was an area of ocean northeast of Guam and was established by the customary intercept area the Russians were normally encountered in throughout the Cold War. Typically, this was done by them for USN Battle Groups and capital ships arriving from the West Coast and Hawaii during their transit to WestPac. Each deployment I made while aboard the *Connie* had experienced the "Bear Box" and our BG preceding us for this WestPac had experienced it ahead of us. Normally, one Bear Delta would make the intercept, but on occasion two would show up with one flying "up top" and the other flying very low and within visual range of the carrier. CAP was always launched and maintained for the expected period of the "fly-by" and they would make their intercept with each of the Russian aircraft at specifically planned ranges from the carrier. Each CAP for this occurrence consisted of two fighters, one stationed "in trail" and the other stationed below the bomber. Of course, this was changed if the bomber was in a "low-e" (low elevation) approach.

During *Long Beach's* transit it wasn't really expected that the Russians would put on the show for a lone ship, but we had planned for it should they decide to make an appearance. Which they did! As soon as we got "tipper" information that a flight had left Vladivostok, we entered "Line of Bearing" (LOB) data to the tactical data display and calculated the range, bearing and time of intercept using updated inputs from our "remote source." While our "opponent" was still hours away, the ship was placed in EMCON Alpha, which was a total blackout of all ship's transmissions. Frequent updates to his bearing from us showed that he remained on his prescribed course for the duration of the transit. Eventually our track data showed that he had passed his closest point to us, which our own internal "tennis shoe" types verified, and was now opening range. Shortly after this aspect was reported to the Tactical Action Officer (TAO), who forwarded the information to the CO, orders were passed to "light 'em up" and the ship came out of EMCON, all radios and radars "shining." When our radar picture came up, we were immediately able to locate and established track on the Bear Delta, who even at that moment was in a turn and coming back towards us, because he had detected our emissions. He made his overflight, we made our point, and everyone was satisfied!

The usual encounters with overflights occurred during every WestPac and for each BG, as well. As is evidenced with the photos, below!

29 Feb 1984 @ Sea of Japan   *19 March 1987 & F-14 Tomcat Escort*

TEAM SPIRIT '84

Our first scheduled port call was Yokosuka Naval Base and we were only there for three days (2-4 March). Leaving Yokusuka, we made our way south, around Kyushu and into the Sea of Japan. Exercise Team Spirit would be our next evolution and we had been assigned as AAWC for our first portion of the joint exercise with the South Korean Navy (6-14 March). Upon completion of this segment of our assignment, we pulled into Inchon, South Korea for liberty call (15-17 March). The approach to Inchon is tricky and there are many islets and mudflats to avoid. The tidal change is drastic here, creating added difficulty to navigation for deep draft vessels such as *the Beach*. To allow for that, the ship had to drop anchor a considerable distance from the port itself. For liberty transport, the local water taxis provided service and each could carry around 30 to 40 people. After the initial surge of personnel leaving the ship, getting back and forth was fairly quick and easy. The port had been constructed using huge blocks forming a 30-foot sea wall to compensate for the tidal shifts, which exceeded 20 feet. So, the launches carrying us back and forth to town would tie up to floating piers that were moored to pilings rising over 30 feet out of the water — the piers moved up and down with the radical tidal shifts. The only other port I saw with such radical tidal swings would be a couple years later, in Anchorage, Alaska.

Naturally, one of the days in port I had duty! There was a planning conference being held aboard the carrier that day and because I had duty and was also one of the three qualified AAWCs aboard ship, I was tagged to attend. The weather had been cold, so I dressed accordingly, thermals underneath my dress blues and my overcoat, with gloves. To get to the conference, I would have to take a MWB (Motor Whale Boat) across the bay to the carrier and as I climbed down the A-comm (accommodation) ladder I could see it wasn't going to be a fun ride. There was already a good chop on the water and the wind was coming from the direction the boat would have to take to get to the carrier. Sure enough, once we got going, the wind was right on our nose and the chop was coming over the bow, so I moved further aft to avoid the spray. The double layer of clothing was quickly overcome by the biting cold wind and by the time we got there, I was numb. There was a petty officer waiting to take me up to the conference, which was in a space adjacent to CIC and as we walked through that space, I spotted the coffee pots and stopped to grab a cup, my hands still shaking from the freezing cold trip. Now, I was ready for the meeting!

Later I was able to make a trip up to Seoul for some sightseeing. We spent the night, and the next morning we were eating a late breakfast in a 3rd floor restaurant in the Itaewon district when suddenly sirens began to wail outside. We all craned our necks looking out the window and watched in amazement as the people below cleared the street in less than a minute. Just like that, the streets were devoid of life! We asked the waiter what was going on and he casually told us it was a regularly scheduled air raid drill and would be over soon. Sure enough, a short time later another siren wailed (all clear) and people started to emerge back into the street as if nothing had happened. Living under the ever-present reality of possible attack from the NORKs is not something a non-resident would even consider! Until you witnessed an event such as this! Our topic of discussion the rest of breakfast was how seriously everyone took the drill and the fact that "you'd never see that in the States" until after the bombs or missiles started falling!

One other item of interest was that while making our way to the train station in Inchon, I was duly impressed by a huge statue in a round-about, of Douglas MacArthur. Fitting, given the locale!

COLLISION-AT-SEA (21 MARCH 1984)

Back out to sea for the conclusion of Team Spirit 84-1, the ship had been operating in the Sea of Japan, north of the Tsushima Strait and off the south coast of Korea. There had been numerous encounters with the Russians, both surface and aircraft, mostly north of the strait.

During the course of our participation in the joint exercise, the Battle Group had been collaterally tracking a Soviet V-3 submarine located to the north in our battle space. We had conducted tracking and hold-down tactics to let the sub know that we knew he was there. But after the point had been made, the BG proceeded to reorient its assets and prepare to conduct the next scheduled event in support of Exercise Team Spirit. Accordingly we had stopped tracking the V-3. The sub skipper, on the other hand, had not lost interest in the BG!

The BG was operating in a dual environment: support of Exercise Team Spirit and doing the "cold war shuffle" with the Soviets. Although we had stopped tracking the V-3, there were a number of other Soviet assets we encountered daily. As part of "the game" a DECOPs (Deceptive Operations) period was scheduled for the late evening/early morning hours of 21 March 1984. DECOPs is the attempt to confuse and mislead the opponent about the identification and location of your assets. This particular period, the carrier and CGN-9 would be the players in this ruse, which consisted of altering our visual, acoustic and electro-magnetic signatures while steaming in close proximity and then, when the affects had been made, to open range and bearing and monitor the response of the opponent.

Shortly after 10PM and as the two ships commenced opening range and bearing, we received a report from the carrier that it had experienced what it suspected was a collision. Almost instantly, on an internationally monitored distress frequency, which was on an open speaker in CIC, we could hear an obviously excited voice, in Russian. Our intel personnel were told to patch into the voice circuit and monitor what was being transmitted. *Kitty Hawk* was listening to the same thing and both ships recognized that *Kitty Hawk* had been involved in a collision with a submarine. One could suspect that, confused by the change in our acoustic signatures and not realizing that the carrier was effectively in his "baffles" and may have been operating below cavitation speed, the Russian skipper had decided to come up to periscope depth to "take a look see." A costly mistake on his part!

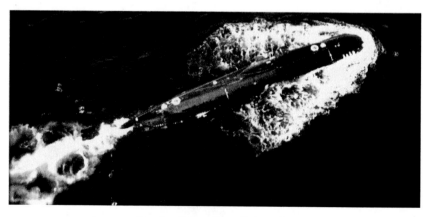

Russian Victor Class Submarine

It was quickly decided that the BG should displace south, passing through Tsushima Strait and clear the area so the Russians would realize there would be no interference of their rescue operations from us. One of our escorts was detached and directed to stand off at an appropriate distance in case the Russians requested outside assistance or until such time as their rescue vessels reached the area and also to meet our required international obligations of rescue at sea.

By the time the exercise was over and the BG had transited to our next port-of-call, Subic Bay Naval Base, R. P., the incident was widely known. To what extent, we didn't realize until out on liberty when we saw clothing shops up and down the street with T-shirts on display blaring CV-63 1, V-3 0 and other variations to that effect.

Also, while in port, *Kitty Hawk's* hull was inspected. A portion of the sub's propeller had lodged in the *Kitty' Hawk's* hull near the bow and a portion of the subs "anechoic coating" was found. The propeller was cut into pieces and one piece went to the CO of *Kitty Hawk*. The destination of the other two pieces was speculated upon and rumors abounded.

To those of us who were aware about the extent of the damage to the submarine, it was a sobering reminder of how deadly our "game" could be and how costly a mistake might prove.

Fifteen sailors died that night!

"GOO" & 75 DAYS AT SEA
UNDERWAY: 8 APRIL TO 21 JUNE 1984

After spending the first week of April in port at Subic Bay, the ship departed for the Middle East. It would be over two months later before our next port call. We proceeded south and made passage through the Malacca Straits. The straits were so heavily trafficked that CIC and the Bridge had to set a modified Navigation Detail — added personnel were available to handle the increased "traffic" that we were required to plot and maneuver through.

CGN-9 was assigned as AAW Picket station in the Gulf of Oman ("GOO"), outside the Arabian Sea but including the Straits of Hormuz and key Iranian military sites within our sensor and missile ranges. And, there we stayed! The first couple weeks were spent familiarizing ourselves with our assigned duties and our "neighbors." One of our key communications links and our "air support," should it be necessary, was a secure communications link with the Omani Air Force. The officers and pilots we spoke with were all graduates of the British RAF Academy at Cranwell, and spoke fluent Oxford English. And we could also call upon any available U.S. military aircraft should that opportunity arise. One of our other early efforts was directed at familiarizing ourselves with the large numbers of civilian air traffic and identifying their various routes within our "controlled air space." We soon noticed that when the Arab "weekend" arrived, there was a heavy increase in civilian air traffic originating in the Gulf States (UAE) en route to India. At the beginning of the weekend, there were hundreds of flights going east and at the end of the weekend there were hundreds of flights going west. The "locals" were going there to do what they were forbidden to do at home! Party like a rock star!

We were there primarily to keep tabs on the Iranians, and we had been briefed on some of their routine activities, which we would be involved in monitoring. One of these was their established routine of conducting "maritime air patrols" in their U.S.-built P-3 Orion aircraft. After all, we had trained them in this process and all the Iranian pilots spoke fluent American English. We knew when they were airborne and when one of their maritime patrol aircraft was within our airspace we kept constant track of their progress. We also had a procedure to conduct when they came too close. A warning was issued, in the clear over IAD (International Air Distress) calling them by their IFF "squawk," giving them their location in relation to an established navigational aid and informing them that they were "standing into danger" and to conform to a specific flight profile to clear our area. Without fail, they would acknowledge our call and make the required change to their route. With current variations applied, this procedure is still used in the Gulf today!

After the first few weeks, everything was pretty much routine and the daily grind had set in. Because my sleeping compartment was on the third deck, the mess decks were on the second deck and CIC was on the fourth deck, the opportunity did not present itself for me to regularly see sunshine. It would be over a month before I finally had to make it a point to go topside and actually witness that daylight still existed! Rather like a mole, I suspect! The days crept by, eight hours on watch in CIC, a couple hours spent working at the ever-present task of personnel management (paperwork, paperwork and more paperwork)! Then a few hours in my rack sleeping, before starting the routine all over again. By the second month, the men were complaining, asking for any break in the routine or watch rotation. After some deliberation and consultation with the command, we were able to institute a rotation of personnel that allowed us to gradually shift men from one watch rotation to the other (port & starboard being our scheduled rotation). This was accomplished by "dogging the watch" and moving small numbers of men from one watch section to the other and vice versa until all personnel had made the switch. As the guys all realized, this was about the only possible solution, given our manning requirements and our current duties. So realizing we had done what we could, the griping fell off to its usual level and everyone got on with it!

The ship had been at sea and on-station for more than a month when we were ordered south to the Omani island of Masirah. There, we dropped anchor off the coast! We were taking advantage of the airfield there for transshipment by helo of some needed spare parts and for mail, the latter being the most appreciated, of course! We only spent the day there before weighing anchor and proceeding back up to our assigned AAW station. We had been back on station a few days when, during the course of the daily routine, CIC picked up multiple and very faint radar signatures on aircraft flying from India toward the Gulf and not on any of the civilian air routes we would normally track them on. Our reaction was to establish their identity by making voice calls on the normal frequencies and by vectoring an air asset to their location for a visual ID. No responses from these aircraft were immediately forthcoming and it wasn't until the fighter under our control pulled up alongside of the three aircraft in question that we learned these were small private planes being ferried to the Gulf by American civilians under contract. One of their pilots finally came up on IAD and declared who he was, his destination and his surprise when the fighter showed up alongside him. We all got a good chuckle out of that as we sent him on his way, and for a short time, under escort!

After two months on station, we finally got our "beer ration." Strictly controlled and monitored, you lined up on the fantail, were issued two "chits" for two beers, your name was crossed off a roster list and you proceeded, in line, to the point where you surrendered your "chits" for two warm cans of beer. Not that any of us minded them being warm! After that length of time, two would do and I for one enjoyed them more so because it was cause for me to be up on deck, in the fresh air and daylight!

Finally released from our AAW station, we proceeded south by south-east, en route for our much-anticipated port call in Australia and our rendezvous with King Neptune and his court of scallywags! I mean shellbacks!

CROSSING THE LINE 6 JUNE 1984

Shellbacks & Pollywogs

The age-old custom of mariners when crossing the equator was upheld when CGN-9 crossed over on its way to Australia. As part of the initiation, us "wogs" spent a good deal of time on our hands and knees crawling along on the deck where the "non-skid" made short work of our dungaree pants and in no-time I was bleeding at the knees from the abrasive surface. Our route took us through the various stations set up by the Shellbacks that ensured everyone was "put through the wringer" in good order. This meant crawling through garbage, getting swatted on the ass with paddles and kissing the greased-up belly of the fattest Shellback aboard! After it was over, I tended to the problem of my abrasions as best I could and hoped that was good enough. But, after both knees scabbed over, the right knee still showed inflammation around the area, and I knew I had a problem. The day before we were to pull into port, I went to see an HM (corpsman) who could fix me up. Officially, if I went to sick call to have it tended to, I risked the chance of being put on the sick list and restricted aboard (no liberty). So after explaining my predicament, the HM gave me some peroxide, gauze and medical tape that I could use for a "DIY" repair job. I waited until the head had cleared out during the morning and went in to make the fix. I was able to remove the scab (I passed out for a brief period when ripping it off) swabbed it out with peroxide (passed out again) and when I came to, was able to put a good, snug dressing on. It healed up nicely and never was an issue during liberty ashore! After 75 days at sea, there was no way I was sitting this one out aboard ship!

A Shellback at Last

HMAS STIRLING 22 - 26 JUNE 1984

While the *Kitty Hawk* BG pulled into Perth, Australia, CGN-9 was directed to proceed to the Australian Navy base at HMAS Stirling. The base was on an island connected to the mainland by a 2.7 mile long causeway, at the end of which was the quaint town of Rockingham, WA (Western Australia) with a population of around 15,000.

Garden Island, HMAS Stirling & Rockingham WA

The reason for our "exile" from Perth was our nuclear reactor and if we were to follow the rest of the BG to Perth, it was feared there would be a large crowd of protestors with attendant media. So, with us neatly tucked away on an island 50 miles removed, that concern was greatly mitigated, but not entirely eliminated. The first two days at HMAS Stirling, there were small crowds of protestors at the mainland side of the causeway, but due to the remoteness from Perth, the detachment from the protestors to the object of their protest and the lack of media interest, their impact was marginalized and they quietly resigned from the effort by the third day.

Every port is different and so is every country, but the differences and the similarities are not always striking in the way I would expect, given the majority of overseas ports that I had been to during my career. After Singapore, Hong Kong, Tokyo and Manila, being in Australia felt almost like I was back in the

States. It was so much like America that, if you didn't count the Aussie accent, you would almost swear you were back in the USA. Even the "smell" of Australia seemed more West Coast U.S. than I was used to overseas. I imagine that this was partly due to the fact that "down under" during that season of the calendar is their winter and after over three months in the heat of GOO and the tropics of PI, this was our first exposure to cooler weather. While Japan is neat as a pin and Singapore is spotless, they still held that foreign scent which was unmistakable to my American nose! I'm sure that any person, returning home from abroad, can relate the same experience regardless of the country he's from.

It had taken three-quarters of my career and a 75-day stint underway to "earn" this port call and I was very excited about the whole idea of "Australia!" Alas, my duty section assignment meant that I would only be able to have two consecutive days ashore before having to report back aboard for my duty day. That meant very limited travel possibilities. I settled for staying in Rockingham and was able to get around town some. The hotel I stayed at had an adjoining restaurant and the locals were most accommodating. I met an Aussie sailor and he took me around to some of the pubs in town, but after a couple of "oil cans" I'd had enough. And, the "meat pies"? Well, for me, it's an acquired taste that I didn't have enough time to spend acquiring!

Leaving Australia, the ship headed north for a transit through Lombok Straits, past Bali and through the Makassar Strait into the Celebes Sea and then the Sulu Sea. This was a part of the world I had never been in or transited through previously and I made several trips topside to get a look at many of the hundreds of islands we were passing. We were headed home, by way of a short stopover in Subic (5-9 July), before transiting the San Bernardino Strait, out into the Pacific and headed north by east for another short stop at Pearl to pick up some "Tigers."

CHAPTER 20

LOADING "TIGERS:" PEARL HARBOR, HI

23 – 24 JULY 1984

WE HAD BEEN INFORMED a considerable time before our port-call in Pearl that a "Tiger Cruise" was to be allowed during our transit from Hawaii to San Diego. This meant that male dependents would be allowed to come aboard while we were there and ride the ship back to San Diego with their kin. So, I had made arrangements for my youngest son Sean to fly over with a group of other "Tigers" and I would meet him when he arrived. Once we hooked up, I checked him in aboard ship, took him to his bunk and showed him how to get around the ship so he would know how to get to chow, CIC and back to his bunk – all this so when we were underway, I wouldn't have to worry about him too much. Because we only had the day of his arrival before the ship departed the following day, we had limited time for me to take him around and do some site-seeing. But the ship had laid on a luau on the grounds of the Hale Koa Hotel in Waikiki for that evening, so we were able to enjoy that event. The first evening of our voyage back to San Diego, I was able to take dinner with him. The chow-hall was serving up the second go-round of our provisions from Australia, which they had saved for this "Tiger Cruise." When Sean saw those huge steaks and lobsters, he was thoroughly impressed. I made sure though, that he understood this was not the norm and from where the food had been procured! Still, that was one of his favorite topics when we arrived back in San Diego!

FLEET WEEK, SAN FRANCISCO, OCTOBER 1984

The ship arrived stateside the end of July and the crew had two months when personnel were rotated onto and off of leave – for those who wanted to do so! No sooner had the end of that period arrived than we were scheduled to partic- ipate with many of the ships from our former Battle Group in San Francisco's annual Fleet Week celebration. The ships assigned sortied from San Diego during the first couple days of October and proceeded north for the festivities. We formed up in a column, with *USS San Francisco* (SSN-711) as the lead ship. During this Navigation Detail, I was not obligated to man a station, so I was able to go topside and be a "spectator" for a change. As was my experience aboard the *Hood* this approach would be through a very dense, low-lying fog bank. However, ap- proaching the headlands to the south of the channel, the fog began to thin and we could just make out the throngs of people standing on the shoreline watching as we slowly proceeded toward the Golden Gate. Just a couple hundred yards short of the bridge the fog bank ended and there was the bridge, absolutely jammed with people. The bridge was so crowded with people, in fact, that the crest of the bridge actually flattened out some from the weight. Then the rest of the shoreline became visible and it seemed as if every square inch was packed with spectators. Just after passing under the bridge, SSN-711 up ahead came to the point in the channel where she would make her turn to the SSE and this was the prearranged signal for the Blue Angels to make their appearance. Bursting over the hills and flying low, they made for the point where SSN-771 was making her turn and just as they arrived at the spot they all went vertical! You could hear the crowd roar in awe and excitement. It was quite the spectacle and all hands that were topside manning the rails were just as impressed as the civilians! The *Beach* proceeded up the Bay and down past the piers of the Embarcadero, where most of the ships were to tie up. But we, being nuclear, were not welcome there and continued on to our assigned berth at NAS Alameda! There was a lot of bitching among the division about being so far removed from the action down- town, but I knew it wasn't all that bad. So, leaving the ship with a few of the guys, I headed over to the BART station, which was not that far from the base. We had to grab a cab for the ride through the tunnel, but it was a short ride from there. Hopping on the BART, we took the ride under the Bay and got off at the station closest to the piers. Walking down the Embarcadero, we realized we had actually caught a break by tying up at Alameda. This was because the following day, the ships tied up along the Bay would all be holding open house. Tour guides, lost kids and endless questions! No thanks!

Although, it was quite a walk, we were soon down around Pier 39. The place was packed. One family even stopped us so they could have their picture taken with some "swabbies" – the first day in port we were all required to wear our uniforms. We all got a chuckle out of that. We spent the day walking through the shops and venues of Pier 39 and moved on to Fisherman's Wharf. There we grabbed a bite to eat; my favorite was a small sourdough roll fresh out of the oven, split open and stuffed with fresh Dungeness crab and washed down with a glass of Anchor Steam beer! Can't beat it!

Early that evening the guys asked me if I knew a good place to "hang out" and knock back some brews. I had heard of a place, but had not been there so we grabbed a cab, told the driver the name of the place and he took us there. The bar was in a neighborhood of old two- and three-story Victorian houses, sprinkled with small mom-and-pop grocery stores, delis and the like. I do recall that over the door hung the front end of a Cadillac! Quite the eye catcher! Anyway, we had only been there a short while when, standing at the bar, my foot up on the rail and elbows on the bar, someone grabbed my ass. Now, being in San Francisco, that always begs the question as to which gender was doing the grabbing. Quickly turning around, I was relieved to find that a female was standing there smiling and asked if I was going to be there awhile as she had to leave for a bit. I told her I hadn't been there long so didn't have plans to go anywhere soon. When she showed up later she took me to a couple of her favorite hang-outs, where she could be seen with a sailor by people she knew. As she was paying, I wasn't complaining!

The third day in port, I bumped into some of the guys from the division who had recently come ashore and they told me that I had been tasked to attend a conference the next day aboard one of the ships tied up at the Embarcadero. I was being sent there as the AAWC representative for an upcoming exercise that was to take place off the coast. Well, the following morning when I arrived at the pier where the ship was tied up, it was pouring rain, I didn't have an umbrella and the ship was a long way down the pier. So, pushing my jacket up over my head, I made a dash down the pier for the gangway and arrived absolutely soaked to the bone! Coming aboard, I asked where the conference was being held and was directed to the Wardroom. As I entered the room, I got a lot of looks from the group because of how drenched my clothes were, but no one said anything. And, I wasn't called upon to provide any input so the entire thing was a waste of time and a miserable trip! When I got back to the ship later that day, no one in the command asked me about the meeting! Did anyone even know whether I'd been there or not?

ANTI-SUBMARINE AIR CONTROLLER (ASAC) SCHOOL
17 DECEMBER 1984 TO 1 FEBRUARY 1985

In preparation for the ship's next deployment overseas and to fill billeting requirements in compliance with the Battle Organization Manual (BOM) and the Watch, Quarter & Station Bill personnel had to be aboard with the requisite training and qualifications to enable the ship to prosecute ASW (Anti-Submarine Warfare) at extended ranges and over-the-horizon. This meant that two currently qualified ASACs were needed. One was ordered in from another command and I was selected to attend the training course for ASAC at the FAAWTC, Point Loma. The curriculum and control time of both synthetic and live aircraft was an FAA accredited course and upon graduation would carry with it an FAA assigned controller ID number. During each successive quarter thereafter, the graduate had to maintain his qualification by logging the necessary minimum control time using either synthetic or live aircraft or a combination of the two. Under MTT (Mobile Training Team) observation, this could also be accomplished aboard a ship that was capable of generating synthetic video into its CDS, which CGN-9 was capable of performing.

During the course, we spent a goodly portion of time in class with instruction in the reference documents and publications that were to be used. About the fourth week, we were introduced to the "mock-up" module, where we were familiarized with use of the equipment installed, because many of us had differing equipment aboard our assigned ships. Once classroom lessons were completed, the remainder of the course consisted of briefings, mock-up simulated control periods and de-briefings. These simulated control periods got progressively more difficult due to the added requirement that the student had to employ proper tactics in the prosecution of a simulated "target," based on data being provided over the R/T net in the headset each of us wore. This continued until everyone had completed the minimum hours of synthetic air-control required. So now you had to be aware of each aircraft's weapons and sonobuoy loadout, its fuel remaining and "bingo" state (time versus fuel remaining for him to get home), and the "target's" capabilities. You also had to be aware of other assets available and time required to bring them into the "engagement" and what to do with them when they arrived, all stacked at various altitudes and awaiting your direction as to where and when they would be employed. Then, there was the weather! Out at sea, in the open ocean, weather was of primary concern regarding even the feasibility of prosecuting the target!

One requirement levied by the Fleet & Type Commanders was that the ship must demonstrate its ability to conduct a Low-level Visibility Approach (LLVA) as a prerequisite to certification of its flight deck. Actually landing a helo during low-level visibility meant that the controller (ASAC) had to talk the pilot through the prescribed flight path and onto the flight deck, providing constant range and bearing and any corrections necessary. The ship could demonstrate this by conducting the event at sea with an actual helicopter or having MTT aboard to observe a simulated, synthetic demonstration. As CGN-9 had no hangar and therefore no air detachment stationed on-board, any aircraft we needed to get this requirement accomplished would have to be "borrowed" from someone else. Time and asset availability ruled out using actual aircraft, so a simulated demonstration was scheduled with MTT. The two ASACs assigned to the ship (me and another OSC) would have to each go through the demonstration successfully or the ship and its flight deck would not be certified for LLVA situations. An LLVA is oriented such that the aircraft commences its approach from a predetermined range and bearing from the ship and aligned relative to the "line-up lines" painted on the flight deck. In real-world scenarios wind speed, barometric pressure and ship's speed are all critical considerations. Although these were simulated and noted during the synthetic run, the import of those conditions not being "live" mitigated much of what was being demonstrated. Two successful runs each (port and starboard approaches) were required from each controller. In the end, both of us were successful and then it was onto our "live" demonstration runs out at sea, conducted with "live" helos and graded by FTG (Fleet Training Group). Although the environment was not in actual reduced visibility, the approach corridor and procedures for LLVAs were required during these runs. After conducting three each, we passed the tests and the ship and flight deck was certified, LLVA's included!

As I will relate later and during a real-world submarine prosecution, I would be controlling and tasking a P-3, H-3 and a pair of S-3 aircraft simultaneously! Granted, some would be under "Positive Control" and others would be standing by, under "Advisory Control." Others would be checking off station and some would be checking in for tasking. All of this would be going on while directing the tactical employment of sonobuoys and attempting to enter all that data into the NTDS console I was using during the prosecution of the target. The sheer volume of input data had overtaken the man-in-the-loop (me) and a solution had to be improvised on-the-spot! This was something not considered by the school curriculum.

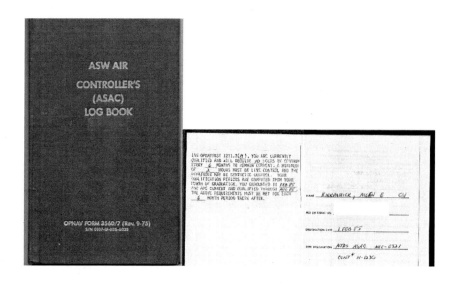

BACK TO PSNSY BREMERTON, WA 5 JANUARY '85

After Fleet Week in October, the ship returned to San Diego for a short stint, but on January 5th 1986, the ship got underway for an encore visit to PSNSY, Bremerton. It was time for the ship to get Tomahawk! Arriving on 9 January, work was soon underway for the TWS installation and a few other key pieces of equipment as well. But, I was not onboard! As related above, I was enrolled in ASAC School and wouldn't' return to the ship until February.

Even then, I would not remain for long because I had been assigned to attend OS "C" School, up on the hill at Point Loma, at FAAWTC (Fleet Anti-Air Warfare Training Center) and completion of the course would not be until 13 September. OS "C" School seats were assigned to senior enlisted OSs (E-6 and above), provided as an advanced curriculum to polish their technical skills as well as a refresher in the more complicated CIC tasks such as progressive maneuvering board problems involving multi-ship formations and station keeping. Many of us spent hours poring over our notes before each weekly quiz and even more hours before the final. But we were all envious of one of our classmates, who seemed immune to our problem. He aced almost every quiz and on the final, scored higher than us all. In the end, he was recognized as having maintained the highest GPA to ever have been attained by an OS "C" school student! And, when I mentioned this to my OSCM, he successfully lobbied the guy to accept orders to CGN-9!

It was toward the end of my studies at "C" school that I found out I had turned in a good score on my exam for chief and that, combined with my evaluations, had led the Selection Review Board to select me for advancement to OSC (E-7). The day the names of the selectees were released, one of the instructors came into our class and bellowed out "Chief Kirkpatrick!" Everyone looked at me, but I knew not to respond because he was baiting me and I wasn't going to bite. I wasn't a chief until the assigned advancement date and until I had been through the "initiation" and had my chief's anchors pinned on! If I responded to his call, he would invariably tell my OSCM and OSCS and that "infraction" would be added to the list that I knew they would be compiling. These "charges" would be levied on me during the initiation and fines and punishment would be meted out accordingly. In the end, the instructor trying to get a rise out of me, gave up and walked out, but now everyone knew I'd made the list and at the end of the day, my classmates helped celebrated the occasion at one of the local watering holes.

I arrived back in Bremerton on the afternoon of the 15th of September, the day before my scheduled advancement date. The "initiation" of the other CPO selectees from CGN-9 was scheduled to be held the evening of the 16th at the base CPO Club and I knew that between the time I got back in town to the start of the initiation, I would have hell to pay for being absent from the hazing that all the other CPO selectees had been going through since the selection list had been posted. I did *not* look forward to going back aboard ship! Instead, I plunked myself down on a barstool out in town at one of OI Division's favorite haunts and debated how to avoid the chiefs that would be out looking for me. It seems everyone I ran into knew I'd made chief and offered up their opinions about how to avoid the search. Shortly, one of my shipmates entered the bar and told me the chiefs were a couple joints down, working their way to where I was sitting. I made a quick exit and, walking down and across the street, put some distance between me and them. As it worked out, that was how I avoided being found for the rest of the evening. Just as the searchers drew close, someone would come into the place I was at and tell me and I would move again. I snuck aboard ship in the wee hours of the morning and was able to get a few hours' sleep before they found me and what I had dreaded most was dished out with a lot more relish than normal! If I thought I had avoided most of the hazing, the chiefs more than made up for it during the initiation. But, that's a story that will remain untold!

Reporting back aboard ship and after getting my anchors "pinned," I found that much of the SRA work in CIC had been completed. The TWS consoles had been landed in CIC as were the ISAR console and the JOTS terminal. Once service hook-ups (power, water and air) had been completed and equipment tests had been run, systems testing was next. Adding TWS meant that many of the OSs would be attending a three-day familiarization course being given by the techreps aboard ship. Even though the TWS console operators would have to complete more formal training in their specialty, it was deemed prudent that a number of other OSs be taught the basics of the weapon and the launch process. Once systems testing commenced, we began the same sequence as during our previous shipyard period in '83. But this time we had the added level of difficulty of TWS being incorporated in the tactical problems we would run through.

CHAPTER 21
WESTPAC '86 - USS LONG BEACH
13 MAY - 24 OCTOBER 1986

Days Deployed: 164 days
Days In Port: 55 days
Days At Sea/Underway: 109 days

BB BG Battle Group ROMEO

During our work-ups and throughout our SOCAL Ops, one of the primary concerns was the technological dissimilarities experienced while operating in proximity of our new arrival to the West Coast fleet and our assigned Battle Group partner, USS *Vincennes* (CG-49). This would be the first time an AEGIS ship would deploy in the Pacific. These interoperability problems had been discussed but until they had been observed in a live tactical environment, problem solving for the BG could not be put into practice. The AEGIS CDS and SPY-1 radar had been designed and configured to manage the tactical data within its sensor range and tailored to those requirements and capabilities. So, when non-AEGIS ships were present in that environment, allowances had to be made for different CDS capabilities so as not to be overcome by the AEGIS CDS operating in its default configuration. Once those "tweaks" had been made and practiced, they quickly became SOP (standard operating procedure).

Another of the unique problems with a BBBG (Battleship Battle Group) was our lack of air support, because we had no carrier assigned to the battle group. In a series of exercises, both simulated and using real-world assets, we practiced employing air assets sent from shore stations and taking up CAP assignments as would be done if we actually were employing aircraft from a battle group carrier. During our deployment overseas, aircraft would actually be tasked, during a period when the battle group would be within range, to support and deploy as would be the case if a carrier were present within our tactical disposition. For instance, if the BG were 300 miles SSW of Japan, flights of CAP would be tasked to dispose themselves at pre-arranged radials and ranges from the BG, checking in with the BG AAWC (CGN-9 or CG-49). Due to the extended ranges of operations, these assets would also be supported with tanker aircraft, enabling them to remain on station for the duration of their assigned support period to the BG. While deployed and when put into practice, this did not always come off as planned and too often we did not get the assigned air assets, they showed up late, or the tanker didn't show up meaning the CAP had to depart earlier than planned. These were contingencies put forward during planning, but which the BG had been assured would not happen.

To extend our capability of gathering data from outside the BG and without a carrier, it was also planned to incorporate ASW information using ASWOC (Anti-Submarine Warfare Operations Center) data and when possible including them in the BG's tactical data link. With ASWOC's spread from Hawaii to Japan and the Aleutians this was a promising asset not normally included in BG deployments. On our way to WestPac and while in port at Pearl Harbor, we managed a briefing with the ASWOC at Barbers Point and were pleased with their enthusiasm to participate. But when attempting to employ the other ASWOCs while deployed in their general vicinities, success varied and results were mixed.

As our time for deployment rapidly approached, a handful of ship's company that did not want to make the trip and would do anything to avoid it. Two of those personnel were from CIC. One was a senior EW whose wife had told the ombudsman (an appointed wife of a senior enlisted crewman and official liaison to the command) that she didn't want her husband to leave and she was threatening action through political channels. The command discussed this with the EW and he was told to deal with it. But, either his heart wasn't in the effort or he and his wife had changed pants! In either case, something had to give and it was the command that blinked. The EW was transferred before we left!

A case closer to home dealt with one of our OS3s! A few days before our scheduled departure, I was called to the division admin office, a space adjacent to and forward of CIC. When I arrived, I was asked by OSCM and OSCS if I had heard anything about this particular OS that would indicate he was gay. I had not! He had just told them he was, which would mean he was not "deployable!" Given the navy's stance back then regarding openly gay men aboard ship, our hands were tied unless we could prove his story was a fabrication. However, without enough time remaining to allow for that, we had no choice but to send him ashore and let them deal with the situation from there. His former shipmates in CIC would have to pick up the slack left by his vacancy and perform the duties he would have been tasked with, which didn't sit well with anyone!

ISAR & INCSEA

(ISAR) Image Sensing Aperture Radar aboard CGN-9 was installed by SPAWAR under contract with Raytheon during the ship's limited upgrade at PSNSY Bremerton, WA in 1985. ISAR used the SPG-55 radar antenna in a "slave" configuration.

By so doing, this allowed for a very high horizon for the acquisition of targets as the SPG-55 antenna was located high enough above the horizon to give ISAR a range of approximately 70 miles. After installation and our departure from the shipyard, the Raytheon tech rep remained onboard for our "work-up" period prior to deployment and also rode the ship to Hawaii. This was in order to allow adequate time to train shipboard personnel on in the use and application of the ISAR Operator Console that had been installed in CIC. Although I sat for the operator training, my other duties didn't allow me to get much "stick time" on the console.

ISAR had been previously configured and installed aboard P-3 Orion aircraft and during flights over and around the northeastern Atlantic had built a library of images taken during that period and in that locale. But due to these images being sourced from an aircraft, their "aspects" could not be applied for our purposes aboard CGN-9. We would have to build our own image library. This was important for the system's capacity for establishing the identity of the target being imaged. If you had a previous target in the library that had been confirmed (by visual or other means) as a specific hull, you saved it in the library and if you imaged a similar hull, the system could recognize it as being the same type and assigning that target an identity of that reference image. So, during our work-ups in SOCAL and our transit to Hawaii, any and all surface contacts within range were imaged using ISAR and these were saved in an effort to build our own library. We continued to do this after we "chopped" to 7th Fleet until we started encountering Soviet Bloc merchants.

It was then that the question arose on whether we would "shine" or "illuminate" a Soviet combatant using ISAR and the fact that ISAR was slaved to a fire control radar. Technically, this would be a breach of INCSEA. The INCSEA (Incidents at Sea) Agreement (25 May 1972) had been established between the USSR and USA in an effort to avoid such confrontational actions as had occurred in the late 1960s between Soviet and USN ships. The concern was with item "f" below. And, so died ISAR aboard CGN-9. To my knowledge, it sat in a SPAWAR warehouse somewhere in San Diego, for years!

Specifically, the agreement provides for:

a) steps to avoid collision;
b) not interfering in the "formations" of the other party;

c) avoiding maneuvers in areas of heavy sea traffic;

d) requiring surveillance ships to maintain a safe distance from the object of investigation so as to avoid "embarrassing or endangering the ships under surveillance";

e) using accepted international signals when ships maneuver near one another;

f) not simulating attacks at, launching objects toward, or illuminating the Bridge of the other party's ships;

g) informing vessels when submarines are exercising near them; and

h) requiring aircraft commanders to use the greatest caution and prudence in approaching aircraft and ships of the other party and not permitting simulated attacks against aircraft or ships, performing aerobatics over ships, or dropping hazardous objects near them.

HARPOON SINKEX EX-GRAYBACK (SSG-LPSS-574)

One of the first events scheduled during the deployment in which we were to participate was titled a "SinkEx," in which the former USS *Grayback* had been designated as the target. *Grayback* had been decommissioned for the second time on 15 January 1984 at Subic Bay Naval Station, R. P. *Grayback* was painted red, towed out to the target area and sunk on 13 April 1986 in the South China Sea.

As I recall there were four designated "shooters" and six designated "Sim-Shooters" that would participate in the exercise. Platforms that would actually fire a Harpoon included the BB, a P-3 and a DDG. Sim-Shooters included CGN-9, a DDG and a B-52.

The "range" designated for the shoot was an open ocean area, out of the shipping lanes but still large enough to warrant employing a range clearance aircraft (a P-3) to patrol daily up to the exercise day to ensure that the area was clear of surface craft. Sure enough, the first few days of the aircraft's efforts revealed that there were surface craft in the area; it reported that the range was "foul!" So it was determined that the target would be hauled out to the southwest and the range moved accordingly. This was successful; the P-3 reported that the range was "clear" and we could commence the countdown for the exercise to commence.

Once the exercise commenced, there were multiple hits observed, including one on the "sail" area. When *Grayback* did not sink within the expected time period, loitering air BDA assets requested that they be cleared "hot" into the target area for their attempt to sink it. Just as they were in position to engage the target, the *Grayback* gave up the ghost and slid beneath the waves — much to the chagrin of the strike aircraft, which dropped their ordnance anyway.

Here's a story that arose during the exercise. While all participants were engaged in maneuvering to their assigned positions and developing their firing solutions in preparation for the "shoot," AAWC *Long Beach* was tasked with ensuring that all air assets were on non-firing bearings and out of range until cleared. A problem was that a B-52 "non-shooter" hadn't showed up yet! We needed to know his whereabouts ASAP and so we tried contacting him on the assigned frequency, but looking at the "Communications Plan" for the exercise, we could find no designated call sign with which to call him. So, turning to "Mikey" I asked him if there was an unofficial call sign I could use for a B-52. Being an ex-Air Force type, he laughed and said yep! "Just call him BUFF!" BUFF??? "What the hell is that?" I asked? As the TAO and the CO were standing over our shoulders, he said he'd tell me later. So, out on the R/T I made the call, "BUFF, BUFF, this is Alpha Whiskey, over!" Short pause, and again "BUFF, BUFF, this is Alpha

Whiskey, over!" Shortly a voice responded with a chuckle, "Alpha Whiskey, BUFF, roger over!" As soon as I finished my directions to BUFF, I turned to "Mikey," and asked him again, what the hell BUFF meant. Then he told me, with a big grin "Big Ugly Fat Fucker!" Even better, the B-52 responded to it! Yep, the CO and TAO overheard "Mikey's" response, but what could they say! We *HAD* established comms with the B-52, right?

"TIME FRAME"

Before our previous deployment, the division received personnel aboard to replace those who had departed the service or had transferred to other commands. One of these was an OS1 who had "converted" from an aviation rating, to OS. A most unusual career path change! He had never been to sea as an OS and here he was as an OS1 on one of the most complex weapons platforms then in existence and in a CIC that reflected as much. He had a steeper learning curve than the more junior OSs and started his tour aboard with this handicap; it fell to many of us in CIC who were his peers and seniors to bring him up to speed. He was provided with all the documentation required and his progress was monitored to ensure he didn't lag behind. But, after quite a few months had passed, it was evident he needed more help. He was getting his paperwork signed off, but when he sat at a watchstation TDS console, it was difficult for him to apply the book learning to the actual functions necessary at the console. So in an effort to afford him the opportunity to contribute and also allow him more time to adjust, he was assigned as Surface Watch Supervisor, which was more of a management position than the various station assignments at a console required. But, again, it was more than he could handle! When things got busy in the "Surface" area of CIC and when he was on watch, he became testy, flustered and ineffective as the Watch Supervisor. Multi-tasking was beyond him! Other, more serious on-watch problems were noted and it was necessary for us to re-think his placement. One of his traits was that, whenever you tried teaching him something, as when it was necessary to change settings on a console, he would invariably ask "What time-frame would that be?" What? "No, it's not driven by time, it's driven by tactical or environmental conditions!" "Yes, so what time-frame should that happen during?" If you were explaining the schedule for the day and an event was conditional, he would ask about the "time-frame" it would occur in. It was also during this WestPac that CIC found out we had a cartoonist in our midst. Or, at least, a person who fancied himself as such. An "underground" comic strip, with all of the CIC gang as occasional cast members, made its rounds among the OSs. Sooner or later we all made our appearance and some more than others were frequent subjects. If you made a boneheaded mistake, you were in. Or, if you were the cause of a certain group's displeasure, you made "the strip." The eight or ten that I saw seemed to feature "Time Frame" more often than not — probably because the OS1 provided so much material to work with. And so, the legend was born and he forever became known as "Time Frame"!

SUBIC BAY 10 - 19 JULY 1986
DIVISION PARTY

USS Long Beach CPO Party, Olongapo R.P.

During our port-call to Subic Bay, I attended two parties. One was the CPO Mess party, given out in town at one of the local establishments. And, as evident by the photo above, a good time was had by all.

The second party I had a personal hand in planning. As was my habit by that stage in my experience with liberty in Subic that I never chose to stay downtown. Rather, I would catch a jeepney and go out to Barrio Barretto up the shore of the bay. It was quieter, more laid-back and slower paced than in town and much, much cheaper! Many establishments had beach access at places like Gaines Beach Landing and White Rock. I would get a room at the Marmont Hotel and then hang out at a little mom-and-pop beachfront bar that took care of me, and made sure no one messed with me, and that I got something to eat without having to go somewhere else. There was even a pool table, somewhat weathered, but still in usable condition and you didn't have to put coins in it to play. I could spend the afternoon there for less than $20! My kind of joint! When my LPO (Steve) and I started discussing putting on an OI Division party, this was the place I had in mind. So, when we pulled into port, we went out to discuss it with the owners. The place was owned by a local Filipina and her husband, an ex-sailor from the Australian Navy. He met us to talk about the party and was very enthusiastic. The place was located adjacent to Gains Beach Landing, so had beachfront access. On the premises, he also had a four- or five-room structure to house overnight guests. The rooms were clean, the showers and toilets worked (not always the case out in the Barrio) and the rates were cheap — if I recall, about $8 per night. So Steve and I reserved one room for each of us and a "crash" room for the others we anticipated would need it. We ordered the letchon (roast pig), pansit, lumpia, beer, etc. for the day of the party. The owner suggested we rent a banca-boat that could take groups of the guys on a short tour of that section of the bay, which we did. The day of the party, Steve and I showed up early to make sure all the arrangements were in place and then settled into a half-assed game of pool . By six that night, the place was packed! The boom box behind the bar was rocking and everyone did their bit to eat all the food we had laid on. The boat tours were busy well into the night. As the party drew to a close, Steve and I made the rounds to ensure that the remaining food had been "donated" to the locals, that the guys who were too soused to make it back to base were bedded down in the "crash pad," and that the last banca-boat run for the night arrived back safely. As the boat approached the shore and the bow ground into the sand, everyone hopped off and waded onto the beach. Just then, one of the guys asked "Where's Time Frame?" He had been on the boat, toward the back and as he wasn't in the group standing before us, had now gone missing. With worried looks out into the water, we started getting antsy that somehow he'd managed to drown in less than three feet of water. Just as that possibility was being nervously considered, out from the edge of the water, crawling on all fours like some prehistoric amphibian, emerges Time Frame, coughing and sputtering and mumbling to himself! We all busted up laughing! The legend grows!

PHATTAYA BEACH, THAILAND
29 JULY – 6 AUGUST 1986

Before beginning Exercise Cobra Gold, the *Beach* made a port call at Phattaya Beach, Thailand on the eastern shore of the Gulf of Thailand. The place is a favorite vacation locale for Australians, with a mix of German and Brit tourists as well. Ex-pat Americans, a hold-over from the Vietnam experience, were also in residence. Many of the mom-and-pop watering holes and small businesses were owned by these as well as other "tourists" who had decided to stay. Of course, ownership of any business required that the ex-pat be married to a local, who retained the majority share of the enterprise.

Because there were no pier or port facilities at Phattaya, getting ashore was a chore. Long, narrow water-taxis would pull up alongside the A-com Ladder and once filled would make the run into the beach. When the bow grounded on shore, you got out and waded the last couple feet onto the beach. On the upside, if you wished, the taxi folks could serve you a cold brew or soda during the ride to the beach!

The first day ashore a group of us had just stepped off the boat and crossed the beach to the boulevard paralleling the beach when we were approached by a few Caucasian tourists who asked if we were off that ship out there. Responding that we were, they asked when we were leaving, because the stores and bars along the waterfront had all raised their prices in anticipation of our arrival. We were pretty peeved at him and someone said "We just f….in' got here, pal," and we all walked away. Welcome to Thailand!

Later that day, four of us were walking down the beach when a pair of locals started trailing us and were attempting to have us hire a speed boat to take us para-sailing, one of the favorite activities in Phattaya. As we walked and they followed, we discussed among ourselves if we wanted to do that and we all agreed we would. But the price the hawkers had started at was way too high, so we kept walking and the price kept falling. They finally dropped it to a point we all agreed was acceptable and we stopped to discuss what we would get for that price. We told them each of us wanted to be taken out and around the *Beach* at anchor about a mile out. When that was agreed upon, one of them took off down the beach to find a boat that would agree to the same "contract," he and his buddy keeping a "finder's fee." A boat soon showed up and one of the other guys in the group was the first to get strapped in for the ride, then off he went. It was my turn, next! Strapped into the harness, I made a running start to help get the lift needed to leave the ground and soon I was about 100 feet in the air headed towards the ship. The tow-boat passed wide of the stern while I passed over the fantail. And, as he ran up the starboard side of the ship, I passed close enough to the Quarterdeck watch-standers to offer them a wave!

During my first couple days on the beach I put together a party for the division. I found a second-floor apartment that had a balcony across the road from the beach, living room, kitchen, and two bedrooms for two nights. Everyone attending kicked in funds for the apartment rental and drinks. A few others and I procured the food. The place was packed and a noisy and a good time was had by all. Well, almost all! One of the guys brought a real looker with him and, unbeknownst to me, had hustled her off into one of the bedrooms. Minutes later, he stormed out of the room in just his skivvies, cussing up a storm as he took his "squeeze" by the arm and threw her out of the apartment. Turns out, her "credentials" as a female did not pass closer inspection! Those in the immediate vicinity got a hoot out of that! Not ten minutes later, there was a knock at the door and two Thai policemen with our shipmate's "benny girl" were standing in the door. Seems that "she" was pissed off about not being paid and the cops were there to make sure that happened. Which it did! Our buddy never, *ever* lived that one down.

The last night I was ashore, I went with a group out to do some "steamin'" and eventually found a place that was *the* hot spot in Phattaya. Inside, the place was large enough to hold 300 or so people. The music was loud and the tunes were good! The place was wall-to-wall with tourists, ex-pats, sailors and locals. We had two or three tables put together to accommodate everyone because many of the guys had paired up. Hours passed and a couple of us left with our dance partners and made our way to a mom-and-pop bar owned by an ex-pat Australian. Sitting at the bar, the conversation was lively and time drifted on. The girl I was with learned that I would be going back to the ship because I had spent the funds I had on-hand — meaning, that she had no hope of making any money off me that night. I learned from her, that she was from northern Thailand and was staying with a bunch of girls who had also traveled down to Phattaya to make some money off the tourists and sailors. Because it was getting very late, she asked if I would like to crash at her place and that there was room on the couch if I did. What the hell, it beat going back to the ship! So, we jumped into a taxi and a few minutes later we were at a large, two-story house on a raised foundation with a wrap-around porch just a few blocks back from the beach. She pointed to the couch, said good night and went upstairs, to bed! When I woke in the morning, it was to the noise and smell of someone preparing breakfast. Well, Thai breakfast, anyway! Three of the roommates were in the kitchen yakking away a mile a minute. I made it to the bathroom and tried straightening out the wrinkles from the night before and making myself more presentable. As I came out one of the girls offered me a cup of coffee, which I gratefully took and I walked out the door and onto the porch. Sitting on one of the railings and leaning back against the upright, I found myself watching a group of people across the street as they cleared the lot of underbrush and jungle growth. What was most interesting was that one of them, appearing to me to be in his early to mid-teens, was riding on an Asian elephant and directing his mount in the clearing process. One of the girls came out with a kit bag in hand, and shyly told me she was hoping to get a job in a beauty parlor and asked if she could practice on me. So, there I sat, in the morning shade, watching the kid on the elephant, sipping my coffee and getting a manicure! Life was sweet!

Later that morning, I returned aboard *Long Beach* because I had work to do before the ship was to get underway. I had been assigned to dissect the OpOrder for the upcoming Cobra Gold exercise and provide a briefing to CIC personnel. The OpOrder was a tome! It was divided into sections detailing all aspects of the exercise: frequencies for voice and data circuits, ship assignments and dispositions, opposing force composition, and any and every detail necessary for the execution of Cobra Gold. So, for the next two days, I studied, took notes and constructed a display that I would use in the briefing. I would like to believe the information disseminated was, in part, instrumental in our successful participation in the exercise. Cobra Gold was held 10 to 13 August in the lower Gulf and comprised a USN CVBG (Carrier Battle Group) and an ARG (Amphibious Readiness Group) as well as a number of Royal Thai Navy vessels. As usual, CGN-9 was assigned as the CVBG AAWC and placed as a "shooter" on the "threat axis."

The second day of the exercise I was manning the AAWC console and my Senior Chief was manning the FAAWC console. Our radar had picked up a south-bound aircraft, "squawking" a broken civilian IFF code and not on any prescribed civilian air route. As it was not part of the scenario and was not conforming to acceptable criteria, we designated it as a "bogey" initially. Senior Chief and I agreed that if the aircraft didn't align with a civilian air corridor by a certain range and bearing from the ship, that its designation would be changed from "bogey" to "hostile" and engaged with missiles (simulated). This came to pass and the tactical data was updated to reflect the progression of the sequence to engagement. About then, our OpsBoss asked Senior Chief why the aircraft had been assigned as "hostile" and taken with missiles. Senior Chief responded, "If it flies, it dies, sir!" Everyone got a chuckle out of that!

ASIAN GAMES
20 SEPTEMBER TO 26 SEPTEMBER 1986

Our next assignment was in support of the Asian Games being held in Seoul, South Korea. Threats from North Korea, to cause an incident during the games, were taken seriously and the South Korean Navy, JNSDF (Japanese Naval Self-Defense Force), and U.S. Navy units were to station themselves at assigned locales surrounding the southern portion of the Korean peninsula as a preemptive measure. For our assigned period of support during the games, and as AAWC for the U.S. naval units, CGN-9 was stationed to the south and west of the peninsula to better utilize our radar sensors and long-range missile capability. Whether North Korea was mollified by the force displayed or the threat was just a bluff that had been called, could not be known by us — that was above our paygrade. What, after the fact, was known is that nothing happened and the show of force did what it was supposed to do!

THE MEETING (27 - 28 SEPTEMBER 1986)

Battle Group "C" (Charlie). *Vincennes* (CG-49), *Long Beach* (CGN-9) and *New Jersey* (BB-62 & escorts)

Before the Asian Games were concluded on 5 October, our BG was detached to proceed to our next operational assignment. We steamed north, through Tsushima Straits. Reaching Tsugaru Straits, between Honshu and Hokkaido, we transited from the Sea of Japan and out into the northern Pacific.

Kara Class Cruiser: North of the Kurile Islands

CGN-9 Water Over the Bow, Northern Pacific 1986

The Battle Group had been assigned to conduct a passage into the Sea of Okhotsk, demonstrating our right to do so, which was in accordance with accepted international agreements (INCSEA). These operations were referred to as FONOPS (Freedom of Navigation Operations). We had made these previously to the east and north of Vladivostok, but this passage had added risk by the nature of its intended route. We were to proceed with a northern passage through the Kurile Island chain and relatively close to the southern shore of the Kamchatka Peninsula, home of the large Russian military base of Petropavlovsk, which was certain to instigate a sharp reaction from the Soviets. The BG steamed north, into the Sea of Okhotsk and to the designated point of 59 degrees north latitude before reversing course and debouching back through the Kurile chain. CIC being an air conditioned space that was normally kept cooler than most other spaces due to the equipment requirements, made for a VERY cold environment during our run up north. You dressed as warm as you could and while sitting at your TDS console you wrapped your legs around it to get some warmth from the console itself while keeping your hands in your pockets unless absolutely necessary to perform your watch station functions.

Shortly after passing north through the Kurile chain, Russian air activity increased, as expected. We were also informed of expected Russian surface forces that had sortied from "Petro" with the expectation that they would become our designated "shadow" for the passage. Before the end of the first day, we met our opposite number, which proceeded to take station on our starboard beam at an uncomfortably close range. As we steamed parallel with our shadow, I had been relieved on watch and I and my Senior Chief proceeded up and out of CIC with the intention of "eyeballing" the opposition. Coming out on deck into the biting Sea of Okhotsk wind was in itself an experience, but there just off our beam was a Kara-class cruiser with Russian sailors, staring back at us and hoping the same thing we were, that no one would make a mistake!

The following excerpt is taken from a webpage regarding our "Sea-of-O" assignment: "According to a declassified command history for the battleship *New Jersey*, during her transit through the Sea of Okhotsk on 27–28 September 1986, 'close passes' were made by Soviet Bear and Badger bombers, a Hormone helicopter, and a May maritime patrol airplane. A *Kara*-class cruiser and two *Grisha III* frigates also shadowed the U.S. ships." There were many other Russian aircraft being tracked by our radar, but remained out of visual range.

This was the only instance during my career when I was eyeball-to-eyeball with a Russian surface combatant while at sea. Ironically, just a couple years later, two Russian destroyers tied up for a visit at San Diego Naval Station and from my shore duty desk I could look out the window and watch their crewman going out on liberty.

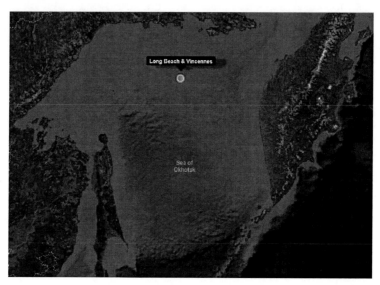

Sea of Okhotsk 27 & 28 September 1986

OFF-RANGE TOMAHAWK SHOOT

Once the "Sea of O" transit was completed, CGN-9 broke away from BG Charlie, to proceed to our next assigned event: the navy's first-ever "off range" Tomahawk shoot. Previous testing during the missile's development — conducted to observe performance for upgrades and to demonstrate tactics during individual ship's CSSQTs (Combat Systems Ship's Qualification Trials) — had all taken place on U.S. Navy designated ranges. PMR, Point Mugu, California and PMTC, Barking Sands, Kauai in the Hawaiian Islands were the two that existed on the Pacific side of the country. Our task was to demonstrate the missile's capabilities under extreme weather conditions – in this case winter weather in the far north Pacific along the

Aleutian Islands. Of course, this would also be a demonstration for the benefit of the Russians who, as expected, showed up for the event. To meet the requirements of the test and to keep the Russians out of the way, this would be a very busy evolution. First, there would be chase planes designated to loiter on station, and once the Tomahawk was in flight they were to follow it down range to the target and observe the impact. This of course would also require a tanker aircraft specifically assigned to the chase aircraft. Then there were designated CAP aircraft assigned to loiter at their designated station with an attendant tanker. When the Russians showed up and if they should get within a set distance from the "shooter" (us), the CAP were to be directed to intercept and warn the Russians they were intruding. So, there were two CAP and two chase planes on station. CAP and chase planes rotated off their respective tankers to enable one to be on station at all times. And, to assist in the management of the air assets, an Air Force E-3C was flown out of Elmendorf AFB and took up orbit WNW between CGN-9 and where the Russians were expected. CAP and chase aircraft launched from Shemya Island. The E-3C would control CAP and its tanker. We would control the chase planes and their tanker. Our target was Kanaga Island to the ENE of our launch position. Back then, to launch a Tomahawk, the launching platform was required to maintain a location within a circle of less than one mile — primitive compared to today's technology.

The first day, the E-3C showed up, CAP and chase planes were on-station and tankers were standing by. The Russians showed up, the CAP intercepted and the Bear drew back under escort. But then it was determined that the weather was below minimums to allow the chase planes to be able to get a visual and maintain it throughout the flight of the missile to impact. The question hung in the air for an hour or so before we were told that the shoot would be delayed until the following morning in the hope that the weather would clear.

Our Captain being an inveterate tourist with a multi-million dollar vehicle, decided, because it was still early in the day, he wanted to do a little sight-seeing. So, off we went to tour some of the nearby islands. I don't know why he expected the weather to be different there than it had been where we tried to launch the Tomahawk, but when we got where we were going, I ran up and out to snatch a peak — all I saw was fog! So, we didn't hang around long before heading back in the general direction toward where we needed to be the following morning.

Much to our disappointment, we went through the entire set-up process again the next morning, only to have the same problem. The weather postponed the event again. As the Russians showed up for our second attempt, I'm sure they were as disappointed as we were because they would have to make that long trip again the next day. The third time's the charm and this was no exception. Everyone and everything was in place (including the Bear) the third morning and this time we had fair weather. The missile was fired, the chase planes followed it to target and reported a hit. We were just as happy the missile performed as advertised, because now we could get out of there and go home! With a couple detours en route.

THE ALEUTIAN CHAIN, SHEMYA ISLAND

After completing our off-range shoot, we proceeded directly to Shemya Island because it had been arranged for our mail to be forwarded there from Elmendorf AFB. We hadn't had mail since departing Japan, coming up on three weeks

Shemya Island is approximately two miles by four miles of relatively flat terrain. In May of 1943, during the Aleutian campaign in WWII, the island was occupied by U.S. troops and an airfield was quickly established. Over the decades, most of the personnel facilities (dining halls, sleeping quarters, etc.) were moved underground to avoid the fierce and frequent Aleutian "williwas" (Alaskan storms between a hurricane and a nor'easter) that delivered so much damage to the previous above-ground infrastructure. Shemya is located about 1,500 miles WSW from Anchorage, Alaska at the end of the Aleutian chain.

As we approached the airbase on Shemya, I was on watch at the AAWC TDS Console and we were discussing how to establish communications because the air base would not be monitoring any of the communications circuits that we used (with the exception of the ones designated for use during emergencies) and vice versa. We agreed that we could probably get near enough to the base to establish VHF communications and so I pulled out our copy of the TACAID, which contained the configuration, operating capabilities and communications frequencies of U.S. Military Airfields. I located the VHF frequency for the tower, contacted our radio room and had them patch the circuit into my console and a speaker over my head. When we were about eight miles NNE of the base, I made the call. "Shemya Tower, this is *USS Long Beach*, over." There was a slight pause and with obvious curiosity in his voice, tower responded, "*USS Long Beach*, Shemya Tower, WHERE ARE YOU?" I gave him our bearing from him to us and he shortly responded that he held us visually (given the normal state of the weather, a rarity in those parts). I explained what we were there for and he told me to stand by while he made those arrangements. Within the hour, he informed us that the helo with our mail would be en route shortly and I informed the TAO who made arrangements for the ship to set "Flight Quarters" and come to a course within the desired "wind envelope" necessary to receive the helo!

There were a lot of happy campers aboard that night as we read our letters from home! And, I'm sure the tower operator had a good story to tell in the mess hall that evening, "No shit, a Navy cruiser, right out there!" Those guys don't get out much!

ANCHORAGE, AK 10 -13 OCTOBER

Steaming east from Shemya, we pulled into Anchorage, Alaska the 10th of October. To allow CGN-9 to make a port call at Anchorage, it was requested that a brow that would accommodate the radical tides in the port be left by the preceding *Connie* BG for our use in early October. Even with the longer brow, we would still need to shift it for every tide cycle, from the main deck to the 01 Level and back. The brow was there when we arrived that morning. The weather was overcast and cool, but we were all glad to be in port for a few days. The first day in Anchorage, we were told that the local VFW posts had arranged a party for any of the crew who wanted to attend. So, the next evening we were graciously welcomed to the VFW Post where the party was being held. There was a long serving line of food and plenty of the VFW members on-hand to ensure we enjoyed ourselves! These were a great bunch of guys! There was only one more day in town and I had duty that day, so I didn't get much of a chance to see the sights. Actually, I was more interested in getting on home, anyway!

GLACIER BAY NATIONAL PARK

USS Long Beach CGN-9 Glacier Bay National Park, Alaska

Our next stop was a surprise to most of us! The CO had arranged for us to take a "tour" of Glacier Bay National Park on our way south to the lower '48! As we came into the mouth of the bay, we hove-to and sent our motor whale boat out to pick up two park rangers that were to act as our "tour guides." Owing to the restrictive passage, we set a modified Navigation Detail to keep us out of harm's way from any large floating chunks of ice as we maneuvered further up into the bay.

The two rangers alternated between providing a running commentary over the ship's 1MC (PA system) and the other one getting a tour of the ship. When it came time for the first one to tour CIC, he told us that all the rangers wanted to go, but that only two would be selected. So, they all put their names into a hat and their boss pulled out the names of the two winners. OSCS and I left CIC to go take a look see and when the frigid air punched us in the face, we made a bee-line for the exhaust blowers amidships in an attempt to keep warm. From there, we could watch as the motor whale boat moved away from the ship to take the photo seen above. We didn't stick around much longer though, as we could only warm one side of our bodies at a time, while the other side rapidly froze!

CHAPTER 22

SURGE-PAC 2 MARCH – 29 APRIL 1987

BATTLE GROUP ALPHA

AS PLANNED, this Surge-Pac Battle Group would be built around USS *Midway* (CV-41). However, she had recently undergone shipyard modifications that added "blisters" which would enhance her stability. This design change was proven to be a problem during her sea trials following the upgrade and she was withdrawn from the Battle Group; USS *Ranger* (CV-61) was substituted. There was another change, and this one directly affected CGN-9 — the DDG (Destroyer Guided missile) originally assigned to this operation had experienced engineering problems and CGN-9 was assigned to take her place. Because we had returned from our own WestPac just five months previously, none of the crew was pleased with the idea of doing another two months overseas.

Even before the griping had subsided, we realized that we had some catching-up to do in preparation for our tasking within the Surge Battle Group. Conferences were held, and the OpPlan was digested, dissected and briefed. What training was available we participated in and what wasn't available, but necessary, we formulated and conducted ourselves, in house. Because some of our scheduled events included anticipated participation by "the opposition," we practiced the expected encounter using "the plan" as it had been presented to us. Ships of the BG were leaving their respective homeports for our rendezvous point far out into the Pacific, well north of the Hawaiian Islands. The game was "on!"

The BG was disposed using what was referred to as an X-ray Grid. This was nothing more than a gridded overlay placed on a chart of the expected area in which we were going to be operating. The advantage was that, using only the GRP (grid reference point), the BG could be shuffled using grid coordinates from the overlay and the GRP could be moved as often as necessary. We could also employ a rather new concept referred to as RTLOS (Remote Track, Launch on Search). This meant that when provided with target data from another unit that had radar "skin," a missile ship could launch a (in this case, simulated) weapon to the designated grid coordinate and when the missile arrived in that square, the seeker on the missile would home on the target. This meant you could fire on a target while in EMCON Alpha (total emission control) and thereby keep from being detected by the opponent. Of course, the question was that, given the seeker parameters of the missile and the area of the grid square it was being launched into, would it even find the target? To my knowledge, this was never demonstrated using X-ray Grid, a live missile and/or a live target!

An additional tool at our disposal and that had been added during our last shipyard period was JOTS (Joint Operational Tactical System), which was a networked terminal located in Flag Plot and in CIC, just to the left of the TAO's console. The ship would receive message traffic that provided data informing us of expected SATVUL (Satellite Vulnerability) periods, when and where Russian satellites could be expected to over-fly the area of ocean the BG might be operating in. Once the data from the message was entered into the terminal, it would display the path and swath of ocean the satellite could be expected to pass over and its coverage. This enabled the staff planners to anticipate the possibility of BG exposure to Soviet satellite tracking. So, now it was just a matter of staying out of the path of the photo satellite to avoid being detected by that resource and of altering our electronic emissions to confuse the Soviets should they employ an ELINT satellite. During this exercise, the Russians would be unable to use their satellites as a means of providing the incoming Bear aircraft with our current force disposition.

We were informed from outside sources that the expected opposition was on its way. A *Bear* was being tracked by U.S. assets in the western Pacific and their projected flight path indicated they were headed in our direction. From previous encounters, we knew the objective of their mission was to do a fly-over of the carrier. Anticipating this, ships of the BG began changing their electromagnetic signatures — radars, radio transmissions and other emissions unique to specific ships were turned off or put into receive-only mode. Every ship was assigned a station within the X-ray grid and conformed to the new disposition. Aircraft patterns within the BG airspace were also changed to give the impression that the carrier was in a location she wasn't. At a pre-arranged time and station (location), all units assigned to the BG "lit off" in their reconfigured emissions "footprint" prior to the arrival of the Bear aircraft. Because this was not expected by the Russians, their first fly-over must have been disconcerting when they didn't find a carrier, but rather one or two other ships of the BG. With them being at such extreme range from base, they didn't have the necessary fuel to remain long, so after a couple passes, they turned for home. We expected them back the next day!

After the Russian's departure, the units of the BG began to re-deploy within the X-ray grid, using total EMCON to mask the movements. The next morning, upon learning that the Bear was again en route, the BG ships came out of EMCON and their electronic emissions again modified for that day's expected encounter. Again, air traffic patterns (CAP, the E-2C Hawkeye, tankers & marshall) were configured to reflect what the Bear would expect to see if oriented from a carrier. Again, the Bear made his flight path conform to an expected intercept that revealed, upon his arrival, the carrier was not there! To further his confusion, CAP intercepts were made on the Bear, where they would be expected from a carrier. And, when any of the BG airborne aircraft were RTB, they would fly a pattern that would appear to be en route a carrier and then descend to a low altitude (to avoid being tracked by the Russians) before making course changes that would take them back to where the carrier actually was. This was done one more day, before finally "allowing" the Bear to "find" the carrier. What I have related does not comprise the entire evolution and certain techniques and tactics have been omitted because they may still be in use today. Did we fool him, or was he playing his expected role? Good question!

A good reference source and a more comprehensive understanding of what similar tactics and techniques were employed, I suggest reading John Lehman's recent work (released June 2018), *Oceans Ventured.*

Our shell game with the Russians concluded, the BG proceeded on its transit west. *The Beach* was positioned out ahead of the projected track of the BG, acting as AAW picket. As we approached the area of the Pacific SSE of Japan, a P-3 Orion aircraft informed the BG that it had obtained a MAD (Magnetic Anomaly Detection) contact on what it believed to be a Russian submarine. To maintain contact when the P-3 was scheduled to depart the area, the BG ASW commander tasked CGN-9 with continuing the prosecution of the contact. An H-3 helo was sent out to us, refueled aboard and then vectored to the location of the P-3's report. All this had taken place while I was off-watch and catching some Zzzzs between scheduled CIC watches. I was awakened early and told what was going on and that the other ASAC had been "on" the contact for the past few hours – also that he needed to be relieved. I rushed to get dressed, grab a quick bite to eat and then reported to CIC. I pulled up a chair next to the console the ASAC was using to prosecute the target and he briefed me on what had happened, what assets were on-station as well as en route or available. He told me what type of tactical prosecution was being employed (taken from the ASW/ASAC TACAID and employed as the situation warranted). After grabbing a cup of coffee, I talked with the OSCM and we discussed with the TAO how we should proceed and then I relieved the OSC as ASAC. I had an H-3 and S-3 on-station, and sonobuoys in the water providing data on the target's location. When the target maneuvered outside the radius of the sonobuoys it was necessary to "fix" him again with MAD or throw a "pinger" in the vicinity and see if contact could be re-established. Once his position had been fixed, I would "sow" more sonobuoys along his expected path. This was done for the next few hours as the situation evolved. The trouble was, when "sowing" these new "'buoy roads" each new sonobuoy had to be entered into the NTDS console. Doing so required a lot of my time, which couldn't be spared because I still had to maintain either positive or advisory control of the aircraft. So on the fly a process was worked out by which one of the other senior OSs on watch manned an adjacent NTDS console, monitoring the R/T circuit I was controlling on. Then, as sonobuoy data was relayed from the aircraft as they were dropped, the other OS would write that data on the console's scope face in grease pencil and then enter it into the system. This freed me to control the aircraft without losing valuable tactical data and allowed for a better and more accurate tactical display of the situation. Between the other ASAC and me, we held contact on the target for close to 12 hours before we were directed by the ASWC BG commander to break it off — there were other scheduled events requiring our time and attention and we had already expended a lot of time, gas and sonobuoys. After the countless hours of controlling aircraft for LOG (logistics) runs, SAR (Search & Rescue) helo training runs, PONY (mail runs) and PAX (passenger helos), I had finally been able to control aircraft in a "real world" tactical anti-submarine prosecution. What a rush!

Upon our arrival overseas and after a few less memorable exercises and events, *Ranger, USS Puller* and *Long Beach* pulled into Sasebo, Japan for a few days R&R (10-14 April). During our stay, a large musical event was scheduled to be held at the U.S. Navy's Park & Recreation Center, adjacent to the U.S. Naval Station, Sasebo. Because the park was open to civilians, it was expected there would be large crowds in attendance. The ships in port were expected to "augment" the Naval Station Shore Patrol, who would provide coordination and transportation. As luck (or lack thereof) would have it, I had duty that night and was put in charge of the ship's shore patrol personnel being provided for the event for one of the shifts. My shift was 6 PM to midnight, when the event was to be over. As it turned out, it had been raining and the rain was expected to continue for some time. Indeed, the rain continued, alcohol started contributing its expected problems, and mud was everywhere! We maintained a continual cycle of Shore Patrol vans shuttling drunks and trouble-makers back to SP HQ. By the end of the event and when I finally turned in my SP Brassard after midnight, I noticed that my uniform, from just above the knees on down, was caked in mud and that my jacket sleeves from the elbows down, were the same. I got a few chuckles from some of the office weenies at SP HQ about the state of my dress, but when they noticed that I didn't share in their humor they quickly went about their business!

Our next scheduled operation was Team Spirit '87, an annual event conducted with ROK (Republic of Korea) forces on, over and around the Korean peninsula. Although we had participated in the previous Team Spirit '86 exercise, this one would be different. *The Beach* was assigned as AAWC (Anti-Air Warfare Coordinator) within the BG and within the naval units assigned in support of Team Spirit. One of our primary tasks during the exercise was to "build" the first fully integrated Battle Force Link-11 tactical network. This would entail the link being fashioned around the capabilities and limitations of such diverse participating units that it would be a monumental coordination effort as well as a continual, hour by hour and day by day management effort. And, the scope of the effort would be unprecedented! This was evident as well in the fact that our Operations Officer was assigned to shore as liaison between the various shore commands involved and those units at sea that would be participants,. During this exercise, participants involved would encompass TOCs (Tactical Operations Centers) from the Air Force and Army. The Marines of the Amphibious BG involved in the exercise would also be tied into the tactical picture once their TOCs had been landed ashore.

There have always been two primary limitations to Link-11 — the limited number of Participating Units (PUs) and the range over which "real time" tactical data could be broadcast. And, these were the two limitations we would have to work through during Team Spirit. First, the PUs allowed to broadcast and receive data was restricted to specific units within the tactical picture and all others were relegated to RU's (receiving units), which allowed for faster data transfer rates. Second, the "over the horizon" limitation of maintaining an accurate tactical picture was overcome by passing link control and management to an on-station Air Force E-3. Once effectively integrated and configured, the tactical picture incorporated over 30 Air Force, Army, Marine Corps and Navy units covering a radius well in excess of 500 miles. From the Chinese/North Korean border, to Vladivostok and from NW Japan to Okinawa, the tactical picture was the most complex ever "built." As it turned out, this was to be the "swan song" for Link-11 — NATO Link-16 was even then being tested.

THE INTERCEPT

One of the more memorable incidents (for me, anyway) that also occurred during the Team Spirit exercise and while I was in CIC manning my assigned watch-station as AAWC on the NTDS console, was an intercept of a Russian Maritime Surveillance flight (a Bear D). The ship had been informed that there had been a Russian launch of an aircraft in the Vladivostok area and we were given its bearing. Entering that information in the NTDS system, I informed the TAO. Shortly, an update to the contact was provided and I updated the LOB (Line of Bearing) in the system. Given the bearing, it appeared the contact would follow the ADIZ (Air Defense Intercept Zone) line between South Korea and Japan, running between the two and down through the Tsushima Strait. Doctrine dictated that we must contact the carrier and request DLI (Deck Launch Intercept) to make an intercept of the aircraft before it reached the strait and ensure it was "escorted" while making that transit. A few minutes after contacting the *Ranger*, we were informed that DLI was not available within the time constraints to enable the intercept to occur at the desired range.

This caused quite a stir, because it was expected that the Russians would not be allowed to follow this flight path without being intercepted and escorted. What was more troubling was that we knew the Russians would be expecting us to do so! We first checked our airspace and message traffic to see if any scheduled JSDF (Japanese Self-Defense Force) aircraft or USAF assets (out of Taegu, S. Korea) were available and in the right airspace to make the intercept. There were none! However, I informed the TAO that we had a P-3 aircraft transiting our airspace, returning from her maritime patrol assignment. Looking at the "set up" (P-3 range & bearing to the Russian aircraft), it was within the realm of possibility for an intercept to occur, but only if the decision to do so was made promptly because the P-3 would not otherwise have the speed to make an overtaking angle to the contact successfully. While the decision was being discussed up the chain-of-command, I contacted the P-3, explained the situation and requested its fuel status to ensure it had enough for what we might ask it to do. The response from the P-3 was quite enthusiastic as their type aircraft were not normally used for this purpose.

Shortly, I received word from the TAO to task the P-3 with the intercept, which I did and gave it range and bearing to the contact. As the P-3 was "off the bow" of the contact, it would only be necessary for the P-3 to alter course about 20 degrees or so and report a visual when the intercept had been made. But owing to the lower speed of the P-3, it would not be able to hold the intercept for as long as we would have liked . . . or, so we thought! Following the two planes' flight path as they closed, I gave the P-3 a final bearing and range, to which it soon followed with a "tally ho" as visual contact was established. The aircraft commander was so excited about being given this opportunity that contact was maintained for much longer than we had expected before the Russian's speed outdistanced the P-3. And, for that amount of time, the P-3 pilot must have had his throttles wide open! Before breaking off, the pilot informed me that he had some real good photos of the Russian and would I be interested in getting some copies! About a week later, a large manila folder was delivered aboard containing the photos! Great stills!

CHAPTER 23
CSAT: COMNAVSURFPAC STAFF
1987 – 1991

I WAS COMING UP ON MY ROTATION DATE to shore duty and it was time to start looking around for what was available in the San Diego area. But before I could start making any plans, I got a call from Senior Chief (he had rotated off CGN-9 a few months previously) asking if I would be interested in following him to a ComNavSurfPac (CNSP) Staff billet. He explained that he was involved in standing-up an assessment team that would go aboard surface combatant vessels and take a "snap shot" of their Combat Systems and their readiness to deploy. It sounded great to me and I readily agreed, if he could see to it that my detailer was informed and the necessary orders were cut to get me in that billet.

Initially, CSAT (Combat Systems Assessment Team) was classed as a shore duty billet, but with the understanding that with the team spending so much time "on travel" and out of our "homeport" area, paperwork would be submitted justifying that it be re-classified as "neutral duty." This came to pass quickly and before we had even gotten up-to-speed with our on-board assessments. Once we did and Hawaii and Japan missions were included, the CSA OIC began working on the necessary paperwork for submission up the chain of command to again change the billets' status from neutral duty to sea duty. About two years later, the decision was delivered and CSAT became a sea duty billet retroactively. This meant we all got back-pay for sea duty, which averaged around $1,400. A wind-fall well deserved!

The CSAT was originally "stood-up" for two reasons. CNSP was upset with ships' performances during INSURV due to a high failure rate of simulated missile launches. And, as ships "chopped" to 7th Fleet, that command was complaining about the poor performance of ships coming from CNSP. CSAT was located in Building 55 (topside, south end) on the Naval Station across from Pier 1. When I reported to staff and the CSAT billet, Senior Chief explained what the goal was and that we had to come up with a plan on how to get there. As we would be assessing so many classes and flights (sub-classes) of ships, we needed to identify those not only by the class but also the "baseline" (i.e. FFG "flight I & II, CG Ticonderoga AEGIS Baseline I, II and later III, etc.) because each of these classes and flights had differences in how the crew employed their system. The only way to correctly identify the necessary data to make an accurate assessment of each platform, class and flight was to know what the crew was expected to know, by using the documents and doctrine that they themselves used for training, configuring and employing their system. And for Senior Chief and me, that meant hitting the books for the first four months, to bring us up to speed on the first ships we would be scheduled to go aboard. Continuation with our studies of further hulls and classes would eventually complete our portion of the assessments' documentation. We would have to build a "package" for each, containing CIC watchstation tests, WQSB manning checks, publications library checks, and a host of lesser check points to quantify the crew and ship's level of readiness. This meant we also had to be as knowledgeable and current as the crew of each ship we went aboard, that is, knowing their latest and most current CDS software upgrades and patches; their latest maintenance system "faxes" (changes); and any changes or deliveries to the CSTOM's (Combat Systems Technical Operations Manuals) and Combat Systems Doctrine. We had to play catch-up on many of the older classes of ship, but because AEGIS was so new to the West Coast, we were able to get ahead of that class early and were able to stay abreast as those ships arrived on the West Coast, "chopping" to their homeports from the builders' yards.

Staff had established a few benchmark criteria for an assessment, and one of those was that each ship we went aboard first had to demonstrate its ability to be able to complete an OCSOT (Over-all Combat Systems Operational Test). If that could not be accomplished, the assessment would not proceed until the problem was resolved. Initially, this proved to be a game-changer because too many of the ships could not do so. Soon a compromise was put in place such that if the ship had CASREP'ed (reported the casualty up the chain of command) a piece of gear or system, then a waiver could be issued and those portions of the OCSOT that were not impacted by the CASREP, could be accomplished. CASREPs were like toilet paper. The fleet was papered with them!

During early considerations of the "flavor" of the assessment team, it had been decided that to ensure the ships realized a CSA was unlike the FTG (Fleet Training Group) RefTra, one of the first differences they would notice was that the team came aboard wearing khakis and not the overalls that FTG wore! Also that each point in the assessment was referenced from their own ship's documentation. Be it their CO's Battle Orders, the class Combat Systems Doctrine, their WQSB, or technical operations manuals, we would only assess them on their level of knowledge from their own source documents. And, we made it a point to never use the justification of "Because I said so!" That was a refrain too often heard from other training and evaluation commands.

Our routine consisted of spending the first three days in port performing OCSOT, giving watch station exams, having the crew perform scheduled PMS checks, reviewing watch bills and checking manning deficiencies. The last two days were devoted to taking the ship out to sea for observation of their NAV detail, simulated ASW using a mobile target, performing a gun shoot at a towed sleeve pulled by a Lear jet, and a simulated missile firing. Depending upon what other weapons were onboard, (such as Harpoon) events were added to the agenda. Owing to added security constraints, we did not involve TWS (Tomahawk Weapons System). When not at sea we worked on reports and submitted recommended changes to FXPs, Tacmemos, and other technical publications. We also built and maintained a computer database for each assessment based on hull and class and that documented our efforts. We wrote summaries for the visit's final report, which was routed up the chain of command to the Chief of Staff, who briefed CNSP (the Admiral).

Later, I was given the collateral duty of Scheduling Officer and attended the scheduling conferences to ensure the assessments occurred at the right time in the ship's pre-deployment cycle and at the expected level of readiness for the assessment — no easy feat! Even if I secured a ship to receive an assessment, I would then have to ensure I could also secure the necessary range time in SOCAL. If I needed to schedule the area for a gun shoot (or any other event requiring additional assets or range time), I would have to attend that separate meeting within the scheduling conference.

Originally Navigation was not part of the CSAT charter, but it had come to the attention of the teams' OIC (Officer in Charge) that this would need to be added. An observation aboard one of the FFGs in San Diego was noted as case in point. Apparently, when getting underway, it had been observed that the ship was navigating without charts on the Bridge and there was no navigation detail in CIC that was engaged in performing what was expected of a radar navigation detail. Thus there was no established NAV track and no one swinging arcs and taking fixes. So, NAV became one of our observed "events" from then on out.

As our "packages" were completed for ship classes and flights, our schedule became busier and we found ourselves aboard ship on average three weeks out of each month. As the process matured, trips out of town were added and we were soon driving to Long Beach Naval Station or flying to Hawaii. As the cost of this bang was more bucks, whenever we were "out of area" we did our best to schedule two or three ships in a row —especially if the trip was to Hawaii or, later, Yokosuka, Japan. An example would be one of our trips to Hawaii: three weeks, three ships and three different classes (FF, FFG & DDG).

We hadn't even been around a year before word came back to us of the fleet's perception of our performance . . . tough but fair! In part, this was also on account of our own level of interest in the ship's performance. Because we came from the fleet and many of us would return to the fleet before retiring, we had a vested interest in assisting any way we could in the resolution of some of the problems we identified during our assessments. If the ship were missing a TACMEMO or TACNOTE, we made note of that in our report, to be sure. But, we would also point out to the crew how that impacted their Combat Systems Doctrine and any other changes that needed to be made and then gave them the name and phone number of the person they needed to call to obtain their copy. Too many times we would find the missing document, but due to its added security classification it had been received onboard and then promptly locked up in a safe where the people who needed to see it weren't even aware of it. Other times, we would note a manning deficiency where a specific NEC (job code) was required prior to the ship deploying and attempts by the crew to secure a body or school house slot were met with frustration. Again, we would note that in our report, but we also made many phone calls and touched base with many of our "contacts" in the pursuit of helping the ship meet that requirement. Although not always successful, we did what we could and the ship recognized the effort.

Ships that did not pass the assessment were not allowed to deploy until they were able to correct the discrepancies, which added increased scrutiny from the DESRON commanders. As the number of ship's completing CSAT grew, if was pretty easy to identify which ships would do well and which would not. If the CO and the CPOs were actively engaged and pro-active during the process, chances were that the ship would pass. A few ships that we boarded were unable to complete the assessment due to equipment issues beyond their control. But, just the fact that CSAT had come aboard and added further validation of their problem would often times result in expediting the problems resolution.

As mentioned, our charter was for us to assess CNSP combatant ships. By our second year, our reputation had become known to the point that notice had been taken by commands outside the realm of our own. PHIBRON was having serious issues with their LHA class and had queried CNSP about the viability of our being employed to provide some "shock value" and added documentation in bringing these issues to the fore. Well, the OIC was told to "make it happen" and the team spent the next few months scheduling the ships to visit and putting together our class "package" for the type. Senior Chief and I quickly discovered that the LHAs would bring their own set of "benchmarks" and problems to the process. One of the first things we did with the other classes of ships was to procure our own set of CSTOMs for addition to our technical library and for our use in the formulation of their assessment package. When I tried obtaining a set of CSTOMs from the LHA combat systems program manager, I was told to come on over and pick it up. When I got the box back to our office and spread it out on the conference room table, I discovered that I had been given an original set and that all the page change updates were loosely piled into the box (about eight years' worth). I spent the next day inserting all the page changes to the original set. Now, we could begin studying each volume, taking notes and building the class assessment package. We were also able to obtain many of the CSTRs

(Combat Systems Trouble Reports) that had been documented on the CDS program over the years as well as which had been corrected and which were still outstanding. This would become very useful during our visit aboard the LHAs, which at the time were based up at Long Beach Naval Station. Arriving aboard for our first LHA for assessment, we met in the wardroom with the command personnel to discuss the intent, focus and end-product of our efforts, based on what was being requested of us by their TYCOM (Type Commander). Then, we went up to CIC to commence the OCSOT, our first benchmark for the readiness condition of the Combat System. When we stepped into CIC we were greeted by the presence of a number of tech reps contracted by the program manager to manage the software development and the CDS. Talking with them, we learned that the program manager wanted his own set of eyes on what was being done and to point out documented issues as they arose and also to write up any emergent problems discovered during the course of the OCSOT. OCSOT was a cluster… …! The software hadn't been upgraded — with the exception of minor "patches" — for years because of lack of funding. The LHA's mission wasn't to put "weapons on target" as a surface combatant but rather marines on the beach. The software was unique to what we had been familiar with on the surface combatants. But we had done our homework and were aware of the program's many special functions dedicated to the accomplishment of the ships' mission. These are what we focused on and paid added attention to during the course of the test. One of the basic requirements was a task to be performed at the TAO console: A grid reference point had to be entered, which oriented the rest of the AOA (Amphibious Operating Area) to the planned Lines of Departure (LOD), Boat Lanes and beaches. During our OCSOT, when this reference point was entered, it did not orient to the desired position. This, in turn, caused the LOD and Boat Lanes to appear where they shouldn't have. So the primary function of the program, during the landing evolution, was a failure. But, we continued with the OCSOT. Another station that proved a problem was the AIC (Air Intercept Controller) console. When the AIC attempted to conduct a simulated intercept of a bogey track, the program should have provided him with the correct geometric display and readout to direct his CAP to intercept. In this instance, the geometry and readout were 180 degrees out from the correct solution. Another failure! And, the list grew! Upon completing as much of the OCSOT as possible, our

OIC informed the command that we would return when they had corrected the deficiencies and we departed the ship. It would be over six months before we could get back, due to their schedule and ours. We performed one more mission aboard an LHA before the TYCOM decided he'd had enough!

CSAT's impact on the waterfront resulted in the CSMTT (Combat Systems Mobile Training Team) commencing what was termed as pre-CSA work-ups for ships in the scheduling window. Although the East Coast was apprised of our efforts, they had not instituted any similar organization to address the issues laid out in our charter. A point of pride was felt by all of us when we were made aware that, during the period CSAs were performed, all but one incident involving a ship and covered by our charter occurred on combatants stationed on the East Coast!

One of the ships we visited was the *USS Kinkaid* (DD-965) and their CO turned out to be the Ops Boss on CGN-9, when OSCS and I were aboard her. He was an odd duck and, on *The Beach*, he garnered a rather checkered reputation. He had a penchant for using quotes from historical figures from the past. During the CSA "in-brief" in the Wardroom he used the opportunity to incorporate a quote from Genghis Khan. I don't recall the actual lines, but we all thought it came across as being out of context for the venue. Anyway, we proceeded with the CSA. One of the checks we normally conducted was ensuring that the Combat Systems Doctrine had been updated to reflect the ship's current capabilities and this included reviewing the Captain's Battle Orders. I was in CIC doing so with the senior OS and the CIC Officer looking on. The opening passage was a quote from "Bull" Halsey, made in the heat of WWII stating "Kill Japs, Kill Japs, Kill More Japs." Odd enough! But, what made it disquieting was the fact that the CIC Officer was of Japanese descent, so I turned to him and it was obvious he knew what I had just read. He gave me a weak grin and shrugged!

When *Kinkaid* was returning from her next deployment overseas and transiting the Malacca Straits, she collided with a merchantman, killing one crewman aboard *Kinkaid*. CNSP called our OIC and asked that a copy of the CSA Report be sent over for review. They were looking for any indication that either we had overlooked something or that the report would reveal a problem that had gone unresolved. In the end, the report revealed nothing out of the norm! Murphy sometimes takes his due!

Another ship scheduled for us for an onboard CSA was an FF (Fast Frigate) tied up at one of the piers aboard NavSta, San Diego. Our group was assembling on the pier before our going aboard when our (FC) Fire Controlman noticed the maintenance panel on the back of the CIWS mount on the fantail was open. While our group was still on the pier, he went aboard ship and took a closer look at the mount. Returning shortly to our group, he told the OIC there was a problem! His inspection of the CIWS mount revealed that it had been "fried" by a fire! This was not a showstopper except for the fact that he stated there was no CASREP that he had seen indicating the mount was "down." We were told to wait on the pier as the FC and the OIC went aboard ship to confer with the CO. It wasn't long before they returned and our OIC told us the CSA was off and he was going back to the office to tell CNSP Chief of Staff why the CSA was being cancelled.

It was while I was stationed with CSAT that my youngest daughter had her first baby! My ex-wife was back East and my daughter's husband was aboard ship, out on local ops. He had requested to stay ashore for the birth, but his CO denied his request based on his being indispensable or a ne'er-do-well who didn't warrant the consideration. Looking back, I would have to say that it wasn't the former. Anyway, I was not out of town on assignment, so I was available to be with her and when she phoned saying she was already at Balboa Naval Hospital, I rushed over. When I arrived, they had put her in a room until she was ready to deliver and when I got there she was already in much pain, her face flushed and muscles straining. She looked at me and said, "Get the nurse, quick!" So, I snatched a nurse out of the hallway and hustled her into the room. When my girl asked for something for the pain, the nurse told her she was too far along and should have taken the offer earlier. I asked the nurse about that and she told me it was a typical mistake made by first time mothers. Apparently, my little rookie was no exception! It wasn't 30 minutes later that they wheeled her into the operating room, my hand now firmly locked in hers! The delivery was quick and soon we were back in the other room with me trying to nurse some circulation into the hand that she had been gripping for the past hour!

I went out into the hall and walked down to where there was a phone and made a call. I had told my daughter that when the baby was born I would make sure that "daddy" knew. So, I placed a call to FACSFAC (Fleet Area Control &

Surveillance Facility) because they were the managing command for the SOCAL operations areas. I got hold of "Beaver" (their call sign on the R/T net) and explained to him who I was and what I wanted done. He told me he'd take care of it. "Beaver" called the ship my daughter's husband was on and they woke him up and told him he was a "daddy!" As the message was sent "in the clear" over an un-encrypted R/T net, every CIC in SOCAL heard it. Not your usual radio traffic, for sure!

A scaled down CSA team was aboard an FFG in SOCAL and I had just completed my final portion of the assessment, but because of our busy schedule, I needed to get back to the office, pick up my next assessment package and get aboard that ship. It was arranged that I would hop aboard an SH-60 back to NASNI and a vehicle would pick me up there. While on the ride in, I was sitting in the SENSO seat with a headset on behind the cockpit and the sliding door had been left open. We were up about 200 feet cruising along when the pilot called out *"whale!"* The aircraft banked and dropped down to about 100 feet as we passed over a spouting gray whale, so close you could almost reach out and touch it. And, me without a camera!

While on one of our trips to Pearl Harbor, we completed two CSAs on ships in that port and had commenced the last one aboard an Adams class DDG before we were to return to San Diego. After completing the in-port portion of the assessment, the ship was scheduled to get underway for completion of the remainder of the CSA. But our underway time was delayed due to a tropical storm passing through the OpAreas we were to be using. Hours before our "drop dead" time arrived, the storm was downgraded to a tropical depression, which meant the ship could get underway, which it did. We had some time to make up and the ship put on a few extra knots in an attempt to do so. Even with the storm abating, it was not a comfortable ride out at sea and on that hull. While conducting our drills in CIC, the ship tossed and turned and we spent much of our time just holding on to keep our feet under us. We didn't finish up until late that evening, but were cutting it close with our arrival time back in Pearl, because we had a flight to catch. To help us, the OIC made arrangements for the ship to offload us over the fantail by Jacobs ladder and into a MWB (motor whale boat). The MWB then took us to a landing at Iroquois Point where we were met by a waiting van to take us to Barbers Point where we would get our gear, check out of the "Q" and then take the same van for a ride to the Honolulu airport to catch our ticketed flights home. When we arrived at the airport, another CSA member and I were told that if we volunteered to take a later flight (they had over-booked ours), the airline would give us a meal voucher and a "domestic" ticket good for anywhere in the continental United States. When we asked what time we could expect to arrive in San Diego, they told us it would be about an hour before the flight we had been originally ticketed on because we wouldn't be changing planes in L.A. We took the offer, of course. Just another day at the office!

One of our other trips to Hawaii occurred while the ships participating in that year's RIMPAC were in port Pearl. The port was jammed with ships from the various participating countries and the base was packed with their sailors everywhere you went. That evening OSCS and I decided that instead of going downtown and fighting the crowd there, we would go to the base EM (Enlisted Men's) club, instead. Well, we were wrong to expect it to be less crowded than downtown and it was certainly a boisterous bunch that filled every nook and cranny of the place. We first started out standing at the bar because there weren't any vacant tables. But, eventually we were able to snag a couple seats at one by sharing with two other Chiefs. Later, as we were about to leave, we made a head call and as we were finishing up our business, we heard a commotion behind us. Turning around, we saw that an Aussie sailor had managed to get a condom over his head and inflated (don't ask me how or why). Everyone in the place cracked up laughing, but the Japanese sailors there, went bonkers! Shouting at each other, gesticulating and pointing to the Aussie as if they couldn't believe each other's descriptions of what they were seeing. OSCS and I wondered out loud if that was how it was applied down-under!

On our first trip to Japan there were three ships scheduled consecutively, to optimize our time spent for the money expended to get us there and keep us there, for three weeks. This was just a few months after the eruption of Mount Pinatubo in the Philippines that caused so much damage at both Clark AFB and the Naval Station at Subic Bay. Some of the ships stationed at Subic had participated in the evacuation of Navy dependents from Subic to Japan, where they were now tied up and awaiting determination of their future homeport assignment. We had monitored the situation to ensure there was not going to be an impact on our schedule, but there were still some issues in doubt when we left to make the flight to Tokyo and the bus ride down to Yokosuka. While in Yoko', most of us were housed in the senior enlisted barracks and others took rooms in the Navy Lodge, making the trip to the ship each morning by bus or cab. We usually took dinner at the CPO Club on base, where we ran into some previous shipmates that had been aboard the ships evacuating the dependents. They filled us in on their experiences and we were all glad we hadn't been there when it happened. What a mess!

Before I left for Japan, Mike told me our former CMC from CGN-9 was now stationed in Yokosuka and he told me to look him up. When I got there and after I had checked into the barracks, I decided to look up "Doc" (the CMC). What better place than the base CPO Club to do that. When I asked the bartender if he knew where "Doc" was, he asked why and I told him about being stationed with him aboard *The Beach*. Immediately, he grabbed the phone and dialed. After a short conversation, he told me Doc was on his way. He and I had a good time that evening reminiscing and before we split up that night, he made sure I was coming to dinner at his house the following night. His wife was a doll and it was a relaxing break from a hectic schedule to spend time with a former shipmate over a good meal! Sea-stories were told that night and I'm sure Doc's were more colorful than mine!

Anyway, the CSAs aboard the three ships scheduled came off without too much drama and the only issue I had was with the detect-to-engage sequence, because our underway schedule limitations didn't give us enough open range to allow for a normal *set-up* and had to be abbreviated.

USS Vincennes (CG-49) showed up on our schedule before her deployment overseas in '88. The crew was extremely arrogant and the CO, Captain Will Rogers, thought himself quite the rogue, wearing cowboy boots with his uniform.

The week passed with us going through our established program, tailored for the AEGIS class cruisers and we finished up the assessment with our usual "out brief" in the wardroom. When it was our FCCS's turn to debrief the CIWS portion of the assessment, he stated that both CIWS mounts were inoperable and being carried as "down" and that he had drawn up a list of the needed parts to fix them both. The CO stated that he didn't care about fixing them. FCCS had a surprised look on his face and our OIC asked the Captain why he wasn't going to fix them. The CO stated that nothing was going to get close enough to use them so why waste the money. The hope expressed among the CSA team was that none of us would be aboard when they did need them.

Roughly six months later they shot down the Iranian Airbus and none of us were very empathetic. Our OIC received a call from 5th Fleet Combat Systems Officer in the middle of the morning asking him questions about the CSA assessment we had conducted prior to the *Vincennes* deployment. One particular question was if we assessed ROE (Rules of Engagement). Our OIC said "No, we only assessed their ability to put a round on target and that it appeared they were able to do that." Fifth Fleet CSO had a mild chuckle at that and the conversation ended. We later found out that during the "green board" investigation one of the 5/54 gun mounts had experienced a mechanical failure and was not operational while they were fighting the Iranian boats. This defect severely handicapped them as they had to maneuver more aggressively to fight the Iranian boats with only one gun-mount operable. This definitely contributed to their "losing the bubble" (situational awareness).

It was near the end of my tour of duty at CSAT that the "Tailhook" affair broke out into the front pages of the news media! The "Tailhook Association" had existed for years (and still does), excessive behavior being tolerated with a wink and a nod by its governing organization.

The Wikipedia account can be found here: https://en.wikipedia.org/ wiki/Tailhook_scandal

In an attempt to address the issue Navy-wide, the entire Navy "stood down" and conducted a day of awareness classes tilted to address the crisis. So, the 99.9% of us who had not been involved in the incident, spent the day twiddling our thumbs while the various HR representatives took their turn on stage to address all of us potential offenders!

The time had come for me to rotate to my next and last duty station and I worked with the detailer to get a shore duty billet in San Diego so I wouldn't need to move out of the area. We worked out that I would be transferring down the street to FCSTUP (Fleet Combat Systems Training Unit, Pacific). OSCS Norrod (my partner at CSA) had departed to his next duty assignment before me, which was FTG over by Point Loma. I missed him already! His replacement, an OSCM, had arrived before he left, but some of his training was left to me before I departed. However, my replacement would be "gapped" and would not arrive before

I had left. This was a point of contention with the CSA OIC, but there was nothing to be done about it.

CHAPTER 24
FCSTUP, SAN DIEGO

Leave & Transit: 9 Sept. – 27 Oct '91
Included IT School 3 Aug '92
Requested transfer to Fleet Reserve 30 Jun '93

IT Class, Author @ Front, Center

I WAS SENT TO IT (Instructor Training) School and graduated from that course on 2 Oct '91. The course was a requirement prior to reporting aboard at FCSTUP as an accredited Instructor.

Upon arriving at FCSTUP, I familiarized myself with the new group of senior enlisted personnel I would be working with and got introduced to the training curriculum that I would need to master before being a qualified member of the command. Included was my UI (Under Instruction) status while learning the position of Team Leader in each of the training vans (20B4 & 20B5). Each type van was configured to support its own specific spectrum of ship types which, during a training mission, would be plugged into the training ship's combat direction system. In the van, the trainers would man stations where the ship's reaction to canned training scenarios injected into their CDS could be observed and evaluated. Observer trainers would include an OS, FC, ST and EW capable of recognizing correct and incorrect reactions from the ship.

During the first couple months while I was learning the ropes at FCSTUP, my previous command would call my current command and request that I "augment" one of their CSAs aboard an AEGIS ship, the reason being that my gapped billet had not as yet been filled. An added reason for the request was that, while at CSA I was the one who had written all the "detect-to-engage" scenarios and had them written to tape. The current level of expertise at CSA wasn't familiar enough with AEGIS CDS to run the scenario tapes and function at the training console in CIC. FCSTUP let me go, but my new OSCM was pissed at having another command appropriate one of his people. I was caught in the middle and unfortunately, OSCM vented on me. Eventually, he managed to bend the ear of the CO and no further requests came from CSA for my services, or if they did, were denied. This was a great relief to me. Hell hath no fury as a pissed-off master chief!

One day I was on a training mission in one of the vans, plugged into a DD alongside the pier. We had been running training scenarios most of the morning and had just started another, when word came from the ship that they were calling a "training time out." As mission leader, I got on the headset and asked why the hold-up. Word came back that anyone wanting to get autographs from some San Diego Padres at a signing on the mess decks was doing so. In a flash, I grabbed some blank paper and made a bee-line aboard ship. Entering the mess deck, I found the line had already played out and there was no waiting. So, I walked right up to Steve Garvey and asked him to autograph my blank sheet of paper, addressed in my dad's name. When I sent dad that autograph, he was thrilled. A baseball "nut" all his life, he'd never been local enough to a baseball stadium to acquire many autographs and Steve Garvey was one of his favorites.

Because I was anticipating this command would be my last before retirement, I had been looking into the possibility of taking some college courses to add to the credits I had acquired while attending the junior college so many years ago. One of the adjoining buildings to the library housed the resident college representatives and after meeting with them, I found that I only needed a Humanities course and one more Math course (I selected Statistics) to accumulate the necessary total credits for my AA degree. But owing to my work schedule and the course schedule, the two courses would have to be completed over separate quarters. My work schedule wouldn't interfere with me attending classes, but it would interfere with my being available for duty days. So, I had to submit a chit up the chain of command, requesting that I be exempted from duty while attending the courses. The first signature necessary was my Master Chief's and he disapproved it. When it got to the XO's desk, he called me and the Master Chief into his office and proposed a compromise, which still didn't sit well with the MC. The agreement was that I would be assigned a collateral duty that could be performed during regular working hours, but not while I was assigned and conducting a mission aboard ship. The collateral duty? Senior enlisted in charge of one of the Navy's Honor Guards for burial detail. Apparently, no one else cared for the task and the command always had trouble filling that requirement. Really, I didn't see what the problem was because I felt it an honor to do this duty and so I had readily agreed. A prerequisite to the duty was that I attend a course at the shooting range up at Miramar Naval Air Station — to become qualified with the sidearm I was required to wear. I hadn't qualified previously because I had never been assigned a duty that would require me to do so. The course was given from about 4PM to just after dark because part of the qualification required a "night shoot." Being left-handed as I am didn't help matters much, but I managed to pass the course and the notation was duly entered into my service jacket. Next, I met up with the person I was taking over for. He explained some of the finer points of the job and introduced me to the personnel making up the detachment. My detail and I were tasked with being available for services one day a week, but some days the schedule would comprise a service in the late morning and another, at a different cemetery, in the afternoon. Some services were more emotional for me than others, especially when there were only one or two people attending. But others, more memorable, were well attended and the service was more upbeat in remembrance of the life past. Two of these stand out!

The first was a ceremony held at Rosecrans National Cemetery on Point Loma. It was being held for a Torpedoman 2nd Class off a WWII submarine. All his living shipmates showed up, dressed in blazers with the ship's patch on the breast and all of them wore a musketeer-style hat replete with feather. Upon completion of the ceremony, I was able to speak with some of the shipmates and immediately was regaled with some of their adventures. By the time I left, I felt I had met the man! The second ceremony I most recall was held at the chapel aboard the Amphibious Base, on the strand south of Coronado. I was to present the flag to the members' family after the service in the chapel and, instead of going to the cemetery, my detail was to render honors as the casket left the chapel. While the service was being given, I had taken up position at the back of the chapel and was able to listen in on what was said. Our honoree was a SEAL and veteran of the Korean War. During the course of the service, one of his team mates got up to speak to the assembled audience. Some of the stories he told were probably, at some point, previously classified and others were plain bawdy and off-color. But, the audience responded with laughter, so it must have been what was expected. He was a SEAL, after all!

As FCSTUP was billeted with senior enlisted, many of them were in the final stages of their careers and would retire from that command. So, as many others were doing, I ran through my numbers, which would give me a rough estimate of what my "retainer" formula would look like. The calculation would include number of active duty years, reserve time and "constructive" time (which was added to my formula as a result of Vietnam service). The numbers looked good and over-all, with 22+ years, I would retire with an added 2.5% applied to my retainer pay. It was referred to as a retainer because I would be retiring into the Fleet Reserve, thus being subject to call-up for the next 10 years. So I wrote up and submitted my request to retire! But, as the numbers I had crunched took me out to the end of May the following year, my transfer to Fleet Reserve date would not be until 30 June '93. So, that was my requested date of retirement!

A couple weeks prior to my retirement date came the obligatory mustering-out classes offered as assistance in your transition from sailor to civilian. There were some whose logic escaped me. I mean, do you really have to sit through a class given by the DMV? Then, there was a class for "Survivor's Benefits," one given by the life insurance company underwriting the program. When they finished explaining the program, I was left to wonder why anyone, with access to an alternative, would want to sign up. I surely didn't! All this was well intentioned, but I found most of it to be boring and only relevant for certain circumstances and to certain personnel.

The command offered to use their usual source to commission my "Shadow Box" (with the folded flag flown over the Capitol Building in Washington, D. C.), medals, ribbons and small metal name plates with duty stations and dates. Instead, I knew a buddy of mine had done those and when I talked with him he offered me a better choice of the finished product and for less. The command also offered to hold a "Retirement Ceremony" where the CO would get up and tell everyone what a swell guy I was, etc. I declined! But, I did want to go out with a bang. So, a few close shipmates helped me put together a retirement party that would be tough to top. We put up posters around the command to make sure everyone got the word and when the day of the party arrived, there wasn't any parking available within four blocks of my house! What a blast!

Taking terminal leave, house hunting, travel time, proceed time, etc. I was still collecting pay through the end of July. And, with what my wife and I had put aside for this day, I wasn't going to be looking for work until the following year. So, I dove into my "honey do" list with a vengeance – it kept me busy for a couple months, anyway. I also started doing more volunteer work at my VFW post two days a week. By the following year, I was doing courier work for a local company, to keep me busy and unavailable for more "honey do's." Sitting idle was unbearable and this was totally out of the realm of anything else I had ever done , so I was actually enjoying the whole experience. The money was just a bonus!

About a year after I had officially retired, I got a call from Mike Norrod. He told me one of our mutual acquaintances had called asking if he wanted a job. But, Mike had left California to take care of his mother after his father had passed and wasn't on the job market. When he told me who I would be working for and what the contract was, I told him it sounded interesting. He gave me a number to call, which I did and a couple weeks later, I drove up to Port Hueneme for an interview. As I was parking my truck next to the mobile I was going to, I saw four or five guys standing out on the stoop smoking and shooting the breeze. I recognized half of them! Turns out this was a Martin Marietta AEGIS contract for new-construction ships and follow-on contract work aboard AEGIS during upgrades and overhauls. After the interview, I went to lunch with my sponsor, who was the person who had called Mike. I asked him what he thought my chances were and he assured me it was "in the bag." Although, I was hired, I was told I still had to fly back East, to Cherry Hill, New Jersey for an interview with one of the higher-ups, but that this would be more of a formality. I was returning to the Navy as an ISEA (In-Service Engineering Agent) and would remain working under that AEGIS contract for five years, before receiving a better offer from BAE Systems. I would witness and participate in some of the Navy's newest, cutting edge, technological developments in the field of Combat Systems. I would also ride dozens of ships and participate in a half-dozen CSSQTs, including a new-construction FMS (Foreign Military Sales) JMSDF (Japanese Maritime Self-Defense Force) AEGIS destroyer.

I was back! Making a contribution to the Navy! *My Navy!*

Acknowledgments

To begin with, I am obliged to mention the numerous website references that, while not constituting the breadth of material necessarily requisite in the composition of a book, are nevertheless important and relevant to the inclusion in this work. The story of PIRAZ, the Collision at Sea with the V-3 submarine, liberty in Subic back in the late '60's and early '70's and others were referenced and portions quoted in this work.

I would like to recognize the input, encouragement and support of many of my friends and family. To Rudy Pantoja for his assistance in recalling earlier passages aboard the "Connie". "Mikey" Norrod for his input and encouragement from our days aboard Long Beach and CNSP Staff. My sister, Kathleen! Thanks, Sis! And, my wife for constantly asking me when I was going to finish!

And, to my editor, Brooke Stoddard, for all the enlightenment provided in acquainting me with the numerous processes and pitfalls of attempting to publish a book of this nature!

I find that this work would be incomplete if I did not list my shipmates, whom I have known over the years and who provided me with friendship, wisdom, guidance and understanding. Their ranks, as listed, are from when I knew them and not necessarily indicative of their final rank.

RM1 Rudy Pantoja
OS1 "Pappy" Sarver

OSCM (SW) Michael Norrod
OSCM (SW) Jess Mahon
OSC (SW) Tommy Thompson
OSCS (SW) Richard Shykes
OS1 (SW) Steve Bobbitt
OS1 Al Smith
AW1 Todd Gilbert
AW1 Jim Burt
OS1 Wylie Dupree

References

Maps generated at Maptive.com

USS Constellation Association website: http://www.ussconstellation.org

https://en.wikipedia.org/wiki/MIL-STD-6011

http://www.ussgoldsborough.com/final-weeks-of-the-gunline/

Naval Tactical Data Systems Employment During the Vietnam War:
http://ethw.org/First-Hand:The_Naval_Tactical_Data_System_in_Combat_-_Chapter_7_of_the_Story_of_the_Naval_Tactical_Data_System (PIRAZ;NTDS & BVP)

"One Day in a Long War", Jeffrey Ethell & Alfred Price ISBN 0 - 394 - 57622 - 5

"Troubled Water", Gregory A. Freeman ISBN 978-0-230-10339-9

On Yankee Station: The Naval Air War over Vietnam (Bluejacket Books); by John B Nichols & Barrett Tillman

https://www.amazon.com/Nixons-Trident-Bombardment-Operations-Linebacker-ebook/dp/B013ZWM4KS/ref=sr_1_1?s=books&ie=UTF8&qid=1485751780&sr=1-1&keywords=Haiphong+Harbor

http://www.history.com/this-day-in-history/racial-violence-breaks-out-aboard-u-s-navy-ships

https://en.wikipedia.org/wiki/USS_Constellation_(CV-64)

http://www.history.com/this-day-in-history/mining-of-north-vietnamese-harbors-is-announced

http://navysite.de/cvn/cv63ri.htm

http://www.navy.mil/navydata/nav_legacy.asp?id=69

http://www.hullnumber.com/CV-64

https://en.wikipedia.org/wiki/USS_Mount_Hood_(AE-11)

https://en.wikipedia.org/wiki/USS_Mount_Hood_(AE-29)

http://www.hullnumber.com/AE-29

http://ww2today.com/10-november-1944-the-crew-of-uss-mount-hood-disappear-in-massive-explosion

http://www.cvan-cvn-65.org/

http://www.usslongbeach-assoc.org/

https://www.globalsecurity.org/military/ops/pocket_money.htm

https://en.wikipedia.org/wiki/USS_Long_Beach_(CGN-9)

https://www.navalhistory.org/2011/03/21/soviet-sub-collides-with-uss-kitty-hawk-21-march-1984

http://www.upi.com/Archives/1986/08/10/US-Thai-forces-hold-largest-maneuvers-since-Vietnam-War/5583524030400/

http://www.navy.mil/navydata/nav_legacy.asp?id=69

http://w https://navalmatters.wordpress.com/2014/05/27/new-jersey-battle-group-westpac-1986/ww.hullnumber.com/CGN-9

https://en.wikipedia.org/wiki/USS_New_Jersey_(BB-62)

https://en.wikipedia.org/wiki/SOSUS

http://www.public.navy.mil/subfor/underseawarfaremagazine/Issues/Archives/issue_25/sosus2.htm

https://navalmatters.wordpress.com/2014/05/27/new-jersey-battle-group-westpac-1986/

https://en.wikipedia.org/wiki/Synthetic_aperture_radar

http://www.uscarriers.net/

http://www.hazegray.org/faq/slang1.htm

https://en.wiktionary.org/wiki/Appendix:Glossary_of_U.S._Navy_slang

goatlocker.org/resources/nav/navyterms.doc

https://en.wikipedia.org/wiki/Identification_friend_or_foe

http://www.dean-boys.com/extras/iff/iffqa.html

http://steeljawscribe.com/2007/08/11/the-long-war-russian-bears-back-out-of-hibernation

https://dennisclevenger.wordpress.com/2012/02/21/liberty-call-olongapo-city/

https://www.youtube.com/watch?v=ft-99VbGjaM

https://planesandstuff.files.wordpress.com/2014/05/samplejwn.pdf

https://en.wikipedia.org/wiki/Mikoyan-Gurevich_MiG-17

https://fas.org/man/dod-101/sys/ship/weaps/an-wlr-1.htm

http://hazegray.org/faq/slang1.htm

http://www.hullnumber.com/ALL-HANDS/what-goes-on-in-cic-navymen-
find-out-at-school

https://en.wikipedia.org/wiki/PIRAZ

http://babesinopen.blogspot.com/2008/09/naval-gunfire-support.html
(NGFS Explained)

http://www.public.navy.mil/fltfor/ewtglant/Documents/courses/cin/J-113-
0045.html   (MTT for NGFS)